BRAVE COMPANIONS

PORTRAITS IN HISTORY

David McCullough

SIMON & SCHUSTER PAPERBACKS
New York   London   Toronto   Sydney

SIMON & SCHUSTER PAPERBACKS
Rockefeller Center
1230 Avenue of the Americas
New York, New York 10020

SIMON & SCHUSTER PAPERBACKS and colophon are
registered trademarks of Simon & Schuster, Inc.
For information about special discounts for bulk purchases,
please contact Simon & Schuster Special Sales:
1-800-456-6798 or business@simonandschuster.com
Designed by Irving Perkins Associates
Manufactured in the United States of America

33 35 37 39 40 38 36 34 32

Library of Congress Cataloging-in-Publication Data is available.

ISBN-13: 978-0-671-79276-3 (pbk)
ISBN-10:   0-671-79276-8 (pbk)

Grateful acknowledgement is made to the following for permission to reprint previously published material:

American Heritage: "The Lonely War of a Good Angry Man," December 1969; "The Unexpected Mrs. Stowe," August 1973; "Steam Road to El Dorado," June 1976; "The Treasure from the Carpentry Shop," December 1979; "I Love Washington" (titled here, "Washington on the Potomac"), April–May 1956.

Audubon: "The Man Who Rediscovered America" (titled here, "Journey to the Top of the World"), September 1973; "The American Adventure of Louis Agassiz," January 1977.

The Brooklyn Museum: "The Builders," from *The Great East River Bridge, 1883–1983,* 1983.

Blair & Ketchum's *Country Journal:* "Cross the Blue Mountain," February 1977.

Geo: "Glory Days in Medora," October 1979.

Life: "Extraordinary Times," 1986, Vol. 9, No. 12, Time Inc.

The New York Times Magazine: "Aviator Authors" (titled here, "Long Distance Vision"), October 12, 1986.

The Saint Louis Art Museum: "Remington," from *Frederic Remington: The Masterworks,* Harry N. Abrams, Inc., 1988.

Smithsonian: "A Rothschild Who Is Known as the Queen of the Fleas" (titled here, "Miriam Rothschild"), June 1985.

Viking Press: "South of Kankakee: A Day with David Plowden," from *An American Crenology* by David Plowden, 1982.

For Rosalee Barnes McCullough

Contents

Introduction

THERE IS a story that goes with the painting of Theodore Roosevelt by John Singer Sargent that hangs in the White House.

Sargent, it is said, had been waiting about the mansion for several days, hoping for a chance to see the president and talk to him about doing his portrait, when one morning the two met unexpectedly as Roosevelt was descending the stairway.

When might there be a convenient time for the president to pose for him, Sargent asked.

"Now!" said the president.

So there he is in the painting, standing at the foot of the stairs, his hand on the newel post. It is a great portrait, capturing more of the subtleties of the Roosevelt personality than any ever done of him.

And it's a good story. Moments come and go, the president was telling the painter. Here is the time, seize it, do your best.

•   •   •

My earliest ambition was to be an artist. When I was ten or so, our art teacher at Linden School in Pittsburgh, Miss Mavis Bridgewater, demonstrated two-point perspective on the blackboard, and it seemed to me a miracle. I don't think I would have been much more amazed had she caused her desk to levitate.

I began to draw and paint. At Yale later, though an English major, I studied under an artist named Dean Keller, who, because of the rather old-fashioned portraits he did (largely for the university of its prominent professors) and his insistence on understanding anatomy, was anathema in a department then dominated by Joseph Albers, the German cubist known for his paintings of squares. I wanted to be a portrait painter.

As a writer I am still drawn to the human subject, to people and their stories, more often than to large current issues or any particular field of academic inquiry. The explorer interests me more than geography, the ichthyologist more than his fish, Theodore Roosevelt before, say, the Progressive Movement.

Nor have I ever been able to disassociate people or stories from their settings, the "background." If character is destiny, so too, I believe, is terrain.

Seeing how the light falls in a marble room on Capitol Hill, or smelling the coal smoke in the air on a winter night in Pennsylvania, helps in making contact with those who were there before in other days. It's a way to find them as fellow human beings, as necessary as the digging you do in libraries.

At times I've not known for certain whether I wanted to go ahead with a story until I have been where it happened.

"The sun was scorching hot and we should have had hats, but we dipped our hands in the water and the farther we went the cooler it got and especially when we hit the rapids," I read now in a letter I wrote to my wife from Panama years ago, after a first reconnaissance of the Chagres River wilderness made in a dugout canoe with two young sons, two Cuna Indians, and an American hydrologist, Frank Robinson, who knew the names of every tree, most birds and insects, and all about the stupendous cycle of Panama rainfall. A day or two in such country goes far in stirring your sympathy and admiration for those intrepid souls, the pioneer builders, who came there in the last century, first to build a railroad.

Surroundings are essential to contemporary subjects no less. To spend time with someone like Miriam Rothschild in the fervently bizarre atmosphere of the family estate north of London, for example, or to follow David Plowden through the cornfields and small towns of Illinois, is for me the only way to see them clearly.

So the portraits here are often figures in a landscape.

Most of these essays were written for magazines. That they might one day be companion pieces in a book was a thought that never occurred at the time. Each was an individual undertaking. Several of them, for reasons personal or professional, had to be done on short notice, "Now," as Roosevelt said. They were produced over a period of nearly twenty years, at very different times in my life, and about subjects as dissimilar as Alexander von Humboldt and Conrad Richter. Two of the stories, one set in

Panama, the other in the Badlands of North Dakota, resulted from research I was doing for books. Another represents a return to a subject I had already covered in a book, but about which I found I had some new things to say. It was written as a way of honoring the 100th birthday of the Brooklyn Bridge.

In the final section, I've included two speeches written for such different occasions as a college commencement in Vermont and the ceremonies celebrating the bicentennial of the United States Congress.

Yet I find my subjects are more closely connected than I knew. Reading these essays again, selecting and arranging them as a book, I am struck by how much they have in common. In my way, I see now, I have been writing about the same kinds of people all along. And I see, too, the extent to which they have revealed the world and times past for me, and things about myself, that I would not have known otherwise.

Because of the ichthyologist, the incomparable Louis Agassiz, I was introduced not only to his world of fish, but to his way of seeing.

"Look at your fish!" Agassiz admonished his students in what for me remains one of the most valuable of all lessons. "Look at your fish!" are the words of the small, framed reminder I've since kept by my desk: discoveries are as likely to be found in material already in hand, before your eyes, as anywhere.

Agassiz was one of the greatest of the great teachers of the nineteenth century. His influence reverberates down to our own day. But then it's fair to say my subjects are nearly all teachers. They are writers, civil engineers, men and women of science, aviators, wives and mothers, politicians. One of them, Frederic Remington, is a painter and sculptor; another, Harry Caudill, is a small-town lawyer; David Plowden is a photographer. Yet each in his or her own way is teaching us to see, and to experience the exhilaration, or magic, or outrage, or understanding they feel from what they see.

"What a grand and solemn spectacle! The very sight of it renewed our strength," writes Humboldt of the moment in 1802 when, exhausted, gasping for air at an elevation of nearly fifteen thousand feet, he and his partner, Aime Bonpland, catch a sudden glimpse through the clouds of the summit of Mount Chimborazo.

"My microscope is my marijuana," says Miriam Rothschild, who in many ways is Humboldt's present-day counterpart.

"I don't think that the men at the top of those enormous corporations are wicked men," observes Harry Caudill as he and I survey the ravages of strip mining in his native Letcher County, Kentucky. "But you know there's not a one of them that has been down here to see things with their own eyes, to see what is going on here. Not one. And yet the decisions they make have everything to do with how we live here."

Harriet Beecher Stowe sees the evil of slavery and sees her duty plain. From the vantage point of the airplane, Charles and Anne Lindbergh and their fellow pioneer aviators, Antoine de Saint-Exupéry and Beryl Markham, begin to understand their place in the large order of things.

•   •   •

Finding my subjects over the years has been mostly a process of one thing leading to another. Reading about Henry Ward Beecher, as a way to understanding what life was like on Brooklyn Heights at the time the Brooklyn Bridge was being built, I came upon his sister Harriet, as described in Constance Mayfield Rourk's vivid book, *The Trumpets of Jubilee*. Reading about early explorations of Central America for background on Panama, I encountered Humboldt for the first time, and research for an article on Humboldt led me to Agassiz, one of whose star students, Nathaniel Southgate Shaler, was Theodore Roosevelt's professor of geology at Harvard. It was to understand Roosevelt and his time in the Badlands that I looked into the life and influence of Remington. And so it has gone.

The research has rarely been dull, for the farther one goes in the pursuit, the more fascinating it becomes, like being on a detective case. Conrad Richter once told me he was seldom happier than when working at a big library table, with books, notes, and old letters all about him. It was later I found out what he meant.

How can I spend so much time on one subject, I am sometimes asked. The answer, of course, is that no subject is ever just one subject, but ten, twenty, more. You never know.

What is your theme, is another familiar question, and I rarely can say, not at least in the early stages of a project. "I can't tell as yet," I have to reply. To find the answer is one of the chief reasons for undertaking the story.

Reading about the lives of such great figures of the nineteenth century as Mrs. Stowe, Agassiz, the Roeblings, one is struck again and again by how much they accomplished in a lifetime. Where did they find the time or energy—if only to write all those letters? Or to keep such diaries? I wonder if perhaps it was because tuning out boredom had not yet been made so easy as in our day, before commercial entertainment took over in American life.

Those I have written about here nearly all led lives of active discovery and right to the last. They are immensely charged, renewed by what they do. Their work and interests are inspiriting forces. Harriet Beecher Stowe felt obliged to make herself useful. But then, I see now, they nearly all do in these stories. With the books they write, their bridges, pictures, their breakthroughs in science, the children they raise, their record journeys, the risks they take, they are the givers of civilization.

But I know the primary reason why I write about them: the great pull after all, is that they are good stories, even the few I don't like, such as the Marquis de Morès. Many of their lives are deeply moving. To me they themselves are often very glamorous, in the old, true sense of the word.

If there is a prevailing, unifying theme, I suppose it is the part courage plays. The exuberant daring of the Humboldt expedition is one kind. The moral resolve of Harry Caudill is another. Young Teddy Roosevelt's determination to remain himself in the Wild West, in the face of ridicule, is another kind still.

Courage, moreover, is communicable. It was not Humboldt alone, but he and Bonpland together, who set off on the Orinoco; not one railroad builder who went into the Panama jungle in the 1850s, but a force of many. She flew as her husband's copilot across thousands of uncharted miles, remembers Anne Lindbergh, knowing sheer terror much of the time. These are brave companions.

·   ·   ·

Every writing task involves new problems, some larger than others. Mainly writing means a great deal of hard thinking, the popular impression notwithstanding. (Paul Weis, who taught philosophy at Yale, once remarked, "I'm not as bright as my students. I find I have to think before I write.") Yet sometimes the very struggle of getting the words down on paper does result in unexpected discoveries or clarifications.

In 1986 I was called by an editor of *Life*. The magazine, he said, would soon be fifty years old and he wanted me to do an essay for a special anniversary issue.

Would I sum up the importance of world history since 1936 in five thousand words?

I could hardly believe he was serious. The world since 1936 indeed! I stalled, said I would have to get back to him.

When I put the phone down and explained what he wanted to my wife, she said quietly, "You must do it."

The article, "Extraordinary Times," different in focus from others here, is included because I think it still stands on its own, for all the tumultuous change since 1986, in Eastern Europe, the Soviet Union, and the Middle East, but also because the experience impressed on me as nothing before had the extent to which the little-known events of a given time, and people who are not in the headlines, can be what matter most in the long run. And the long run is the measure of history.

In writing history, to catch the feeling as well as the "truth" of other times, it is of utmost importance, I believe, to convey the sense that things need not have happened as they did. Life in other times past was never on a track, any more than it is now or ever will be. The past after all is only another name for someone else's present. How would things turn out? They knew no better than we know how things will turn out for us.

The problem, as Thornton Wilder said, "lies in the effort to employ the past tense in such a way that it does not rob those events of their character of having occurred in freedom."

·   ·   ·

It is a shame that history is ever made dry and tedious, or offered as a chronicle almost exclusively of politics, war, and social issues, when, of course, it is the full sweep of human experience: politics, war, and social issues to be sure, but also music, science, religion, medicine, the way things are made, new ideas, high attainments in every field, money, the weather, love, loss, endless ambiguities and paradoxes and small towns you never heard of. History is a spacious realm. There should be no walls.

What history is chiefly about is life, and while there are indeed great, often unfathomable forces in history before which even the most exceptional of individuals seem insignificant, the wonder is how often events turn on a single personality, or the quality called character.

I have been going through some of the research files for the stories that follow, remembering not only the work and where it was done, but much else about my own life at the time. I had ventured into the serious business of the historian as an amateur, and with a growing family to support, I was often near the end of my rope financially. But again and again, there were my subjects to lend encouragement, setting a standard by example. How could I not have taken heart from finding that it was as an amateur that Agassiz did his work on glaciers? Or from the picture of him descending by rope's end into one of the "blue wells" on the Aar and surviving to tell the tale?

These, as I have said, are brave companions, the best of companions. Humboldt never reached the summit of Chimborazo. Agassiz's star faded. Washington Roebling endured the painful effects of his work on the Brooklyn Bridge for the rest of his days. Harry Caudill did not live to see an end to strip mining or poverty in Kentucky.

Yet, as I recognize now, these are all success stories. The key is attitude. I hope the reader will remember what Agassiz says to young William James as they lie sleepless in their hammocks on the deck of a steamer on the Amazon, on still another expedition, and how it was that Simon Willard made his clock and why it keeps ticking.

—David McCullough
West Tisbury, Massachusetts
April 8, 1991

I

PHENOMENA

CHAPTER ONE

Journey to the Top of the World

ON A MORNING in May 1804, there arrived at the White House by Baltimore coach, and in the company of the painter Charles Willson Peale, a visitor from abroad: an aristocratic young German, age thirty-four, a bachelor, occupation scientist and explorer. And like Halley's comet or the white whale or other such natural phenomena dear to the nineteenth century, he would be remembered by all who saw him for the rest of their days.

He had come to pay his respects to the president of the new republic, Thomas Jefferson, a fellow "friend of science," and to tell him something of his recent journeys through South and Central America. For the next several weeks he did little else but talk, while Jefferson, on their walks about the White House grounds; or James Madison, the secretary of state; or the clever Mrs. Madison; or Albert Gallatin, the secretary of the treasury; or those who came to dine with the president or to do business with him, listened in awe.

The young man, they found, was a naturalist, an astronomer, a geographer, a geologist, a botanist, an authority on Indian antiquities, a linguist, an artist—an academy unto himself, as the poet Goethe would say. He was at home in any subject. He had read every book. He had seen things almost impossible to imagine. "We all consider him as a very extraordinary man," Gallatin told his wife, speaking apparently for Jefferson's entire official family, "and his travels, which he intends publishing on his return to Europe, will, I think, rank above any other productions of the kind." He also talked at double the speed of anybody Gallatin had ever met before and would shift suddenly from English, which he spoke superbly, into French or Spanish or German, seemingly unaware of what he was doing, but never hesitating for a word, apparently to the very great confusion of his newfound American friends, Jefferson and the Swiss-born Gallatin not included.

Gallatin, a man not easily impressed, found the extent of the visitor's reading and scientific knowledge astonishing. "I was delighted," he said, "and swallowed more information of various kinds in less than two hours than I had for two years past in all I had read and heard."

In a letter to Jefferson written from Philadelphia a few days earlier, the young man had said, "[I would] love to talk to you about a subject that you have treated so ingeniously in your work on Virginia, the teeth of mammoth, which we too discovered in the Andes." Jefferson had responded immediately and most cordially. "A lively desire will be felt generally to receive the information you will be able to give." In the new capital city, Jefferson wrote, there was "nothing curious to attract the observations of a traveler," which was largely so, save, of course, for Jefferson himself. Upon arrival the young man had found the presidential mansion anything but imposing—crude wooden steps led to the front door, rooms were still unplastered—and at one point he had inadvertently encountered the chief executive sprawled on the floor, wrestling with his grandchildren.

But there they were in Washington for several days, two of the most remarkable men of their time, fellow spirits if ever there were, talking, talking endlessly, intensely, their conversation having quickly ranged far from fossil teeth.

The young man's name was Humboldt, Alexander von Humboldt—Friedrich Wilhelm Karl Heinrich Alexander von Humboldt—or Baron von Humboldt, as he was commonly addressed. He had been born in Berlin on September 14, 1769, the second son of a middle-aged army officer, a minor figure in the court of Frederick the Great, and of a rather solemn, domineering young woman of Huguenot descent who had inherited a sizable fortune. He was a baron in about the way some Southerners are colonels.

William Burwell, Jefferson's private secretary, described him as looking considerably younger than his age, "of small figure, well made, agreeable looks, simple unaffected manners, remarkably sprightly." And Humboldt's passport, issued in Paris in 1798, has him five feet, eight inches tall, with "light-brown hair, gray eyes, large nose, rather large mouth, well-formed chin, open forehead marked by smallpox." However, in a portrait by Peale, done shortly after the trip to see Jefferson, the eyes are as blue as Dutch tiles.

Years later, when the phenomenon of Humboldt had become known the world over, the learned and curious would journey thousands of miles for the chance to see him, and his published works would be taken as the gospel of a new age. He would be regarded as the incomparable high priest of nineteenth-century science—a towering godlike inspiration to such a disparate assortment of individuals as John Charles Frémont, John James Audubon, John Lloyd Stephens, Sir Charles Lyell, Simón Bolívar, W. H. Hudson, William Hickling Prescott, Edward Whymper, Charles Darwin, Louis Agassiz. Darwin, during the voyage of the *Beagle*, would carry with him three inspirational books—the Bible, Milton, and Humboldt.

But at this point the name Humboldt meant very little. The honorary citizenships, the countless decorations, were all still to come. No Pacific Ocean current, no bay or glacier or river had been named for him as yet, no mountains in China. Humboldt, Kansas, and Humboldt, Iowa, were still prairie grass, part of that incomprehensibly vast piece of the continent purchased by Jefferson from Napoleon only the year before and that Jefferson had just sent Meriwether Lewis and William Clark to investigate. So it was the young man himself, not a reputation, and the story he had to tell that captivated everyone. After nearly five years he had returned from one of the great scientific odysseys of all time. It was a journey that would capture the imagination of the age, but that has been strangely forgotten in our own time. It is doubtful that one educated American in ten today could say who exactly Humboldt was or what he did, not even, possibly, in Humboldt, Iowa, or Humboldt, Kansas. Perhaps this is because his travels were through *Spanish* America. Perhaps his extraordinary accomplishments were simply overshadowed by the popular impact of the Lewis and Clark expedition. In any event, his was a journey of enormous scientific consequence (far more so than the Lewis and Clark expedition) and a fascinating adventure by any standards.

•　　•　　•

In the company of a young French medical doctor turned botanist, Aime Bonpland, Humboldt had departed from La Coruña, Spain, in June 1799, on a Spanish frigate, slipping past a British blockade in the dark of night, in the midst of a storm, and carrying with him a unique document from the Spanish government. He and Bonpland had been granted complete freedom to explore—for scientific purposes—any or all of Spain's largely unexplored American colonies; to make astronomical observations, maps; to collect; to go wherever they wished, speak to whomever they wished. The whole arrangement was quite unprecedented (prior to this Spain had rigorously denied any such travels by foreigners), and it had come about quite by chance.

Humboldt, after completing his education and serving as a government inspector of mines in Prussia, had decided to lead his own far-flung scientific expedition. Just where was an open question, but both of his parents had died, with the result that he had become a man of ample private means and was free to do whatever he wished. His impulse had been to go to Egypt, to catch up with Napoleon's troops there. But he and Bonpland (whom he had met by chance in Paris) had proceeded no farther than Spain when Humboldt, during an audience with Charles IV, expressed an interest in His Catholic Majesty's overseas empire. An expedition, to be paid for by Humboldt, was immediately and most unexpectedly sanctioned, and the two young men were on their way.

The ship followed Columbus's route, going first to the Canary Islands, and though it was Humboldt's intention to commence his scientific discovery of the New World at Cuba, the Spanish captain, after an outbreak of typhoid fever on board, decided to put the two explorers ashore at Cumaná, on the coast of present-day Venezuela, or New Granada, as it was then known.

They landed, bag and baggage, on July 16. Their gear included forty-odd scientific instruments, the most versatile and finest available at the time and just the sort of thing Thomas Jefferson would have found fascinating. Included were a tiny, two-inch sextant (a so-called snuffbox sextant), compasses, a microscope, barometers and thermometers that had been standardized with those of the Paris observatory before departure, three different kinds of electrometers, a device for measuring the specific gravity of seawater, telescopes, a theodolite, a Leyden jar, an instrument by which the blueness of the sky could be determined, a large and cumbersome magnetometer, and a rain gauge. Their excitement was enormous. No botanist, no naturalist or scientist of any kind, had ever been there before them. Everything was new, even the stars in the sky. "We are here in a divine country," Humboldt wrote to his brother. "What trees! Coconut trees, fifty to sixty feet high, *Poinciana pulcherrima*, with a foot-high bouquet of magnificent, bright-red flowers; pisang and a host of trees with enormous leaves and scented flowers, as big as the palm of a hand, of which we knew nothing . . . And what colors in birds, fish, even crayfish (sky blue and yellow)! We rush around like the demented; in the first three days we were quite unable to classify anything; we pick up one object to throw it away for the next. Bonpland keeps telling me that he will go mad if the wonders do not cease soon."

And then they were on the move. For three months they explored and mapped the coastal plain, collecting some sixteen hundred plants— palms, orchids, grasses, bamboos—among which they were able to identify six hundred new species. They witnessed a total eclipse, an earthquake, and, on a night in November, a spectacular meteor shower that went on for hours. They paddled up the Apure River to its confluence with the Ori- noco and there commenced what was to be their major effort: they would trace the Orinoco to its source, something no one had done before, and establish that there is a connection, by the Rio Negro, between the Orinoco and the Amazon.

In all—on the Apure, the Orinoco, the Atabapo, the Negro, and Casiquiare—they spent seventy-five days in open boats or canoes, travel- ing an estimated 6,443 miles through one of the most difficult and little- known places on Earth. Sometimes, on the Casiquiare, for example, they could make almost no headway against the current, they and their Indian guides rowing strenuously for fourteen hours to go all of nine miles. The smothering humidity and torrential rains destroyed most of their provi- sions. For weeks they lived on bananas and ants, or an occasional fried monkey.

They went as far as Esmeralda, a tiny mosquito-infested village, which Humboldt put on his map and which, curiously, remains on most every map of South America to this day despite the fact that there is no longer a single trace of the place. By September 1, 1800, when they again reached Cumaná, they had beheld, examined, sketched, collected, and classified more plants than any botanist before them (some twelve thousand, by their count). They had gathered rock samples, fishes and reptiles placed in phials, the skins of animals—enough in fact to keep Humboldt occupied for the rest of his life. Yet they had been barely able to collect a tenth of what they had seen, and the humidity and insects had destroyed more than a third of what they had in their plant boxes.

They themselves, miraculously, held up very well. For two such thor- oughly inexperienced, ill-prepared young Europeans to have plunged ahead as they did, knowing nothing of life in the jungle, virtually unequipped by modern standards, had been both amazingly presumptuous and reckless. Bonpland did not even know how to swim. Yet they withstood the broiling climate and every other kind of tropical discomfort with little more to protect them than their own "cheerful character," as Humboldt noted. "With some gaiety of temper," he said, "with feelings of mutual good will, and with a vivid taste for the majestic grandeur of these vast valleys of rivers, travelers easily supported evils that become habitual." The mosquitoes he described as being an atmosphere unto themselves, covering the face, the hands, filling the nostrils. Invariably, he said, they "occasion coughing and sneezing whenever any attempt is made to speak in the open air"—terrible punishment for someone who so loved to talk.

To avoid the suffocating heat, he and Bonpland often started the day at two in the morning. Their only salvation from the mosquitoes was to bury themselves in sand.

Toward the end of their journey back down the Orinoco, both men came down with typhoid fever. Bonpland very nearly died, but Humboldt, who had been troubled by ill health most of his life, made a rapid recovery and except for that one instance remained perfectly fit throughout, healthier than at any time in his life. He seemed made for the tropics. The days were never long enough. His spirits soared. This for him was life at its fullest and best. "I could not possibly have been placed in circumstances more highly favorable for study and exploration," he wrote to his brother. "I am free from the distractions constantly arising in civilized life from social claims. Nature offers unceasingly the most novel and fascinating objects for learning."

He believed, this brilliant, determined young man being eaten alive by mosquitoes, that there is a harmony of nature, that man is a part of that harmony, and that if he himself could observe things closely enough, collect enough—if he *knew* enough—then the forces that determine that harmony would become apparent.

Nothing seems to have escaped his notice. His physical energy was boundless—incredible really. Literally everything seems to have interested him. He sketched, he made astronomical observations, magnetic observations. He gathered up rocks and minerals and Indian artifacts. Above all, he kept the most copious notes imaginable—on tides, soils, petroleum, chocolate, rubber; on missionaries; on the physique of the Carib Indian, the anatomy of shellfish; on turtle eggs, howling monkeys, alligators (one found sunning itself on a sandbank on the Orinoco measured twenty-two feet); on vampire bats and poison darts and electric eels (wonder of wonders); on the nighttime cacophony of the jungle and the sudden silence imposed by the roar of the jaguar (an observation that would intrigue Audubon); on a tribe of Indians, the Otomaco, that overcame annual seasons of famine by eating a particular kind of dirt; on a dark, ugly nocturnal bird called the guacharo (the oilbird), a bird about the size of a chicken, which he encountered in screeching hordes inside a gloomy grotto; on the ravages of termites; on an exotic tree that gave milk (it was actually an *Artocarpus*, which had been brought to America by the Spanish only a score of years earlier); on the great grass fires that lit up the night on the llanos, the sweeping plains that reach southward from Caracas; on Indian legends, Indian diet, Indian apathy, Indian languages. (W. H. Hudson, the great English author whose classic *Green Mansions* is set in the same general locale, would tell a story that Humboldt acquired a parrot from which he was able to produce the vocabulary of an extinct tribe, and that Humboldt later took the bird back to Paris, where it became something of a sensation. Humboldt makes no mention of such a bird in his own writings, but he did include the vocabulary in question in his discussion of comparative native tongues.)

Few Europeans had ever responded with such fervor to an equatorial wilderness as Alexander von Humboldt. Sir Walter Raleigh, two hundred years earlier, on his own famous and abortive expedition up the Orinoco, wrote that he had never seen a more beautiful country and described "all fair green grass, deer crossing our path, the birds toward evening singing on every side a thousand different tunes, herons of white, crimson, and carnation perching on the riverside . . ." Humboldt had read every word Raleigh had written, and his response was no less to a world that had changed not in the slightest in all the intervening time. Often he found himself emotionally overwhelmed by his surroundings, and his notebook entries were set down with a depth of feeling that had little to do with science. There was, for example, the moment on April 15 when he and his party first reached the mouth of the Apure and beheld the Orinoco:

> In leaving the Rio Apure we found ourselves in a country presenting a totally different aspect. An immense plain of water stretched before us like a lake, as far as we could see. White-topped waves rose to the height of several feet, from the conflict of the breeze and the current. The air resounded no longer with the piercing cries of herons, flamingos, and spoonbills, crossing in long files from one shore to the other. . . . All nature appeared less animated. Scarcely could we discover in the hollows of the waves a few large crocodiles, cutting obliquely by the help of their long tails the surface of the agitated waters. The horizon was bounded by a zone of forests, which nowhere reached so far as the bed of the river. A vast beach, constantly parched by the heat of

the sun, desert and bare as the shores of the sea, resembled at a distance, from the effect of the mirage, pools of stagnant water. These sandy shores, far from fixing limits of the river, render them uncertain, by enlarging or contracting them alternately, according to the variable action of the solar rays.

In these scattered features of the landscape, in this character of solitude and greatness, we recognized the course of the Orinoco, one of the most majestic rivers of the New World.

Or there was this extraordinary description of the jungle at midday:

How vivid is the impression produced by the calm of nature, at noon, in these burning climates! The beasts of the forests retire to the thickets; the birds hide themselves beneath the foliage of the trees, or in the crevices of the rocks. Yet, amidst this apparent silence, when we lend an attentive ear, we hear a dull vibration, a continual murmur, a hum of insects, filling, if you may use the expression, all the lower strata of the air. Nothing is better fitted to make man feel the extent and power of organic life. Myriads of insects creep upon the soil, and flutter round the plants parched by the heat of the sun. A confused noise issues from every bush, from the decayed trunks of trees, from the clefts of rocks, and from the ground undermined by lizards [and] milli-pedes. . . . These are so many voices proclaiming to us that all nature breathes; and that under a thousand different forms life is diffused throughout the cracked and dusty soil, as well as the bosom of the waters, and in the air that circulates around us.

"This aspect of animated nature," he would add, "in which man is noth-ing, has something in it strange and sad."

It was such passages that would so stir the soul of the nineteenth century, when they appeared in Humboldt's *Personal Narrative* of the expedition.

Darwin would confide that Humboldt's descriptions of the tropics, read over and over again during his youth, had inspired his entire career. Darwin also liked Humboldt's account of an earthquake at Caracas enough to have lifted some of it, pretty much intact, for his *Voyage of the Beagle*.

From Venezuela, Humboldt and Bonpland sailed for Cuba, arriving at Havana and the comforts of civilization in November of 1800. Humboldt wandered about Havana's botanical garden, made more maps (the first accurate maps of Cuba), and observed with sinking heart the institution of slavery ("no doubt the greatest of all evils that afflict humanity"). He and Bonpland also divided up their collections three ways, shipping one part to France, another to Germany, and leaving the third with friends in Havana.

Their anxiety over the safety of these treasures was very great indeed, and one gets the impression that Humboldt now had certain misgivings about their own chances of survival. "It is really quite uncertain, almost unlikely," he wrote, "that both of us, Bonpland and myself, will ever return alive."

The following spring they sailed for the coast of present-day Colombia, to the mouth of the Magdalena, by which, for the next fifty-odd days, they headed south again, deep inland for hundreds of miles against the current, as far as an outpost called Honda. Before them stood the cordillera of the Andes. They left the river and went overland to Bogotá, where a brightly dressed cavalcade of distinguished citizens rode out to escort them into town.

All told they spent nearly two years in Colombia, Ecuador, and Peru. From Bogotá they went over the Andes on foot, picking the more difficult of two possible routes. They were in the Andes, crossing and recrossing, from September 1801 until October 1802, and they must have made a picturesque caravan, with their guides and mules and scientific instruments. Mountains were measured, valleys sounded, the distribution of vegetation traced on windswept upland slopes. Humboldt was struck by the distinct variations in plant life, according to elevation. The vegetation on the mountains was stratified, he found, and that stratification, he concluded, was dependent on soil, temperature, and weather conditions. There were vertical zones, in other words, and these were characterized at a glance by their plant life. It was a new concept and an extremely important one. As a latter-day biographer was to write, "He began to see what nobody had understood clearly before him: that life's forms and their grouping with one another are conditioned by physical factors in their environment, that atmospheric and geologic conditions need to be known if we are to learn the meaning behind organic life. As in his student days he had described rocks and minerals in relation to plants, he now realized more fully that to classify and identify counted for little unless you understood how to relate such information to integrated natural processes."

•   •   •

He would be called the second Columbus. He had rediscovered America, it would be said. He was also seeing relationships and interrelationships between the Earth and life on Earth in a way that others before him had failed to do. So it would be perfectly fitting also to say that he was among the first ecologists.

They arrived at Quito, Ecuador, on January 6, 1802, and spent the next several months sorting out the new collections acquired along the way. In May, Humboldt and an Indian whose name is unknown climbed an active volcano called Pichincha, something only one man had done before as near as Humboldt could determine. Then on June 9, 1802, he, Bonpland, a number of Indians, and a young Spanish naturalist named Carlos Montufar, who had joined the expedition in Quito, set out to climb Chimborazo, the extinct, snow-capped volcano, elevation 20,561 feet, the highest mountain in Ecuador and then thought to be the highest mountain anywhere on Earth.

Humboldt and Bonpland had by now been in the mountains long enough to know what they were about and to be in exceptional physical condition. They were very likely the finest mountaineers in the world, since mountaineering as a sport and the whole philosophical concept of mountain "conquering" had yet to dawn on the nineteenth-century mind. But again, as on the Orinoco, they set off with little in the way of equipment as we know it, no special clothing, and with little or no knowledge of the mountain itself. Yet "by dint of extreme exertion and considerable patience" they very nearly made it all the way to the top.

How Humboldt and his companions went up, the route they took, is not at all clear from his account. But in many places, he writes, the ridge was no wider than eight or ten inches. On their left a snow-covered precipice shone like glass, on their right "a fearful abyss" dropped away a thousand feet or more. "At certain places where it was very steep, we were obliged to use both hands and feet, and the edges of the rock were so sharp that we were painfully cut, especially on our hands." Much of the time they were shrouded in mist so thick they were unable even to see their own feet. Then all at once the air would clear for an instant and the dome-shaped summit would stand out before them, gleaming in the sunshine. "What a grand and solemn spectacle! The very sight of it renewed our strength."

At 15,000 feet Bonpland captured a butterfly. At 15,600 feet the Indians, with one exception, refused to go any farther. At 16,600 feet Humboldt spotted an ordinary housefly. Above the snow line, at about 16,900 feet, rock lichens were the only sign of life. The next reading was taken at 17,300 feet, at a spot where the ridge was just barely wide enough to set up the barometer and two of them could stand side by side in safety.

They were stopped finally by an impassable ravine. Nauseated by the thin air, they were all so dizzy they could barely stand. Their lips and gums were bleeding. The time, Humboldt says, was an hour after noon. Again the barometer was set up. The temperature, they found, was three degrees below freezing, which both Humboldt and Bonpland, "from our long residence in the tropics," found "quite benumbing." The altitude where they stood was 19,286 feet, higher than anyone had ever been before, even in a balloon.

They had attained the top of the world, they thought. For Humboldt it was a supreme, indescribable moment. Nearly thirty years later, in 1828, when the surpassing magnitude of the Himalayas, long a subject of much conjecture, was verified by the first reliable instrument surveys, Humboldt was noticeably stunned. To a friend he wrote, "All my life I prided myself on the fact that of all mortals I had reached the highest point on Earth."

Chimborazo itself would not be climbed for another seventy-eight years. In 1880, Edward Whymper, the British mountaineer and artist, the first man to climb the Matterhorn (in 1865), would reach the top of Chimborazo, following what he figured to be Humboldt's route. That Humboldt had come as far as he did, Whymper found extraordinary. Darwin, after a brief hike in the Chilean Andes, at an elevation of about 13,000 feet, would write that it was "incomprehensible" to him how Humboldt had done it.

Humboldt and the others in his party descended from Chimborazo in a great hurry—the first 3,600 feet in all of an hour, according to Humboldt, a claim Edward Whymper would declare preposterous. And like our own men on the moon, they busily gathered up all the rocks they could carry. "We foresaw that in Europe," Humboldt said, "we should frequently be asked for a fragment from Chimborazo." Whether he had such a memento with him when he arrived at the White House is not known.

From Chimborazo the party pushed farther south, into the valley of the upper Amazon. Then they were climbing again into the rarefied air of the Andes, traveling now, on occasion, along the "wonderful remains of the Inca Roads" and taking, as it happens, about the same route as the present-day Pan-American Highway. The Inca Road and the thought of the effort and ingenuity it represented left the two Europeans feeling strangely humbled. Nothing built by the Romans had ever struck Humboldt as so imposing, and at one point, according to his calculations, *this* road was at an elevation of thirteen thousand feet. At Paramo and Cajamarca they examined Inca ruins. No ignorant savages were these, he concluded.

He was immensely taken, too, by the giant condors that circled overhead, high above all the summits of the Andes. How was it possible—physiologically—he wondered, for a creature to fly in circles for hours in air so thin, then descend all at once to the level of the sea, "thus passing through all gradations of climate."

Then, on a western slope of the Andes, they saw the sea. The sky brightened suddenly, as a sharp southwest wind came up, clearing the mist and revealing an immense bowl of very dark blue sky. The entire western slope of the cordillera, as far as the eye could carry, was spread at their feet. "Now for the first time," he wrote, "we had our view of the Pacific. We saw it distinctly in the glitter of a vast light, an immeasurable expanse of ocean." Humboldt was so excited that for once he forgot to take a barometric reading.

On October 23, 1802, they arrived at Lima, where they spent two uneventful months. The collections were carefully gone over and repacked; Humboldt made notes on the local use of guano, the fertilizing properties of which were still unknown in Europe. In late December they sailed north for Mexico, and it was during this voyage, as they skirted the shores of Peru, that Humboldt took soundings, temperature readings and the like, in that icy, north-flowing Pacific current so rich in marine organisms that now bears his name. He would insist always that he had simply studied it, never discovered it, that it had been known to sailors and fishermen for centuries; and on his own maps he would label it the Peruvian Current. He could protest as much as he liked, however. The Humboldt Current it would be, and ironically, it is probably the thing for which he is now best known.

They spent a year in Mexico, from March 1803, when they landed at Acapulco, until March 1804, when they sailed from Veracruz for Havana again. It had been a long time since Mexico was a wilderness, and there was little of the natural splendor and mystery of the Orinoco or of the Andes to entice the explorers. But Humboldt's zest for the place seems to have been none the less for all that. He was seldom still. He worked mainly on a map that, once finished, would be the finest thing ever done on Mexico until then. So at variance and imperfect were most maps of the day that the position of Mexico City, for example, differed as much as three hundred miles from one map to another. His was not only geographically accurate, being based on astronomical observations, but would include quantities of political, economic, and ethnological information.

He also studied silver mining, climate, volcanic action, meteorological phenomena. And again he was absorbed in remnants of the pre-Columbian past. With Bonpland in tow, he took a day's ride out to Teotihuacán and the two of them stood spellbound before that ancient temple city. He made measurements of the great pyramids and later sketched Aztec codices and the Aztec calendar stone. Humboldt was, in fact, the first European to sense the scale and greatness of America's ancient civilizations, to take their religious traditions seriously, and his subsequent writings on the subject would open an entire new world for scholars, inspiring, in particular, such latter-day giants in the field as Stephens, who discovered the Maya temples of the Yucatán, and Prescott, author of *The History of the Conquest of Mexico.*

Humboldt and Bonpland stayed only a short while at Havana when they stopped there the second time. After gathering up the collections they had left for safekeeping, they sailed for Philadelphia, where Charles Willson Peale showed them about his amazing museum of natural history, set up in Independence Hall, where now stood, among numerous other curiosities, a mammoth, the first fossil skeleton ever mounted in America.

There was a banquet in Humboldt's honor at Peale's museum, attended by Alexander Wilson, William Bartram, and, among others, a young guest brought by Wilson, John Bachman, then just fourteen years old, who was to be Audubon's great friend and collaborator (on the three-volume *Viviparous Quadrupeds of North America*). Then came the visit to Washington, followed by a brief trip with Jefferson to Monticello, where their conversations continued during more long walks in the gathering heat of the Virginia summer. A famous lifelong friendship had been founded.

On August 3, 1804, Humboldt and Bonpland arrived at Bordeaux, causing a great commotion, since their death by yellow fever had been widely reported some time earlier. They had been gone five years. In addition to all their instruments and Humboldt's journals and record books, they had brought with them "forty-two boxes, containing an herbal of six thousand equinoctial plants, seeds, shells, insects, and what had hitherto never been brought to Europe, geological specimens from the Chimborazo, New Granada, and the banks of the river of the Amazons." It was a very different kind of loot from the New World.

•   •   •

But the journals and the collections were only part of what had been accomplished, only a beginning. Humboldt would spend the next thirty-odd years and virtually all his personal fortune publishing thirty monumental volumes under the general title *Voyages aux Régions Equinoctiales du Nouveau Continent, Fait Dans Les Années 1799 à 1804.* These colossal works were issued in folio and quarto size and contained well over a thousand illustrations and maps, many of them hand-colored. Humboldt did most of the text, but others, specialists of one kind or another, were also enlisted, among them Georges de Cuvier, the zoologist. The books appeared between 1807 and 1839. The complete set cost somewhere in the neighborhood of $2,000. How much the entire enterprise cost is impossible to say, since Humboldt kept secret all his expenses, as well as the total number of books published. The one available figure is for paper, plates, and printing, which came to $226,000.

But Humboldt also produced *Views of Nature* (1807), *Political Essay on the Kingdom of New Spain* (1811), and the very popular *Personal Narrative of Travels to the Equinoctial Regions of the New Continent*, which appeared in French first, then English, and in a variety of different editions starting in 1815. The *Personal Narrative* was a smashing publishing success and made his name known everywhere. The overall effect of his writing and the extent of his influence were enormous and in a few instances had some interesting consequences.

The *Personal Narrative*, to give one example, included a long, detailed discussion of a future ship canal connecting the Atlantic and Pacific somewhere on the Central American isthmus—the first such study ever presented in print. Humboldt, during his travels, had never set foot anywhere on the isthmus, and this he plainly acknowledged, but he was taken as the irrefutable voice of authority all the same. He named five likely routes for a canal, and of these he thought Nicaragua the most suitable, everything considered, with the result that his opinion and his name would be used to support one Nicaragua canal scheme after another throughout the rest of the nineteenth century and right up until the spring of 1902, when the United States Senate by an extremely narrow margin decided instead on Panama.

Some of what he wrote was nonsense, based on hearsay or wild guesswork. He was completely taken in by stories told in the Andes of live fish being spewed out of an erupting volcano. He reckoned the Rocky Mountains to be perhaps 3,500 feet high. But many of his calculations, such as the length of the Orinoco, were uncannily accurate. He also made some astonishing, educated guesses that put him years ahead of his time. It had long been thought, for example, that there is a difference between the levels of the Atlantic and the Pacific. The Pacific was believed to be as much as twenty feet higher, and this supposedly would cause overwhelming problems should a canal ever be opened between the two oceans. But from his own observations, Humboldt was convinced there was no difference in levels—only in the size and timing of the tides. Not until the 1850s, during the surveying of the Panama Railroad, was the issue settled by American engineers. Humboldt was proven to be quite correct.

There are also passages in the *Personal Narrative* substantiating the idea that Humboldt must be ranked among the earliest ecologists. In his speculations on a tide-level canal he shows himself to be deeply and uniquely concerned about the effect of such a channel on the whole pattern of the great ocean currents. But even more pointed, more remarkable, considering when it was written, is something he wrote after examining a lake in Venezuela, a lake that had been mysteriously declining, even though it had no visible outlet. The answer to the riddle, Humboldt said, was not in the lake but in what man was doing to the surrounding countryside:

> By felling trees that cover the tops and sides of the mountains, men in every climate prepare at once two calamities for future generations: the want of fuel and a scarcity of water. . . . When forests are destroyed, as they are everywhere in America by the European planters with an imprudent precipitation, the springs are entirely dried up or become less abundant. The beds of the rivers, remaining dry during a part of the year, are converted into torrents whenever great rains fall on the heights. The sward and moss disappear with the brushwood from the sides of the mountains, the waters falling in rain are no longer impeded in their course; and instead of slowly augmenting the level of the rivers by progressive filtrations, they furrow during heavy showers the sides of the hills, bear down the loosened soil, and form those sudden inundations that devastate the country. Hence it results that the destruction of the forests, the want of permanent springs, and the existence of torrents are three phenomena closely connected together.

Humboldt's books were praised on both sides of the Atlantic. Louis Agassiz was to remark that a walk through the largest botanical garden would hardly be more impressive than an examination of the Humboldt plates. But the Spanish American odyssey had resulted in still more. Major contributions had been made to natural science, to man's knowledge of the Earth and its life systems. Humboldt had been the first to recognize the essential relationships that unite the physical features of the planet, the laws of climate for which he originated the system of isothermal lines (his term) that has been accepted as a standard concept for so long that few remember who started it; the distribution of vegetation over the Earth according to climate and elevation (the basis of plant ecology). He had laid the foundations for modern descriptive geography. He had drawn the first geological sections (in Mexico). He had made vital observations concerning the Earth's magnetism, volcanism, and the role it plays in mountain building. Perhaps most important of all, he and Bonpland had demonstrated how relatively little had been known of the richness and variety of life on Earth, the infinite abundance of life's forms, and how infinitely much more there was to know.

•   •   •

Humboldt lived long enough to see most of his ideas become old hat, and he concluded toward the end that his chief contribution had been to influence younger men. The young Latin American intellectual Simón Bolívar had sought him out in Rome one year to talk about political freedom. John Charles Frémont, who regarded Humboldt as a god, had gone off exploring and sprinkled Humboldt's name all over the map of Nevada. John Bachman would say that his own interest in natural history began with meeting Humboldt at the dinner at Peale's museum. An intense young Englishman named Charles Lyell, who was to become the great geologist, wrote after a long interview, "There are few heroes who lose so little by being approached as Humboldt."

Most impressive of all perhaps is the case of Louis Agassiz, who as a struggling young zoologist in Paris received from Humboldt not only encouragement and guidance, but a donation of a thousand francs to assist in the publication of his initial work on fishes. "How he examined me," Agassiz was to write later, describing a dinner with Humboldt in a Paris restaurant, "and how much I learned in that short time! How to work, what to do, and what to avoid, how to live, how to distribute my time, what methods of study to pursue."

In 1869, in Boston, on the 100th anniversary of Humboldt's birth, Agassiz, by then America's most renowned naturalist, would recount in a long speech the incredible life of his mentor, the monumental productivity right up until the end, the trip to the Urals in 1829, the historic series of lectures in Berlin, the friendship with Goethe, the new career in politics as an adviser to the Prussian king, the keen, relentless observation of the natural world that lasted more than seventy years. "But Humboldt is not only an observer," Agassiz would declare, "not only a physicist, a geographer, a geologist of matchless power and erudition, he knows that nature has its attraction for the soul of man; that however uncultivated, man is impressed by the great phenomena amid which he lives; that he is dependent for his comforts and the progress of civilization upon the world that surrounds him."

The final work, the master work, the grand summing up, was something called *Cosmos*. It was to contain all Humboldt knew—of art, nature, history, all branches of science—portraying as never before the grand harmonies of the Earth and universe. He wished to convey the excitement of science to the intelligent nonscientific reader. He had been thinking about such a work for fifty years. He could not accept what he called the narrow-minded, sentimental view that nature loses its magic, "the charm of its mysteries," by a study of its forces.

The first of five volumes appeared in 1845, when Humboldt was seventy-six. (Jefferson by now had been in his grave at Monticello for nearly twenty years.) It was an even greater sensation than his *Personal Narrative*. By 1851, eighty thousand copies had been sold. Indeed, *Cosmos* was one of the publishing events of the age, like *Uncle Tom's Cabin*. It stirred a whole new generation, in America particularly. It popularized natural science as nothing had before and made Humboldt a household word.

He was venerated in America as few Europeans have ever been. "I came to Berlin," wrote Bayard Taylor, the American essayist, near the end of Humboldt's life, "not to visit its museums and galleries, its operas, its theaters, . . . but for the sake of seeing and speaking with the world's greatest living man—Alexander von Humboldt." Emerson was to call him "one of those wonders of the world, like Aristotle . . . who appear from time to time, as if to show us the possibilities of the human mind."

Humboldt died on May 6, 1859. He was in his ninetieth year and still at work, on the final volume of *Cosmos*. He had never returned to Spanish America, unlike Bonpland, who, after serving for a time as the head of the Empress Josephine's gardens, left Paris for South America, where he finished out his days. But for all the years that had passed, for all the honors bestowed upon him, for all the changes he had seen, Humboldt never regarded their epic journey as anything other than the central experience of his life. Once, in the last year of his life, when there appeared to be very little left of the young man who had posed for Peale so long before, Humboldt sat for still one more, final portrait. He absolutely would not wear any of his decorations, he said, but then he quietly mentioned to the artist that it would be quite all right to include Chimborazo in the background.

CHAPTER TWO

The American Adventure
of Louis Agassiz

THROUGHOUT HIS extraordinary career Louis Agassiz was a man of large plans and boundless energy, a spirit emboldened by noble undertakings. He was a pioneer, a worker. And these, it ought to be said at the start, were not the least of the reasons why he loomed so large in the estimate of our forebears and why so much that was painful—the charge of demagoguery, the bitterness over Darwin—would be forgotten in time, or at least left unsaid.

At the age of twenty-one, writing from Munich, where he was studying to become a medical doctor, he had declared to his father, a provincial Swiss pastor: "I wish it may be said of Louis Agassiz that he was the first naturalist of his time, a good citizen, and a good son, beloved of those who knew him. I feel in myself the strength of a whole generation." The letter was dated February 14, 1829, and that same year, still at the University of Munich, he had undertaken his first important work, a study of Brazilian fish, largely because, as he said, it was so immense a task. In Paris later, at the Museum of Natural History (the Jardin des Plantes), with the blessing and counsel of the great Georges Cuvier, he undertook his vast, illustrated *Recherches sur les Poissons Fossiles*, at a time when fewer than a dozen generic types of fossil fish had been named and he was all of twenty-four.

Cuvier, like others to come, warned against overwork. Alexander von Humboldt, who too had perceived amazing resources in the young man, cautioned against spreading oneself too thin. Having attained, with Humboldt's help, a professorship of natural history at Neuchâtel, Switzerland, Agassiz suddenly had turned his attention to Alpine glaciers.

It was Agassiz, at age thirty-three, who first presented to the world the awesome vision of an ancient age of ice. Others had noted the movement of existing glaciers and the consequent disturbances to the landscape, but Agassiz pictured a time past when all of northern Europe lay buried beneath "a colossal ice field," and thus, he contended, numerous geologic mysteries had at last been solved. His immediate plan was for extended, orderly glacial research, something entirely new.

Everything that he undertook had to be done on a grand, heroic scale. His glacial studies included a harrowing solo descent by rope 120 feet into one of the crystal blue "wells" of the glacier of Aar and a successful ascent of the Jungfrau. His publishing projects—the pioneering, two-volume *Etudes sur les Glaciers*, for example, which appeared in 1840—involved the combined efforts of a dozen or more artists, lithographers, and fellow naturalists, whom he took it upon himself to feed, house, finance, and inspirit with his own particular methods of field study. When debts mounted at his headquarters-home-laboratory at Neuchâtel, when his marriage became a shambles, the solution was an overseas expedition. He would go to the United States, enlarge his horizons, meet everyone who mattered, add to his glacial studies, resolve the financial crises with a series of public lectures—all on his own and all in no more than a few months.

And thus it was in 1846 that he embarked on the very different new life which, ironically, had never been part of his plans. He was almost forty. His major contributions to science, as such things usually are judged, were also behind him. Prolific as he was to remain, nothing published afterward would come up to the earlier works; there was to be no further daring leap of the imagination to compare with his glacial vision.

Yet, as a colleague was to write years later, "A great adventure it turned out to be, lasting until death, and one that put America permanently in his debt."

•   •   •

What he became in the New World was the great proselytizer of the natural sciences, a hero, possibly the most invigorating and influential voice ever heard in American education. He would be called "nature's flaming apostle," the man who first made science a national cause. His popularity was unprecedented, instantaneous, and it swept him off his feet. It would be thirteen years before he returned to Europe, and then only for a brief visit.

For weeks at sea, struggling to learn English, he memorized whole sentences that he repeated to anyone on board who would listen.

He reached Boston in October and spent the first three or four weeks traveling up and down the East Coast, as far south as Washington. He saw Benjamin Silliman at Yale (the "patriarch of science in America," as he noted); James Dwight Dana, also of Yale, who was Silliman's son-in-law and the most promising young naturalist in the country; Joseph Henry, professor of physical sciences at Princeton, who would shortly be named the first head of the new Smithsonian Institution; Dr. Samuel George Morton of Philadelphia, a physician and naturalist; Frederick Ernst Melsheimer, the entomologist, who wrote privately that Agassiz, "this big geologico-everythingo-French-Swiss gun," was really quite a likable fellow.

In New York he conferred with William C. Redfield, the meteorologist; at Albany, with the noted geologist and paleontologist James Hall; while much of the journey he was accompanied by Asa Gray of Harvard, a botanist of "indefatigable zeal."

But then none whom he had met was deficient in either zeal or knowledge, he wrote to his mother. "In both they seem to compete with us, and in ardor and activity they even surpass most of our savants." At Philadelphia, Dr. Morton had assembled no less than six hundred human skulls, of Indians mostly, a collection, Agassiz declared, that alone was worth the trip to America.

What a people, he exclaimed elsewhere in the letter. "What a country is this!" The train from Boston had carried him "with the swiftness of lightning" through dazzling autumn scenery. Ancient moraines and transported boulders, all the telltale tracks of the glaciers, were everywhere to be seen, "literally covering the country." On Long Island Sound, between New Haven and New York, the flocks of ducks and gulls rising in advance of his steamer were greater than any he had ever beheld. He had traveled the "magnificent" Hudson River, which yielded fish by the barrel for his studies.

The first public appearance, his American debut, was made back in Boston in December of 1846. Through the British geologist Charles Lyell, Agassiz's most important convert to the glacial theory, a series of lectures had been arranged with the Lowell Institute, a liberally endowed program of "free lectures of the highest type." As Lowell Institute speakers, Silliman, Lyell, and Gray already had distinguished themselves before large public gatherings and earned fees three times what was customary elsewhere.

He spoke "without notes and from a full brain," as Asa Gray remarked, and he was a sensation. Silliman, until then the unchallenged popularizer of science, came on from New Haven just to hear him. Upward of three thousand people turned out, night after night, even in the most difficult weather, and sat spellbound in the huge hall. He was such a triumph that each lecture had to be given again for a second audience. "Never was Agassiz's power as a teacher, or the charm of his personal presence more evident," his American wife was to write.

His subject, the theme he was to expound upon again and again in times to come, was "the great plan of creation," life on Earth from the smallest radiated animal to the ultimate vertebrate, man. He stood alone on the platform, a piece of chalk in hand, a small blackboard his only prop, talking rapidly and often drawing on the board as he talked. His English still was inadequate, but the long pauses, as he searched for the right word, seemed to add appreciably to the effect he had on the audience. The pauses, we are told, "enlisted their sympathy," as meantime the chalk went swiftly on, producing drawings "so graphic that the spoken word was hardly missed." He would lead his listeners through the successive phases of insect development, for example, until, with a few sudden strokes, a superb "winged creature stood forth on the blackboard, almost as if it had burst then and there from the chrysalis." The audience would break into applause, then moan aloud as he wiped the board clean, to proceed to the next subject.

More appearances followed, in Boston and other cities. He charmed everybody, layman and scientist alike. In six months he had earned nearly $6,000 (about $60,000 in today's money). The timing of his entrance into the mainstream of American life had been perfect. The country was in the throes of an educational awakening. It was the heyday of the lyceum, the nationwide movement to increase "the general diffusion" of learning with public lectures. In Massachusetts alone there were well over a hundred local lyceums, of which the Lowell Institute was the largest and best known. Libraries were being established in one community after another, even in factories. The first normal schools, schools for training teachers, had been founded in an effort to raise standards in education.

Popular interest in science, moreover, and especially the study of nature, was sharply on the rise, as more and more new theories and discoveries appeared to challenge Biblical versions of creation.

It was from the people of America that he drew his greatest inspiration, Agassiz said. He sensed something new beginning on this distant continent. "Naturalist that I am," he explained in the letter to his mother, "I cannot but put the people first." Their look, like his own, was "wholly toward the future."

His change in plans, the decision to stay, came one year after his arrival, in September 1847, when he was offered the chair of natural history at the Lawrence Scientific School, an institution newly established at Harvard partly for the purpose of keeping him in the United States.

Harvard at this point numbered less than four hundred students. Harvard professors "drudged along in a dreary humdrum sort of way" (we read in the recollections of Charles Francis Adams II) and taught virtually everything by rote. Students had no say in the subjects they studied. The classics held the supreme place of honor; science was something to be memorized in fourteen weeks. No one was expected to enjoy any of it.

Agassiz, by dramatic contrast, was a man of insuperable good cheer and apparently boundless energy. He was open, opinionated. He was never dull. "Harvard," he said, "is a respectable high school where they teach the dregs of education."

In appearance, he was still very much in his prime, a physically powerful-looking, handsome man, about five feet ten inches tall, with heavy shoulders, large expressive hands, and a "superb" head that summoned euphoric postulations from the phrenologists. Longfellow, after meeting him at a dinner party, wrote of "the bright, beaming face" and later observed, "Agassiz seems to be a great favorite with the ladies."

"His eyes were the feature of his face," one such lady would recall. "They were of a beautiful bright brown, full of tenderness, of meaning . . . I think there was never but one pair of eyes such as Professor Louis Agassiz's!"

Emerson, seeing the new professor on a train, was surprised by how much he resembled a successful politician.

Agassiz strolled through Harvard Yard enjoying a cigar when to smoke in the Yard was considered a grave offense. He refused to limit his wardrobe to the traditional professorial black. He prepared no syllabus. He required no entrance examinations. His students were accepted purely on whether he liked them, which meant that he took just about everyone who applied, including a large number who never could have qualified according to the standard Harvard requirements. Nor, unlike his contemporaries, did he see any reason for excluding young women. He "came into this puritan society like a warm glow in a chilly room," Charles W. Eliot, Harvard's famous president, would remember fondly. "He was a revolutionary spirit . . . an exception to all our rules."

Most unorthodox of all, and crucial as time would tell, was his manner of teaching. He intended, he said, to teach students to see—to observe and compare—and he intended to put the burden of study on them. Probably he never said what he is best known for, "Study nature, not books," or not in those exact words. But such certainly was the essence of his creed, and for his students the idea was firmly implanted by what they would afterward refer to as "the incident of the fish."

His initial interview at an end, Agassiz would ask the student when he would like to begin. If the answer was now, the student was immediately presented with a dead fish—usually a very long dead, pickled, evil-smelling specimen—personally selected by "the master" from one of the wide-mouthed jars that lined his shelves. The fish was placed before the student in a tin pan. He was to look at the fish, the student was told, whereupon Agassiz would leave, not to return until later in the day, if at all.

Samuel Scudder, one of the many from the school who would go on to do important work of their own (his in entomology), described the experience as one of life's turning points.

> In ten minutes I had seen all that could be seen in that fish. . . . Half an hour passed—an hour—another hour; the fish began to look loathsome. I turned it over and around; looked it in the face—ghastly; from behind, beneath, above, sideways, at three-quarters view—just as ghastly. I was in despair.
>
> I might not use a magnifying glass; instruments of all kinds were interdicted. My two hands, my two eyes, and the fish: it seemed a most limited field. I pushed my finger down its throat to feel how sharp the teeth were. I began to count the scales in the different rows, until I was convinced that that was nonsense. At last a happy thought struck me—I would draw the fish, and now with surprise I began to discover new features in the creature.

When Agassiz returned later and listened to Scudder recount what he had observed, his only comment was that the young man must look again.

> I was piqued; I was mortified. Still more of that wretched fish! But now I set myself to my task with a will, and discovered one new thing after another. . . . The afternoon passed quickly; and when, toward its close, the professor inquired: "Do you see it yet?"
>
> "No," I replied, "I am certain I do not, but I see how little I saw before."

The day following, having thought of the fish through most of the night,

Scudder had a brainstorm. The fish, he announced to Agassiz, had symmetrical sides with paired organs.

"Of course, of course!" Agassiz said, obviously pleased. Scudder asked what he might do next, and Agassiz replied, "Oh, look at your fish!"

In Scudder's case the lesson lasted a full three days. "Look, look, look," was the repeated injunction and the best lesson he ever had, Scudder recalled, "a legacy the professor has left to me, as he has left it to many others, of inestimable value, which we could not buy, with which we cannot part."

The incident of the fish marked the end of the student's novitiate. At once Agassiz became more communicative, his manner that of a friend or colleague, now that the real work could begin.

The way to all learning, "the backbone of education," was to know something well. "A smattering of everything is worth little," he would insist in the heavy French accent that he was never to lose. "Facts are stupid things, until brought into conjunction with some general law." It was a great and common fallacy to suppose that an encyclopedic mind is desirable. The mind was made strong not through much learning but by "the thorough possession of something." In other words, "Look at your fish."

Most important, one must become capable of hard, continuous, original work without the support of the teacher. A year or two of natural history, studied as he understood it, would be the best kind of training for any serious career.

What the student needed above all was the chance to learn to think for himself. So he ought to pursue the line of investigation that interested him most, just as, conversely, a professor ought to be perfectly free to devote his own efforts however he chose. One term, a course of twenty-one lectures was offered on sharks alone, a favorite topic of the professor's, which, as one student remembered, "inspired him to unusual energy and eloquence."

The customary procedure, however, was to spend the first term in zoology (problems of classification, the basics of comparative anatomy), the second on geology (with roughly a third of the time devoted to the glacial age). The material varied little year to year, Agassiz as always "leaning over the lecture desk and hurling whole paragraphs of his lectures with great vigor full in the faces of his students in the front row." And no matter how many years they stayed with him, he remained "the master." To have doubted or criticized anything he said would have been, as one of them said, equivalent to heresy or high treason.

The magic of his personality appears to have mattered above and beyond everything. "His individuality was a subject of continual observation by all.

... Agassiz himself was more interesting than his works," reads one recollection. A contagious enthusiasm surrounded him like an atmosphere, reads another. The "personal quality of Agassiz was the greatest of his powers," the geologist Nathaniel Southgate Shaler wrote in later life, after he too had become a Harvard luminary.

> By far the greater part of the instruction I had from my master was in divers bits of talk concerning certain species and the arrangement of the specimens. He would often work with me for hours unrolling fossils, all the while keeping up a running commentary which would range this way and that, of men, of places, of Aristotle, of Oken. [Lorenz Oken, German naturalist and mystical philosopher, had been one of Agassiz's professors at Munich.] He was a perfect narrator, and on any peg of fact would quickly hang a fascinating discourse. Often when he was at work on wet specimens while I was dealing with fossils, he would come to me with, say, a fish in each hand, that I might search in his pockets for a cigar, cut the tip, put it between his teeth, and light it for him. That would remind him of something, and he would puff and talk until the cigar was burned out, and he would have to be provided with another.

Merely to lecture and inspire was not enough, Agassiz preached fiercely: It was a professorial duty to investigate, discover—*to collect*. So there were summer sojourns in New Hampshire's White Mountains, fishing expeditions off Nantucket. At government expense he went to Florida to examine coral reefs.

He led his first wilderness expedition, across Lake Superior by canoe, the summer of 1848. The party included students, naturalists, two doctors, and an artist. At evening, camped on Superior's northern shore, they would gather to hear him elucidate on the day's findings and observations. A portable blackboard (a piece of canvas painted black) would be unrolled and pinned to the side of his tent, and the lecture would begin, mosquitoes and black flies notwithstanding. Come morning, he would take his place in the lead canoe, which had a big frying pan lashed to the prow as a figurehead. Then once under way, the Indian guides would strike up a song, singing in French the same two or three songs over and over and with a terrible, incongruous sadness that greatly amused Agassiz. What they were singing, he explained to his companions, were in fact the lewd *chansons* of the ancien régime, which doubtless their ancestors had heard sung by young officers in remembrance of distant Paris.

Glacial phenomena of the kind he had encountered in New England were even more pronounced here on the Great Lakes. He saw at once the singular geographic scale of the North American ice sheet, and the expedition returned with a store of geologic samples, as well as eight enormous casks of fish.

•   •   •

The existing collections at Harvard when he first began teaching there were pitiful, a few minerals which never had been arranged properly, the barest beginnings of a botanical garden. Now the rock samples, fossils, the fish and plants and insect specimens began gathering everywhere and anywhere he could find storage space. An old bathhouse on the Charles River was converted into a temporary museum, his students indoctrinated with the omnivorous spirit that had propelled him since boyhood. In his own student days at Munich he had hauled a pine tree into his living quarters and kept as many as forty birds flying about.

Once, when a stable burned a mile from the Harvard campus, killing a number of prize racehorses, the professor himself rushed to the scene, took charge of tending to the surviving animals, consoled their owners, then "skillfully came to the point of his business," which was to ask for the skeletons of all the dead horses. The incident, it would be explained, was illustrative of both his zeal and his ability to charm support from anyone, anytime, under any circumstances; he got the skeletons.

Smaller specimens, including live snakes, frequently were transported to and from class in his coat pockets, and the fenced yard behind the house he had rented contained, among other things, a live eagle, an alligator, a family of possums, and a tame bear known all over town. (One surviving story of the Agassiz household is of the night the bear got drunk at a student-faculty gathering.)

Just when Agassiz began planning seriously for a great, permanent working collection—a proper zoological museum befitting a great university—is not clear. But as his fame spread, people everywhere began shipping him things they had found—some nameless fish from the ocean depths, shells unearthed in a cornfield. The zeal with which some of his minions would serve in the cause become nearly as legendary as his own. To provide Agassiz with freshly laid turtle eggs—these essential to his research in embryology—one young man, the principal of a nearby academy, hid beside a pond for hours before dawn every morning for three weeks, awaiting his chance. Then, the bucket of precious eggs finally in hand, he flagged a passing freight train so as not to delay delivery, an explanation the engineer is said to have understood perfectly.

His peers found him an unfailing inspiration, a virtuoso without equal.

A dissertation on the mathematical arrangement of leaves delivered before a small gathering in Cambridge was acclaimed by the botanist Asa Gray as "most excellent and spirited." In Philadelphia, rising to address the first meeting of the American Association for the Advancement of Science, Agassiz spoke not of glaciers or sharks or embryology, as might have been expected, but on the phonetic apparatus of the cricket.

He was coauthor of a textbook, *Principles of Zoology*, his first American work, which went through sixteen editions during Agassiz's lifetime. For a second series of Lowell Institute lectures a reporter was assigned to transcribe his every word, so the full text could be carried daily in one of the Boston papers.

In 1850 an account of the Lake Superior expedition was published with wide success. Beautifully illustrated, it was at once a fascinating narrative (one of the party had kept a daily journal), a major contribution to American geology, an invaluable guide to Lake Superior birds, fish, and, to the tremendous satisfaction of countless readers as well as reviewers, it was another emphatic declaration by the master naturalist that there need be no conflict between the revelation of science and Genesis. "Agassiz belongs to that class of naturalists who see God in everything," wrote a reviewer in the *Watchman and Christian Reflector*. Agassiz had described the whole of creation as an expression of "divine thought."

He held center stage through the 1850s; he had overshadowed them all—Silliman, Dana, Henry, Hall, Gray. The voice of Charles Darwin was still to be heard.

He was beloved by the transcendentalists, both for his own adoration of nature and for his "huge good fellowship," as Emerson said. Emerson in his private journal listed him number two among "my men," second only to Thomas Carlyle. Henry David Thoreau gathered up turtles and a black snake for him from the shores of Walden Pond. At the Parker House in Boston, when the celebrated Saturday Club dined—Emerson, Hawthorne, Longfellow, the elder Oliver Wendell Holmes—it was Agassiz who sat at the head of the table. Holmes's description, in part, was as follows:

> The great professor, strong, broad-shouldered, square
> In life's rich noontide, joyous, debonair
> His social hour no leaden care alloys
> His laugh rings loud and mirthful as a boy's
> That lusty laugh the puritans forgot
> What ear hath heard it and remembers not?

His writings and lectures on the Ice Age lent a whole new aura to the New England landscape just at the time when the New England landscape was being "discovered" by poets and painters, and White Mountain hotels had become the rage. "Connoisseurs of landscape from Boston and Hartford, parties from Worcester and Burlington, drove on the tops of stages or in private buckboards through Franconia Notch, observing Mounts Webster and Lafayette as if they were two pictures in different styles by the same master," the historian Van Wyck Brooks would write. "They studied the slopes and the cliffs . . . and longed for a little talk with Agassiz. For Agassiz had made these scenes exciting."

Professionally and personally these were the best of years. The old entourage from Neuchâtel, the artists and other assistants, came to join him in his American adventure, to enlist in his latest projects. Following the death of his first wife in Switzerland, he remarried and sent for his three children. Socially, he and the new Mrs. Agassiz—the former Elizabeth Cabot Cary, daughter of a Boston banker—became bright stars in the Cambridge firmament. She was tactful and good-humored and fifteen years younger than he. For years she would handle his correspondence in English, edit his papers and publications, and take notes on all his lectures.

They built a big, square house on Quincy Street that was the setting for famous dinner parties. Summers were spent at fashionable Nahant. Money remained a problem—the large house had a large mortgage, for example—but Agassiz was quoted as saying he had no time to waste making money (which further endeared him among his admirers), and the private school for girls that his wife opened on the top floor of the house helped not only to make ends meet but to put the Agassiz stamp on still another side of community life. "I, myself, superintend the methods of instruction," he wrote in the brochure for the school. "I shall endeavor to prevent the necessary discipline from falling into a lifeless routine, alike deadening to the spirit of teacher and pupil."

So, in addition to everything else, he taught at the girls' school for the next eight years.

The most ambitious publishing effort of his career was launched, a work of ten volumes encompassing the entire natural history of the United States. It was his "endeavor to make myself understood by all." Ten thousand circulars were issued, and twenty-five hundred subscribers enrolled. Proofs of the first two quarto volumes, including his *Essay on Classification*, were received by Agassiz on May 27, 1857, the day before his fiftieth birthday.

The plan for the museum was announced—the Museum of Comparative Zoology, as he wished to have it called. A benefactor, with Agassiz's guidance, had provided in his will that Harvard should receive $50,000 toward the project, but for zoological research only. If no suitable building were provided, then the bequest would be lost. Agassiz, in a manner never dreamed of before, campaigned for additional funds among members of the Massachusetts legislature. "I don't know much about museums," one of them is said to have remarked, "but I, for one, will not stand by and see so brave a man struggle without aid." The legislature voted an appropriation of $100,000. A group of local businessmen raised over $70,000. Harvard provided the site, and in June 1859 the cornerstone was laid.

Acutely aware of his own prominence, acutely conscious of "how wide an influence I already exert upon this land of the future," Agassiz wanted the museum to stand forever as a monument to his whole vision of a true university and of what an education in natural history ought to be about. He had been offered an exalted position at the Jardin des Plantes in Paris, with a salary of 50,000 francs, but he had turned it down, explaining, "I prefer to build anew here."

• • •

It was that same summer of 1859, with the cornerstone in place, that he returned to Europe, accompanied by his wife, and it was in England the autumn following, in November, that *On the Origin of Species by Means of Natural Selection* appeared, a volume bound in green cloth and priced at fifteen shillings. The first copy to reach Cambridge, one sent by the author to Asa Gray, arrived just before Christmas. Agassiz also received a copy, with a note from Darwin asking that Agassiz at least give him the credit for having "earnestly endeavored to arrive at the truth."

He was thunderstruck by the book, as all Cambridge learned soon enough. It was "poor, very poor," he told Gray at first chance, before, in fact, he had read all of it. If Darwin was right, others were saying, then clearly Agassiz was wrong. "Now, John, stop and think of it for a moment," one student, still a believer in Agassiz, wrote to a friend, "and don't you perceive that if his [Darwin's] theory were true it would leave one without a God?"

Gray, who had been impressed at once with the "great ability of the book," became its most outspoken champion this side of the Atlantic. Yet Gray, as everybody appreciated, was the most pious of men, a steady attendant at church. Agassiz, who seldom went to church, denounced the book and its theory as atheism.

The lines were drawn. In no time he and Gray, friends for years, were barely speaking. Among his students Agassiz talked disparagingly of Gray's ability; Gray exploded that Agassiz was a "sort of demagogue" who "always talks to the rabble."

For Agassiz, as for Silliman and others, to study nature was to study the works of God. He had little use for formal religion because, as he once wrote to Dana, he had seen too much in his life of overbearing clerics and religious bigotry. But there could be no evolutionary process as depicted by Darwin for the simple reason that all species were special, distinct, fixed creations. Species—caterpillars, caribou, Lake Superior pike, or Darwin's finches—were the immutable aspects of the divine plan, which from the start had a specific final purpose, mankind. "It can be shown that in the great plan of creation . . . the very commencement exhibits a certain tendency toward the end. . . . The constantly increasing similarity to man of the creatures successively called into existence makes the final purpose obvious."

Progress there had been, the long record of life on Earth was indeed an upward path. The changes, however, had been achieved, he insisted, in great creative stages, these divided by momentous catastrophe. His doctrine, the cataclysmic theory of his own great master, Cuvier, was that all life on the planet had been destroyed repeatedly in order to start afresh with new forms. Evidence of such destruction was abundant in the fossil record, while all present inhabitants of the planet were the latest and final stage. It was as if God, like Louis Agassiz, wiped the board clean again and again to arrive at a grand intended finale, with man the crowning creation.

Several times in his book, to substantiate one point or another, Darwin had referred to observations by Agassiz (on embryological succession, for example). But Darwin's conclusions were "the sum of wrong-headedness," Agassiz told his students. Darwin's theory, Agassiz instructed the members of the Boston Society of Natural History, was "ingenious but fanciful." "The resources of the Deity," he wrote, "cannot be so meager that in order to create a human being endowed with reason, He must change a monkey into a man."

John Amory Lowell, guiding spirit of the Lowell Institute, lent Agassiz his support as the battle got under way. Harvard stood behind him. When the new museum was opened in November 1860, Harvard President Cornelius Felton declared it altogether appropriate that the building stood face-to-face with the theological school, "God's word and God's works mutually illustrating each other."

Agassiz produced a stream of articles for *Atlantic Monthly* and carried the fight to the lecture circuit, his popularity soaring to new heights. The articles, published as a book, *Methods of Study in Natural History*, went through nineteen editions. To know that Agassiz of Harvard decried the theories of Charles Darwin, that he, of all learned men, marched foremost in the assault on the new godless vision of life, brought solace to a degree later generations would never be able to comprehend. He was quite literally adored. He was "the prince of naturalists."

Still, a certain uneasiness spread among his students. Colleagues had begun to question his powers of reason. Admirers were saddened to see him stumble over facts, contradict himself, or stubbornly refuse to give the other side a fair hearing. Gray, with whom he had broken completely, became convinced that the illustrious Agassiz mind was in a state of rapid deterioration. "This man," wrote Gray, "who might have been so useful to science and promised so much here has been for years a delusion, a snare, and a humbug, and is doing us far more harm than he can ever do us good."

To give credence and grandeur to catastrophe's role in creation, Agassiz returned again to his glacial visions, writing now with perhaps greater power than ever before, as can be seen in these lines from still another series in the *Atlantic Monthly*:

> The long summer was over. For ages a tropical climate had prevailed over a great part of the Earth, and animals whose home is now beneath the equator roamed over the world from the Far South to the very borders of the Arctic. The gigantic quadrupeds, the mastodons, elephants, tigers, lions, hyenas, bears, whose remains are found in Europe from its southern promontories to the northern limits of Siberia and Scandinavia, and in America from the southern states to Greenland and the Melville Island, may indeed be said to have possessed the Earth in those days. But their reign was over. A sudden intense winter, that was also to last for ages, fell upon our globe; it spread over the very countries where these tropical animals had their homes, and so suddenly did it come upon them that they were embalmed beneath masses of snow and ice, without time even for the decay which follows death . . . If the glacial theory be true, a great mass of ice, of which the present glaciers are but the remnants, formerly spread over the whole Northern Hemisphere.

In an odd, paradoxical way he became obsessed with an apocalyptic world of ice, the entire globe frozen in death—he who had given himself so wholeheartedly to the study of life, he who was such an exuberant life force. It remained only to find the familiar traces in the Southern Hemisphere as well.

So while Darwin, gray, stooped, two years younger than Agassiz, kept to his country place in England, puttering about in a little greenhouse,

Agassiz announced plans for a trip to Brazil. Another benefactor had supplied the wherewithal; the trip in theory was to provide the professor with a long-needed rest.

He sailed on April 1, 1865, at the head of a large, widely publicized expedition and returned the following year with some eighty thousand specimens and a triumphant announcement: the valley of the Amazon itself with all its fecund tropical splendors once had been obliterated beneath rivers of ice. He had found the proof.

His proof, however, turned out to be exceedingly thin and open to question. His peers were skeptical, or worse. In truth it was the end of his own "long summer." A shadow fell over the brilliant career, for all the popular acclaim, for all the devotion he inspired. He grew increasingly dictatorial with students and with his museum assistants, unpleasantly intolerant of any divergence from his own views. He "not infrequently lost his temper." And numbers of his brightest students revolted, or quit in despair.

A breakdown from nervous strain and overwork in 1869 left him incapacitated for nearly a year. Yet the headlong life resumed. The museum building was doubled in size. He embarked on still another venture, around Cape Horn to California with a Coast Survey expedition, and returned this time with some one hundred thousand specimens. And in the final year of his life he founded still another school of his own, a summer school of science for teachers on Penikese Island in Buzzards Bay.

The epic work *Contributions to the Natural History of the United States*, of which only four volumes had been produced, was never completed. The last published work, an article for the *Atlantic Monthly*, was one titled, "Evolution and Permanence of Type."

He died December 14, 1873. Eight days earlier he had returned from the museum feeling tired and had lain down on the couch to rest awhile. He never spoke again.

Obituaries were carried in every paper. Learned societies held special meetings to pass memorial resolutions. No death since that of Lincoln, wrote the editors of *Harper's Weekly*, had elicited such heartfelt expressions of sorrow.

•   •   •

The legacy was truly amazing. His work on fish, the initial research on glaciers, the impact of his writing on the Ice Age, the zest and glamour he brought to American culture at a critical moment, were all contributions of the first order. His beloved Museum of Comparative Zoology—the Agassiz Museum, or simply the Agassiz, as it came to be known in Cambridge—was without question one of the finest, most important such institutions in the world, which it remains to this day. (In the hall of North American birds, for example, is displayed every species to be found north of Mexico.)

Mistaken as he may have been about evolution, he was by no means alone. Nor do intellectual brilliance and a life in science necessarily mean that it is any easier to break from cherished convictions, not to mention the prevailing views of one's own era. Humboldt had found it impossible to accept Agassiz's theory of glaciers.

Agassiz, besides, had been caught up by a popular success no one in science had to cope with until then. In the eyes of his vast audience he was indeed "the first naturalist of his time, a good citizen . . . beloved of those who knew him," all that he had aspired to so long before in the letter to his father. To have totally reexamined his work after 1859, to have retreated from his own strongly expressed positions on creation, to have abandoned his audience, would have been horrendously difficult. Even someone less inspirited by public acclaim, less dependent by nature on the authority and approval granted by such acclaim, might have found it impossible.

Agassiz, as numbers of students and associates observed, *needed* an audience. On the lecture platform or in the classroom he seemed to draw his energy, his "magic," from the people before him. And this, in a sense, was both his greatest flaw and his greatest strength. It was what, as a scientist, made him something less than a Lyell or a Darwin, and it is what, as a teacher, made him incomparable.

His precepts on the teaching of natural history, certainly a significant part of the legacy, had far-reaching influence. "Never try to teach what you yourself do not know, and know well," he lectured at Penikese his final summer. "Train your pupils to be observers. . . . If you can find nothing better, take a housefly or a cricket, and let each hold a specimen and examine it as you talk. . . . He is lost, as an observer, who believes that he can, with impunity, affirm that for which he can adduce no evidence. . . . Have the courage to say I do not know. . . . The more I look at the great complex of the animal world, the more sure do I feel that we have not yet reached its hidden meaning."

Like Humboldt before him, he took the greatest pride in the influence he had on the next generation of naturalists. And indeed the subsequent careers of his students and museum assistants are as strong a testament to his genius as almost anything else. Nathaniel Southgate Shaler became a popular professor of geology at Harvard (an inspiration to Theodore

Roosevelt, among many others). Samuel Scudder became the country's outstanding authority and most prolific writer on butterflies. Theodore Lyman was an accomplished zoologist who also became a congressman. There was William James, the philosopher; Albert S. Bickmore, who decided to found his own museum—the American Museum of Natural History in New York. Frederic Putnam became a Harvard professor of American anthropology and was instrumental in the growth of most of the country's anthropological museums. Alpheus Hyatt, who is said to have learned all of Agassiz's *Essay on Classification* by heart, became a professor of zoology and paleontology at M.I.T. and was one of the founders of the famous marine biological laboratory at Woods Hole, Massachusetts. Alpheus S. Packard, one of Agassiz's student-assistants and later a teacher at Penikese, wrote *Guide to the Study of Insects*, the first major American textbook of entomology. Edward Sylvester Morse, one of those students Harvard would never have taken under normal circumstances, introduced modern methods of classification to Japan, became a sparkling lecturer, writer, museum director, and with Putnam, Hyatt, and Packard founded the *American Naturalist.*

Agassiz's son, Alexander, who was trained by his father and served as his principal museum assistant, became a leading zoologist, a pioneer in oceanography, and made a fortune in copper mining, much of which he ultimately devoted to the museum and other work begun by his father. Elizabeth Cary Agassiz, in less than a decade after her husband's death, became a founder of Radcliffe College, and was its first president.

In all the surviving accounts in which those who knew Louis Agassiz strive to describe and explain the hold he had on his time, the enthusiasm he generated, his charm and powers as expositor and leader, one theme remains constant: the quality of the man's commitment. Silliman used the word *engaged.* William James told a story.

James had been a member of the expedition to Brazil and had his hammock slung next to Agassiz on the deck of the steamer that carried the party up the Amazon. Late one night, lying sleepless as the engines throbbed and the jungle slipped by under a full moon, he heard Agassiz whisper, "James, are you awake?" then continue, "I cannot sleep. I am too happy; I keep thinking of all those glorious plans."

CHAPTER THREE

The Unexpected Mrs. Stowe

SHE HAD been brought up to make herself useful. And always it suited her.

As a child she had been known as Hattie. She had been cheerful but shy, prone to fantasies, playful, and quite pretty. After she became famous, she would describe herself this way: "To begin, then, I am a little bit of a woman—somewhat more than forty—about as thin and dry as a pinch of snuff; never very much to look at in my best days, and looking like a used-up article now." She wasn't altogether serious when she wrote that, but the description was the one people would remember.

She was born in Litchfield, Connecticut—in a plain frame house that still stands—in 1811, when Lincoln was two years old and when Dolly Madison was in the White House. She was the seventh of the nine children Roxana Foote bore Lyman Beecher before being gathered to her reward, and she was such a worker, even when very small, that her preacher father liked to say he would gladly have given a hundred dollars if she could have been born a boy.

As a child she had found most of his sermons about as intelligible as Choctaw, she wrote later, and never would she be at peace with his

religion. But she loved him, and for all his gloomy talk of sin and damnation it is not hard to understand why. He was a powerful, assertive figure
who had an almost fiendish zest for life—for hunting and fishing with his
sons, for listening to all music, and for playing the violin, which he did
badly. But could he only play what he heard inside him, he told them all,
he could be another Paganini. Best of all he loved to go out and "snare
souls," as he said. In a corner of the cellar he kept a pile of sand, and if his
day was not enough to use him up, and stormy weather kept him from
outdoor exercise, down he would go, shovel in hand, to sling sand about.

Sunday mornings he would come bounding along through the sunshine,
late again for that appointed hour when weekly he brought down Calvinist
thunder upon the heads of upright Litchfield people. He had a special
wrath for drunkards and Unitarians, and he believed passionately in the
Second Coming. But something in him made him shy away from the
strictest tenet of his creed—total predestination—and its logic. Once
when he had agreed to exchange pulpits with another pastor, he was told
that the arrangement had been preordained. "Is that so?" he said. "Then I
won't do it!" And he didn't.

The happiest times in her childhood, Hattie would write later, were the
days spent away from him, visiting an Aunt Harriet in Nutplains, Connecticut, in a house filled with books and pictures gathered by a seafaring
uncle and a wonderful old Tory grandmother, who in private still said
Episcopal prayers for the king and queen.

At twelve Hattie often wandered off from the noisy parsonage to lie on a
green hillside and gaze straight into a solid blue sky and dream of Byron.
One month she read *Ivanhoe* seven times.

In 1832, when Hattie had turned twenty-one, Lyman Beecher answered
the call to become the first president of the Lane Theological Seminary in
Cincinnati. He packed up his children and a new wife and set off for what
he called "the majestic West." A New Jerusalem was to be established on
the banks of the Ohio. The family spirits were lifted; and crossing the
Alleghenies, they all sang "Jubilee." A Philadelphia journal likened the
exodus of the Reverend Mr. Beecher and his family to the migration of
Jacob and his sons.

The following summer the Lane Theological Seminary's first (and at that
time, only) professor, Calvin Ellis Stowe, a Biblical scholar and Bowdoin
graduate, traveled west in the Beechers' wake. For all his learning and
devotion to the Almighty, Stowe was a very homely and peculiar worker in
the vineyard.

He was accompanied by a beautiful young bride, Eliza, who soon became

Hattie Beecher's best friend in Cincinnati but died not very long afterward. Apparently it was a shared grief over Eliza that brought Hattie and Calvin Stowe together. Years later, with some of the proceeds from *Uncle Tom's Cabin*, they would commission an artist to do a portrait of Eliza, and every year thereafter, on Eliza's birthday, the two of them would sit before the portrait and reminisce about Eliza's virtues.

The wedding took place in early January 1836. What exactly she saw in him is a little hard to say. The night before the ceremony, trying to describe her emotions in a letter to a school friend, she confessed she felt "nothing at all." But Lord Byron had not appeared in Cincinnati. At twenty-four she may have felt she was getting on.

Calvin was thirty-three, but he seemed as old as her father. He was fluent in Greek, Latin, Hebrew, French, Italian, and German; he was an authority on education; he knew the Bible better than her father. Also, it is recorded, he had a grand sense of humor. But he was as fat and forgetful and fussy as an old woman. In the midst of a crisis, as she would soon discover, he had a bad habit of taking to his bed, and he had absolutely no "faculty," that Yankee virtue she defined simply as being the opposite of shiftlessness.

He also had an eye for pretty women, as he admitted to Hattie, and a taste for spirits, but these proclivities, it seems, never got him into any particular trouble.

But there was more. Calvin, from his boyhood until his dying day, was haunted by phantoms. They visited him most any time, but favored dusk. They appeared quite effortlessly out of the woodwork, the floor, or the furniture. There was a regular cast of characters, Calvin said, as real and familiar to him as anyone else he knew. Among his favorites were a giant Indian woman and a dark dwarf who between them carried a huge bull fiddle. There was a troupe of old Puritans from his native Natick, all shadowy and dark blue in color, and one "very pleasant-looking human face" he called Harvey. They performed music for Calvin Stowe, and somehow or other they talked to him without making any sound at all, or so he said. He had no reluctance about discussing the subject, and there is no indication that any of his circle thought the less of him for it.

Still, the marriage proved difficult soon enough. Hattie became pregnant almost immediately, and just about then Calvin was asked by the state of Ohio to go to Prussia to study educational systems there. Professing a profound fear of the salt sea, he told her he would never see her again in this life. She insisted that he go, and had given birth to twin daughters by the time of his return. There was a third child two years later, then another, and another, and two more later on. A professor's wages were never enough, even when old Lyman could pay Calvin in full, which was seldom. Hattie's health began to fail. "She lived overmuch in her emotions," one son would explain years later.

"It is a dark, sloppy, rainy, muddy disagreeable day," she wrote once to Calvin when he was in Detroit attending a church convention. ". . . I am sick of the smell of sour milk, and sour meat, and sour everything, and then the clothes *will* not dry, and no wet thing does, and everything smells mouldy; and altogether I feel as if I never wanted to eat again."

She began going off on visits to relatives, leaving Calvin and the children behind. The visits grew longer. She went to the White Mountains, then to Brattleboro, Vermont, to try the water cure. The expenses were met by gifts from distant admirers of the family: the Stowes felt that the Lord had a hand in it. Hattie stayed on for nearly a year at Brattleboro, living on brown bread and milk, enduring the interminable sitz baths of one Dr. Wesselhoeft, and writing home exuberant letters about moonlight snowball fights. And no sooner did she return to the cluttered house in Cincinnati than the professor hauled himself off to Brattleboro, there to stay even longer than she had. When a cholera epidemic broke out in Cincinnati and more than a hundred people a day were dying, she wrote to tell him to stay right where he was. She would manage.

In all they were separated a total of three years and more, and their letters back and forth speak of strong, troubled feelings. The hulking, clumsy Stowe, bearded, nearsighted, complained that she never folded his newspaper properly and that her letters of late were too uninteresting for him to read aloud to his friends. She in turn would run on about her own miseries. The house depressed her, she worried about money, she hated the climate in Cincinnati. She thought too much about death.

But she also told him, "There are a thousand favorite subjects on which I could talk with you better than anyone else. If you were not already my dearly loved husband I should certainly fall in love with you."

And Calvin would write to her when she was visiting her sister in Hartford, "And now my dear wife, I want you to come home as quick as you can. The fact is I cannot live without you and if we were not so prodigious poor I would come for you at once. There is no woman like you in this wide world."

In this same letter Calvin proclaimed to her—and apparently he was the first to do so—"My dear, you must be a literary woman. It is so written in the book of fate." He advised her to make all her plans accordingly, as though she had little else to do. "Get a good stock of health and brush up your mind," he declared. And he told her to drop her middle initial, *E* (for Elizabeth), from her name. "It only incumbers it and interferes with the flow and euphony." Instead: "Write yourself fully and always Harriet Beecher Stowe, which is a name euphonious, flowing, and full of meaning."

She had already written quite a little—temperance tracts, articles on keeping the Sabbath, New England "sketches," for which she drew heavily on Calvin's seemingly inexhaustible fund of childhood reminiscences. Once she had done an article about a slave. She had been selling these pieces to *Godey's Lady's Book* and one or two other magazines. She got two dollars a page on the average, which was more profitable than taking in boarders, she decided. But no one in the family, other than Calvin, had taken her writing seriously.

She worked at the kitchen table, confusion all around, a baby in a clothes basket at her feet. She couldn't spell very well, and her punctuation would always be a puzzle for her publishers. She dreamed, she said in a letter to Calvin, of a place to work without "the constant falling of soot and coal dust on everything in the room."

Then in July of 1849 she was writing to tell him that their infant son Charley was dead of cholera. The summer before she had nearly died of it herself, with her father praying over her all through one terrible, sweltering night, the room alive with mosquitoes. She had been unable to do a thing for the child, she told Calvin. For almost a week she watched him die, with no way to help, she said, no way even to ease his suffering.

Calvin returned to her very soon after that, determined to leave Cincinnati for good. He had accepted a professorship at Bowdoin College, in Brunswick, Maine, and before he could settle up his affairs in Cincinnati, he characteristically sent Harriet and three of the children off to Maine ahead of him.

She left Cincinnati in the early spring of 1850, a shabby little figure, perfectly erect, perhaps no more than five feet tall, nearly forty, and pregnant once again. She boarded a riverboat at the foot of town, saying farewell with no misgivings. She was going home, she felt.

She was also heading for a sudden and colossal notoriety of a kind never known by any American woman before, and very few since; but of that she had no notion whatever. Nor did she or anyone else alive have any idea how important those seventeen years in Cincinnati had been to her and, as things turned out, to the course of American history.

She sailed up the Ohio to Pittsburgh, where she changed to a canal boat. Already she was feeling so good she got out and walked the towpath between locks. At Johnstown the boat and all its passengers were hoisted up and over the Allegheny Mountains by that thrilling mechanical contrivance of the nineteenth century, the Portage Railroad. East of the mountains she went by rail to New York and there crossed by ferry to Brooklyn to see her younger brother, Henry Ward, pastor of Plymouth Church. As children they had sometimes been taken for twins, only Henry Ward had been thick of speech and considered the slow one. Now she took note of his obvious success, and they went out for a drive in a spotless six-hundred-dollar carriage, a recent gift from his parishioners.

In a few days she went on to Hartford, still looking after the children and all their baggage. Her spirits were soaring. At Hartford she stayed with her sisters Mary and Isabella; in Boston with her brother Edward, who was growing ever more militant over the slavery issue. All the Beechers were growing more militant over one thing or another. For Isabella it was women's rights; for the brilliant Catherine, education; for Charles, freedom from theological authority. From Boston, Harriet took the Bath Steamer to Maine, sailing headlong into a northeaster.

On the day they were scheduled to arrive at Brunswick, one story goes, the president of Bowdoin sent a professor named Smith down to greet the new faculty wife, but Smith returned disappointed, saying she must have been delayed. Nobody got off the boat, he said, except an old Irish woman and her brats.

Brunswick offered precious few of the Eastern civilities Mrs. Stowe had longed for, and the house Calvin had taken in advance turned out to be deserted, dreary, and damp, to use her words. She went straight to work, refinishing floors, putting up wallpaper—the pioneer again. When Calvin wrote from Cincinnati to say he was sick and plainly dying and that she and theirs would soon be plunged into everlasting debt, she read the letter with humor and stuffed it into the stove.

Calvin showed up before summer, her baby was born, she rested two weeks. When winter came, there were holes in her shoes, and the house was so cold during one long storm that the children had trouble sitting still long enough to eat their meals. It was during the following spring that she began Uncle Tom's Cabin.

People are still trying to interpret the book and to explain just how and why she came to write it. At first she said she really didn't write it at all. She said the book came to her in visions and all she did was write down what she saw. When someone reproached her for letting Little Eva die, she answered, "Why, I could not help it. I felt as badly as anyone could! It was like a death in my own family and it affected me so deeply that I could not write a word for two weeks after her death." Years later she stated cate-gorically, "God wrote it." And a great many of her readers were quite willing to let it go at that.

· · ·

The truth is, the subject of the book had been all around her for a very long time. Old Lyman had been able to make Litchfield farmers weep when he preached on slavery. In Cincinnati she had opened her own Sunday school to black children, and the Lane Seminary had been a hotbed of abolitionist fervor. The Underground Railroad, she later claimed, went directly through her Cincinnati house, which was a bit of an exaggeration; but on one occasion Calvin and her brother Charles did indeed help a black woman and her child elude a slave hunter. The only time she was in an actual slave state, during a visit across the Ohio River in Kentucky, she made no show of emotion about it. But stories she heard from the black women she knew in Cincinnati moved her enormously, particularly those told by a gentle person named Eliza Buck, who helped her with housework and whose children, Harriet Stowe discovered with incredulity, had all been fathered by the woman's former master in Kentucky. "You know, Mrs. Stowe," she had said, "slave women cannot help themselves."

Eliza Buck told her of lashings and of slave families split up and "sold down the river." Once on an Ohio River wharf Mrs. Stowe had seen with her own eyes a husband and wife torn apart by a slave trader.

By the time she came east to Maine, Henry Ward was using his Brooklyn pulpit to raise money to buy children out of slavery. In Boston she and Edward had talked long and emotionally about the Fugitive Slave Bill, then being debated in Congress, which made it a federal crime to harbor or assist the escaped "property" of a slave master. Her duty was plain. There was, she said, a standard higher than an act of Congress.

She did some research in Boston and corresponded with Frederick Douglass on certain details. But for all that, the book would be written more out of something within her, something she knew herself about bondage and the craving for liberation, than from any documentary sources or personal investigation of black slavery in the South. Indeed she really knew very little about black slavery in the South. Her critics would be vicious with her for this, of course, and she would go so far as to write a whole second book in defense of her sources. But *Uncle Tom's Cabin* could never be accounted for that way.

There is probably something to the story that she began the book as a result of a letter from Edward's wife. "Hattie," wrote her sister-in-law from Boston, "if I could use the pen as you can, I would write something that will make this whole nation feel what an accursed thing slavery is." To which Hattie answered, "As long as the baby sleeps with me nights, I can't do much at anything, but I will do it at last. I will write that thing if I live."

The story appeared first as a serial in the *National Era*, an antislavery paper, beginning in June 1851. It took her a year to write it all, and apparently she did Uncle Tom's death scene first and at a single sitting, writing on brown wrapping paper when her writing paper ran out. The finished story was brought out in book form by the publisher, John P. Jewett, in two volumes on March 20, 1852, a month before the serialized version ended.

Calvin thought the book had little importance. He wept over it, but he wept over most of the things she wrote. Her publisher warned that her subject was unpopular and said she took too long to tell her story. On the advice of a friend who had not read the manuscript, she decided to take a 10 percent royalty on every copy sold ins ead of a 50-50 division of profit or losses, as had also been offered to her.

She herself expected to make no money from it; she thought it inadequate and was sure her friends would be disappointed with her. Within a week after publication ten thousand copies had been sold. The publisher had three power presses running twenty-four hours a day. In a year sales in the United States came to more than three hundred thousand. The book made publishing history right from the start. In England, where Mrs. Stowe had no copyright and therefore received no royalties, sales were even more stupendous. A million and a half copies were sold in about a year's time. The book appeared in thirty-seven different languages. "It is no longer permissible to those who can read not to have read it," wrote George Sand from France, who said the author had no talent, only genius, and called her a saint.

•   •   •

The book had a strange power over almost everyone who read it then, and for all its Victorian mannerisms and frequent patches of sentimentality much of it still does. Its characters have a vitality of a kind comparable to the most memorable figures in literature. There is sweep and power to the narrative, and there are scenes that once read are not forgotten. The book is also rather different from what most people imagine, largely because it was eventually eclipsed by the stage version, which Mrs. Stowe had nothing to do with (and from which she never received a cent), and which was probably performed more often than any play in the language, evolving after a few years into something between circus and minstrel show. One successful road company advertised ". . . a pack of genuine bloodhounds; two Toppsies; Two Marks, Eva and her Pony 'Prince'; African Mandolin Players; 'Tinker' the famous Trick Donkey." In the book, for example, no bloodhounds chase Eliza and her baby across the ice.

What the book did at the time was to bring slavery out into the open and show it for what it was, in human terms. No writer had done that before. Slavery had been argued over in the abstract, preached against as a moral issue, its evils whispered about in polite company. But the book made people at that time *feel* what slavery was about. ("The soul of eloquence is feeling," old Lyman had written.)

Moreover, Harriet Stowe had made a black man her hero, and she took his race seriously, and no American writer had done that before.

The fundamental fault, she fervently held, was with the system. Every white American was guilty, the Northerner no less than the slaveholder, especially the churchgoing kind, *her* kind. Simon Legree, it should perhaps always be remembered, was a Vermonter.

That Uncle Tom would one day be used as a term of derision ("A Negro who is held to be humiliatingly subservient or deferential to whites," according to the *American Heritage Dictionary*) she would have found impossible to fathom, and heartbreaking. For her he was something very close to a black Christ. He is the one character in all her book who lives, quite literally, by the Christian ideal. And if one has doubts that she could see black as beautiful or that she saw emancipation for the black man as a chance for full manhood and dignity, there is her description of Eliza's husband, George Harris, as straight-backed, confident, "his face settled and resolute." When George and his family, having escaped into Ohio, are cornered by slave hunters, Mrs. Stowe writes a scene in which George is fully prepared to kill his tormentors and to die himself rather than permit his wife and son to be taken back into slavery. ". . . I am a free man, standing on God's free soil," George yells from the rock ledge to which he has retreated, "and my wife and my child I claim as mine. . . . We have arms to defend ourselves and we mean to do it. You can come up if you like; but the first one of you that comes within the range of our bullets is a dead man, and the next, and the next, and so on till the last."

She seems to have been everywhere at once after the book was published—Hartford, New Haven, Brooklyn, Boston. Almost immediately the South began boiling with indignation. She was a radical, it was said. All the Beechers were radicals. She began receiving threatening letters from the South, and once Calvin unwrapped a small parcel addressed to her to find a human ear that had been severed from the head of a black slave. Calvin grew more and more distraught. They decided it was time to move again, now to Andover, Massachusetts, to take up a previously offered teaching job at the seminary there.

Then they were sailing to England, where huge crowds waited for her at railroad stations, hymns were composed in her honor, children came up to her carriage with flowers. She went about in a gray cloak carrying a paint box. She was a tireless tourist. And she worried. "The power of fictitious writing, for good as well as evil, is a thing which ought most seriously to be reflected on. No one can fail to see that in our day it is becoming a very great agency."

When war came, everyone told her it was her war, and she thought so too. In South Carolina, as the war commenced, the wife of a plantation owner wrote in her diary that naturally slavery had to go, but added, "Yes, how I envy those saintly Yankee women, in their clean cool New England homes, writing to make their fortunes and to shame us."

Harriet Stowe never saw the Civil War as anything but a war to end slavery, and all her old Beecher pacifist principles went right out the window. "Better, a thousand times better, open, manly, energetic war, than cowardly and treacherous peace," she proclaimed. Her oldest son, Frederick, put on a uniform and went off to fight. Impatient with Lincoln for not announcing emancipation right away, she went down to Washington when he finally proclaimed that the slaves would be free, and was received privately in the White House. The scene is part of our folklore. "So this is the little woman who made this big war," Lincoln is supposed to have said as he shook her hand.

•   •   •

She was sitting in the gallery at the Boston Music Hall, attending a concert, on January 1, 1863, the day the Emancipation Proclamation became effective. When an announcement of the historic event was made from the stage, somebody called out that she was in the gallery. In an instant the audience was on its feet cheering while she stood and bowed, her bonnet awry.

After the war she kept on writing. In fact, as is sometimes overlooked, that is what Harriet Beecher Stowe was, a writer, and one of the most industrious we have ever had. Unwittingly she had written the abolitionist manifesto, although she did not consider herself an abolitionist. She agreed with her father that abolitionists "were like men who would burn down their houses to get rid of the rats." She was not a crusader pure and simple. She never considered herself an extremist, and she seldom took an extreme position on any issue. She was a reformer, and there was an evangelical undercurrent to just about everything she wrote. But writing was her work, her way to make herself useful.

Her life was about half over when she wrote *Uncle Tom's Cabin*, but for thirty years more she wrote almost a book a year on the average, plus innumerable essays, poems, children's stories, and magazine articles, many of which she did under the pseudonym Christopher Crowfield. Perhaps her most artful novel, *The Minister's Wooing*, ran to fifty printings, and a magazine article, "The True Story of Lady Byron's Life," which appeared in the *Atlantic Monthly* in 1869, caused more furor than anything published in America since *Uncle Tom's Cabin*.

During a second visit to England she had become fast friends with the widow of Lord Byron, who confided the terrible secret that the great Byron had committed incest with his half sister and that a child had been born as a result. Mrs. Stowe kept the secret for thirteen years, but when Byron's former mistress, Countess Guiccioli, published her memoirs and portrayed Lady Byron as a self-righteous tyrant who would drive any mortal male to excesses, Harriet Stowe decided it was time to strike a blow in her friend's behalf, Lady Byron by this time having been dead for nearly a decade. So she told the whole story.

All kinds of accusations were hurled at her, some quite unpleasant. She rode out the storm, however, and again, as with *Uncle Tom*, she wrote a book to justify what she had written. But her standing with the American public would never be the same.

She could write in all kinds of places, under every kind of condition. She was always bothered by deadlines, and it seems she was always in need of money. The royalties poured in, but the more she had the more she spent— on a huge Gothic villa in Hartford that was all gables and turrets and was never finished completely; on a cotton plantation in Florida where she intended to provide blacks with a program of work and education; and later, when that failed, on an orange and lemon grove at Mandarin, Florida, "where the world is not," she said, and where she hoped her unfortunate son Frederick might find himself.

Frederick had trouble staying sober. His problem had started before the war, but at Gettysburg he had been hit in the head by a shell fragment, and, his mother would always believe, he had never been himself again.

"After that," one of her grandsons would write, "he not only was made drunk by the slightest amount of alcohol but he could not resist taking it."

•   •   •

Calvin grew enormously fat, ever more distant, and of even less use than before when it came to the everyday details of life. Moreover, Harriet found fame increasingly difficult. She had become a national institution. Her correspondence alone would have drained a less vigorous spirit.

Tragedy struck repeatedly. In 1857, upon returning from Europe, she learned that her son Henry, a student at Dartmouth, had drowned while swimming in the Connecticut River. In 1870, Frederick, unable to endure his mother's Florida experiment any longer, wrote her a touching apology and went to sea, shipping around the Horn. It is known that he got as far as San Francisco, but after that he disappeared and was never heard from again. She would go to her grave with every confidence that he would return one day.

But it was the Brooklyn scandal that hurt her worst of all, she said. In November of 1872 a New York paper reported that her beloved brother Henry Ward, by then the most popular preacher in America, had been carrying on an adulterous affair with one of his parishioners. His enemies swept in for the kill. For all the Beechers the gossip was agonizing. A sensational trial resulted, the husband bringing suit against Beecher for alienation of his wife's affections. It dragged on for six months and was the talk of the country. Whether Beecher was guilty or innocent was never proved one way or the other. He denied everything, the jury was unable to agree on a verdict, and as far as his sister was concerned his character was never even in question.

The whole story was a slanderous fabrication, she said, and she stood by him through the entire grisly, drawn-out business, as did all the Beechers except Isabella Beecher Hooker, who was only a half sister, it was noted, and was regarded by many as just a little unbalanced. (Isabella, who called herself "*the* inspired one," wanted to take charge of a service at Plymouth Church herself and "as one commissioned from on high" declare her brother's guilt from his own pulpit. Years later, when he was dying, she even tried to force her way into his house to get a deathbed confession.)

But it would be mistaken to suggest that Harriet's life became increasingly burdensome. Quite the contrary. As time passed she seems to have grown ever more liberated from her past. She drew further and further from the shadow of her harsh Calvinist heritage, eventually rejecting it altogether. She had long since discarded the doctrine of original sin. Neither man nor nature was necessarily corrupt, she now held. Hers was a faith of love and Christian charity. She had a seemingly limitless love for the whole human family. Years before, Catherine, her spinster sister, had been the first of the Beechers to rebel against the traditional faith when a young man she was engaged to marry, a gifted Yale professor of philosophy, was lost at sea and Catherine had had to face the terrible Calvinist conclusion that the young man was consigned to eternal damnation because he had never repented. In time all of Lyman Beecher's offspring would desert the faith. Henry Ward would even go so far as to preach that there is no hell.

For Harriet, Calvinism was repugnant, a "glacial" doctrine, although she admired enormously the fervor it had given the Puritan colonists of her native New England and the solid purpose and coherence of the communities they established. Like many of her time she sorely lamented the decline of Christian faith in the land. It was the root of the breakdown of the old order, she believed. Mostly, it seems, she admired the backbone the old religion gave people. "They who had faced eternal ruin with an unflinching gaze," she wrote, "were not likely to shrink before the comparatively trivial losses and gains of any mere earthly conflict." If she herself could not accept the articles of the Puritan faith, she seemed to wish everybody else would. And once from Florida she wrote: ". . . never did we have a more delicious spring. I never knew such altogether perfect weather. It is enough to make a saint out of the toughest old Calvinist that ever set his face as a flint. How do you think New England theology would have fared, if our fathers had landed here instead of on Plymouth Rock?"

• • •

Like numerous other literary figures of the day she tried spiritualism and claimed that her son Henry had returned from somewhere beyond to pluck a guitar string for her. She became an Episcopalian, and she developed an open fondness for such things as Europe (Paris and Italy especially), Rubens, elegant society, and Florida, in particular Florida (". . . this wild, wonderful, bright, and vivid growth, that is all new, strange and unknown by name to me"). The theater and dancing were no longer viewed as sinful. She rejected the idea that "there was something radically corrupt and wicked in the body and in the physical system." She took a little claret now on occasion. An account of a visit to Portsmouth, New Hampshire, suggests that once at least she may have taken a little too much claret.

She was asked to give readings, to go on the lyceum, as the contemporary lecture circuit was called, like Robert Ingersoll, P. T. Barnum, and the feminists. She needed the money, so at age sixty-one, having never made a public speech before, she embarked on a new career with its endless train rides, bad food, and dreary hotels. She was very shy at first and not much good at it. But she got over that and in time became quite accomplished. "Her performance could hardly be called a reading," reported the Pittsburgh *Gazette*, "it was recitative and she seldom glanced at the book. Her voice betrayed the veritable Yankee twang. . . . Her voice is low, just tinged in the slightest with huskiness, but is quite musical. In manner she was vivacious and gave life to many of the pages, more by suggestive action than by utterances. . . . She seemed perfectly possessed on the stage, and read with easy grace."

She found she could move her audiences to great emotional heights, but to laughter especially. And she loved the life. Her health picked up. "I never sleep better than after a long day's ride," she wrote.

Her appearance never changed much. She put on no new airs. Nothing, in fact, good or bad, seemed capable of changing that plain, earnest, often whimsical manner. She acquired a number of new friendships that meant a great deal to her, with Oliver Wendell Holmes and Mark Twain particularly. Henry Drummond, the noted Scottish religious writer, wrote, after a visit to Hartford: "Next door to Twain I found Mrs. Harriet Beecher Stowe, a wonderfully agile old lady, as fresh as a squirrel still, but with the face and air of a lion." And he concluded: "I have not been so taken with any one on this side of the Atlantic."

Her affections for Calvin seem to have grown stronger, if anything. He had become absorbed in Semitic studies, let his beard grow, and took to wearing a skullcap. She began calling him "My Old Rabbi." His apparitions took up more and more of his time, and for a while he was having nightly encounters with the Devil, who came on horseback, Calvin said. But otherwise his mind stayed quick and clear until the end, and she found him exceedingly good company.

In their last years they seem also to have had few financial worries. Among other things a book of his, *The Origin and History of the Books of the Bible*, had a surprisingly large sale. And their affairs in general were being capably managed by their twin daughters, Eliza and Harriet, who apparently had considerable "faculty."

Calvin died peacefully enough, with Harriet at his bedside, on August 6, 1886. She lived on for another ten years, slipping off ever so gradually into a gentle senility.

In a letter to Oliver Wendell Holmes she wrote: "I make no mental effort of any sort; my brain is tired out. It was a woman's brain and not a man's, and finally from sheer fatigue and exhaustion in the march and strife of life it gave out before the end was reached. And now I rest me, like a moored boat, rising and falling on the water, with loosened cordage and flapping sail."

She was eighty-two. She spent hours looking at picture books, bothering no one, or went out gathering flowers, "a tiny withered figure in a garden hat," as one writer described her. On occasion she took long walks beside the river, an Irish nurse generally keeping her company. Sometimes, Mark Twain would recall, she "would slip up behind a person who was deep in dreams and musings and fetch a war whoop that would jump that person out of his clothes."

And every now and then, during moments of astonishing clarity, she would talk again about *Uncle Tom's Cabin*, the book that had just "come" to her in visions. Once, years earlier, when she was having trouble writing, she had said: "If there had been a grand preparatory blast of trumpets or had it been announced that Mrs. Stowe would do this or that, I think it likely I could not have written; but nobody expected anything . . . and so I wrote freely."

She died near midnight on July 1, 1896.

II

THE REAL WEST

CHAPTER FOUR

Glory Days in Medora

P ART OF what is enshrined in our collective memory as the "real West" had its origins in a little town in the Badlands of North Dakota—a place called Medora, which by all rights ought to be as celebrated as Dodge City or Tombstone. And the fact that Medora was founded by a "crazy French-man" only serves to make it quite as authentic a bit of Western Americana as does the fact that young Theodore Roosevelt once rode high, wide, and handsome down the main street. It's the "Heart of Rough Rider Country" the truck drivers read as they roar by on I-94, resplendent in their $150 Tony Lama boots.

The setting is best seen from Graveyard Butte, out on the windy point on the west side of the river, where they buried Riley Luffsey. The river and the railroad and the little town are spread below. There is a steep gray cliff behind the town that turns pink in the late afternoon light, and in front of town, in a grassy picnic ground, a brick smokestack, prominent as the point on a sundial, marks the spot where the packing plant stood.

The château, as everyone in Medora still calls it, is nearer at hand, on a bare, high bluff this side of the river, just back from the railroad bridge. Except for the big box elder beside the back door, the house looks no different today from the way it does in the old photographs.

Whether Theodore Roosevelt ever stood here, I can't say. But his friends the Langs did—it was they who "planted Riley" the day after the shooting—and so doubtless did the Marquis de Morès, if only to enjoy the panorama, nearly all of which he owned.

The view has suffered scarcely at all in the intervening years. The light on the landscape is no less extraordinary, the immeasurable North Dakota sky is something to take your breath away. In early fall the cottonwoods are a blaze of gold beside the mudbrown river, and with the disappearance of the summer tourist traffic, Medora might still be the end of the world.

Come winter, it *is* the end of the world. Only about one hundred and thirty people, including the staff of the Theodore Roosevelt National Park and their families, hang on in the town itself, while on outlying ranches, as snowbanks grow and temperatures drop to 20 below and worse, the isolation and hardships of daily life are compounded a hundredfold.

Winter is what ended the cowboy dream for Roosevelt, as for so many others along the Little Missouri River. When the thaw came in the spring of 1887, the carcasses of dead cattle surged downstream past Medora like cordwood. But I am ahead of my story, and it is the story, the odd little history that goes with the place, that makes it something considerably more than just scenery. Harold Schafer, who owns the Badlands Motel, the Rough Riders Hotel, and much else in Medora, likes to tell visitors that the charm of the Badlands is their scaled-down grandeur. "These aren't faraway mountains you can't get to, that you can't feel under your own feet," he says, pointing to the surrounding hills. "This is scenery you can reach out and touch." And then he adds, "Teddy's here, too, of course . . . and so is the Marquis."

The beginning was in 1883, when the cattle boom had hit its peak on the Great Plains. The Northern Pacific had also pushed on through the Badlands by then, and this coming of the railroad coincided with the discovery by the Texans and the Eastern and European money people that the Badlands themselves were not all the name implied. To French-Canadian fur trappers penetrating the area a hundred years before, it had been *les mauvaises terres à traverser*—bad lands to travel across. It is as if the rolling prairie land has suddenly given way to a weird otherworld of bizarrely shaped cliffs and hummocks and tablelands, these sectioned off every which way by countless little ravines and draws and by the broad, looping valley of the Little Missouri, which, unlike the big Missouri, flows north and in summer is not much more than a good-size stream.

Extending along the Little Missouri for nearly two hundred miles, the area is a kind of Grand Canyon in miniature, the work of millions of years of erosion on ancient, preglacial sediments. Stratified layers of clay, clays as pale as beach sand, are juxtaposed against brick-red bands of scoria or sinuous, dark seams of lignite. Some formations have the overpowering presence of ancient ruins, of things remembered from unpleasant dreams. The leader of an early military expedition against the Sioux described the landscape as hell with the fires out. George Armstrong Custer, who spent several days snowbound in the Badlands on his way to the Little Bighorn in 1876, called it worthless country.

The cattlemen knew differently. Unlike the other Badlands to the south (those of present-day South Dakota, which are geologically quite different), these of the uppermost reaches of what was then the Dakota Territory were green along the river bottoms and green above, on the tops of the tablelands. It was "wondrous country" for grass, wrote one veteran cattleman, remembering that summer of 1883. There was "grass and more grass" in the bottomlands and up along sweeping valleys: little bluestem grass, "good as corn for fattening," and curly buffalo grass, "making unexcelled winter feed." Veteran cattlemen and greenhorn money people alike were "dazzled by the prospects." The grass was all free for the taking; there was water; and the very outlandishness of the terrain promised shelter from winter storms. Possibly fifty thousand cattle were driven into the Little Missouri basin that summer alone.

The Texas outfits included the big Berry-Boice Cattle Company (the "Three-Sevens" brand) and the Continental Land and Cattle Company (the "Hashknife"). The smaller ranchers were nearly all from the East or from Canada or Europe, young men primed on such newly published, authoritative works as *The Beef Bonanza; or How to Get Rich on the Plains.*

The main attraction, however—the man of the hour—was one Antoine Amédée-Marie-Vincent Manca de Vallombrosa, Marquis de Morès, recently of the French cavalry, who planned, he said, not just to raise cattle but to found an enterprise unlike any in the West. "It takes me only a few seconds to understand a situation that other men have to puzzle over for hours," declared this altogether humorless young aristocrat in his nearly perfect English. Roosevelt's arrival on the scene, several months later, was by contrast a minor occurrence.

De Morès was Roosevelt's age—twenty-five—and like Roosevelt he was a passionate lover of the hunt and the kill and of the great outdoors. But beyond that, the two had little in common. About six feet tall, spare and wonderfully fit, the Marquis was inordinately handsome, with black eyes and a tremendous black mustache that he kept waxed to perfection. It was the handsomeness of a Victorian stage villain, to judge by the few photographs we have. There is something vaguely unpleasant in the face, not arrogance only, something more threatening than that—but possibly I am influenced by the knowledge of what he became later in life.

Included with his baggage as he got off the train at the Badlands was a silver-headed bamboo walking stick filled with ten pounds of lead—to exercise his dueling arm. One was supposed to hold the stick straight out at arm's length for several slow counts, a trick I myself have tried unsuccessfully at the château, where the stick still stands in a corner of his bedroom.

In duels in France the Marquis had already killed two men, and on his forays along the Little Missouri he looked like a mounted arsenal—weighted down as he was with two huge Colt revolvers, two cartridge belts, a heavy-caliber French rifle cradled in one arm, a bowie knife strapped to one leg. A Roman Catholic of vigorous piety, a royalist, and an anti-Semite, the Marquis liked to tell his new neighbors of his aspirations to the French throne and how the fortunes he would make in the Badlands were to be applied to that specific purpose.

His plan was to revolutionize the beef industry by butchering cattle on the range, there in the Badlands beside the railroad, and thus eliminate the whole costly process of shipping live animals all the way to Chicago. That dressed meat could be shipped almost any distance in the new refrigerator cars without spoilage had already been demonstrated. So why not put the packing plant where the cattle were? It would do away with the Chicago middlemen, which would mean lower prices for the consumer, which in turn would produce an ever-greater demand for beef.

On April Fools' Day, 1883, the Marquis cracked a bottle of champagne over a tent peg to found Medora, which was to be the center of his operations. He had picked the eastern side of the river for his site. The name Medora was in honor of his American wife, the former Medora von Hoffman, whose father, a Wall Street banker, had provided her with an income of about $90,000 a year (which would be roughly a million in present-day dollars). This plus his own family backing gave the Marquis, as he said, little worry over finances. He would spend whatever was needed. He himself would be president and general manager of the new Northern Pacific Refrigerator Car Company, while his father-in-law, Louis von Hoffman, was listed as treasurer.

The young Frenchman was suddenly everywhere at once, seeing to plans, hiring carpenters, masons, ordering equipment for the packing plant, issuing statements to reporters. He bought up all the land he could lay his hands on, twenty-one thousand acres before he was through. He bought cattle; he brought in twelve thousand sheep. He announced plans to raise cabbages, these to be fertilized with offal from the packing plant and shipped east in his refrigerator cars.

There was nothing slack about his imagination. Another idea was to produce pottery from Badlands clays. Yet another was to ship Columbia River salmon from Portland to New York (at a profit of $1,000 a carload, he figured). As for living quarters, he had originally intended to make do with a tent, pending completion of his own Château de Morès, on the bluff across the river, and the arrival of Madame de Morès. But finding tent life a bit more inconvenient than he expected, he had a private railroad car brought in and placed on a siding. "I like this country," he wrote to his wife, "for there is room to move about without stepping on the feet of others."

Yet since arriving, he had done little else but step on feet and sensibilities. The West, for all its aura of freedom, its apparent absence of rules and regulations, was a place—an economy, a way of life—founded on very definite rules and regulations, most of them unwritten. If there was nothing illegal or even illogical about bringing in sheep or buying up land in country where nobody else owned any or believed in owning any, it was all contrary to local tradition and thus, by the prevailing ethic, highly dangerous. Worst of all, the Marquis began fencing his land, and when the fences were promptly cut, as he had been warned they would be, he as quickly replaced them. When three drunken cowboys named O'Donnell, Wannegan, and Luffsey shot up the town and vowed to kill him on sight, he prudently left town for nearby Mandan to ask the territorial justice of the peace what he ought to do. "Why, shoot!" he was told.

So the next time the three cowboys went on a rampage, the Marquis and his men were waiting for them by a bend in the river outside of town. It may have been an ambush, pure and simple—cold-blooded murder, as the Langs insisted—or the Marquis may have been acting in self-defense, as he said. Either way, Riley Luffsey was dead, one slug in the neck, another in the chest.

There were two formal hearings at Mandan, during which witnesses had free run of the saloons, and as things wound to a close, the prosecuting attorney let fly with a scathing burst of frontier oratory, a speech so offensive to the Marquis that he pulled a revolver on the attorney that night at the hotel, aimed, fired, and would have had another killing to answer for had not a bystander struck his arm.

The outcome was an acquittal, and so back to Medora the young Frenchman went, to resume his business in the manner of a man who considered the issue closed and who assumed others did too. Probably he never knew how close he came to being lynched—which is how things stood in early September, when Roosevelt arrived.

•   •   •

Roosevelt got off the train about three in the morning, when it was still cold and dark. He was alone and he looked very little like the man he was to become. At most he weighed 135 pounds, "a little feller" with a wispy mustache and large, metal-rimmed eyeglasses. That he was the classic child of privilege, the very essence of the era's gilded youth by all appearances, escaped no one once day came and he made his presence known. There was something faintly comic about him. He talked in a thin, piping voice and with the swallowed broad *a*'s of an upper-class New Yorker. Later, in an effort to head off some stray calves, he would immortalize himself along the Little Missouri by calling out to one of his cowboys, "Hasten forward quickly there!"

He had come, he said, to shoot a buffalo while there were still one or two left to shoot. He had also come for his health, but of this he said nothing. His vocation was politics. He was an assemblyman from New York's safely Republican Twenty-first District.

He put up at the Langs' ranch south of town, and in a matter of days— having talked to the Langs, having talked to Howard Eaton and a couple of young Canadians named Ferris and Merrifield—he decided to join forces with the Canadians, whose rude cabin, also south of town, was known as the Chimney Butte or, alternatively, the Maltese Cross ranch. What this meant for the moment was money only. He gave Ferris and Merrifield a check for $14,000 to buy some 450 head of cattle, which represented a small start (the Marquis was running something over three thousand head by then), but the direct, trusting manner in which he did it made an impression. He bought no land. Like nearly everybody except the Marquis, he would remain a squatter.

In two weeks Roosevelt was heading home again to West 57th Street and the lovely young wife who was pregnant with their first child. He had killed his buffalo, but only after seven days that had all but killed his guide, Joe Ferris, brother of one of his new partners in the cattle business. The chase had carried them pell-mell over some of the wildest, most difficult terrain in the Badlands. Twice they found a buffalo for Roosevelt to shoot, and each time Roosevelt shot and missed. Exhausted by the pace set by the little Easterner, Ferris kept praying things would get so bad they would have to give up. It rained incessantly, but Roosevelt's joy was not to be extinguished; every new adversity seemed a refreshment. Awaking one morning to find himself lying in several inches of water, Roosevelt exclaimed, "By Godfrey, but this is fun!" For two days he and Ferris had nothing to subsist on but biscuits and rainwater.

Remembering the expedition a lifetime afterward, Ferris was still incredulous. "You just couldn't knock him out of sorts . . . and he had books with him and would read at odd times." When at last Roosevelt shot his buffalo, just across the Montana line, he broke into a wild facsimile of an Indian war dance and handed Ferris a hundred dollars.

He returned in June a changed man. He would stake his future on the Badlands, he said; he would become a cattle baron. There would be time as well to think and to write and to make himself whole again. For by then he had suffered the worst tragedy of his life. Three and a half months earlier, his wife had died of complications resulting from the birth of their daughter, and his mother—the same day, in the same house—had died of typhoid. He saw his political career leading nowhere. He was plagued by stomach trouble, insomnia, and asthma, the torture of his childhood. Added to that was what he called his "caged wolf" feeling. Craving change, craving release from everything in the East, everything in his past, the conventions, the confinement, he was bent on a new life in the open air. New clothes, new work, new companions. Had he been able to change his name as well, as so many others did—there were three men named Bill Jones in Medora alone—he might have done that too, one suspects, given his frame of mind.

The very haunted, often foreboding spirit of the Badlands appealed to him powerfully now. The light in his life had gone out forever, he wrote in a tribute to his dead wife. The Badlands, he said, looked like Poe sounds.

Still . . . something within him refused to be subdued. His depression was serious, but it was also highly sporadic and never, so far as we know, was it immobilizing. He had spent a small fortune on his cowboy getup—big sombrero, fringed and beaded buckskin shirt, horsehide chaps, cowhide boots, silver belt buckle, fancy tooled-leather belt and holster, custom-engraved Colt revolver, fancy monogrammed silver spurs. The works. He gloried in dressing up and having his picture taken. "You would be amused to see me," he wrote to his stuffy Boston friend Henry Cabot Lodge. Truth was, he himself was amused—and unabashedly proud. "I shall put on a thousand more cattle and make it my regular business," he informed his sister Anna. He was in the saddle all day, "having a glorious time here."

Spring mornings were the best, with the mist on the river. He loved the presence of so many birds and animals, the wild roses, the sweet scent of sage and ground juniper. He went off on long early-morning rides on a fiery little horse called Manitou. The dry air and open space and the speed of the horse made "a man's blood thrill and leap with sheer buoyant lightheartedness."

"Black care rarely sits behind a rider whose pace is fast enough," he declared in one of the most self-revealing lines he ever wrote. Get action! It was the old Roosevelt family cure-all—for illness, grief, self-doubt. Seize the moment! In the agony of an asthmatic childhood, the free and open out-of-doors had meant survival, literally life itself.

With very few exceptions, the cowboys took to him from the start. They called him Mr. Roosevelt or Theodore, as he wished; or Four-Eyes or Old Four-Eyes out of his hearing. So far as I know, nobody called him Teddy, a name he never cared for.

He was only an average rider and never much of a roper. He also abhorred foul language and said so, and he did not like to drink. But the cowboys judged him "game to the core." He ate, lived, worked "the same as any man," asking no favors. Besides, he was interesting—he had read a lot, he knew a lot. Once, in a hotel bar in present-day Wibaux, Montana, he stood up and in quiet, businesslike fashion flattened an unknown drunken cowboy who, a gun in each hand, had decided to make a laughingstock of him because of his glasses. The man had chosen to stand foolishly close to him and with his heels too close together, Roosevelt later explained.

He found a beautiful, quiet spot on the Little Missouri some thirty-five miles north of Medora and brought two Maine woodsmen named Sewall and Dow, friends from hunting trips in his college days, to help him establish another ranch, this to be called the Elkhorn. His stake in the Badlands was now up to some $40,000, a fifth of his inheritance.

Bill Sewall, a big, homespun expounder of common sense, arrived from Maine and after looking things over told Roosevelt it was no country for cattle. Roosevelt told Sewall he didn't know what he was talking about. In the privacy of a memorable letter to his family back in Maine, Sewall said, "Tell all who wish to know that I think this a good place for a man with plenty of money to make more, but if I had enough money to start here I never would come here."

The ranch house Sewall and Dow built is gone now. It was a long, low log cabin with a deep front porch where, in the heat of the day, Roosevelt liked to sit in a rocking chair and read poetry or just gaze at the river and the distant plateaus. But the same line of cottonwoods still shades the spot, and there is not another house or road or sign of civilization anywhere in sight.

Roosevelt thought he could write there, and it was as a writer, he had concluded, that the world would take him seriously. In his time in the Badlands, along with everything else, he produced magazine articles, a book on ranch life and hunting, a biography of Thomas Hart Benton, and notes for his epic history, *The Winning of the West*. Most important, he wrote from firsthand experience about the cowboy and the hard realities of the cowboy's life, and this, with but one or two exceptions, was something no writer had done before. Owen Wister, author of the classic western *The Virginian*, called him "the pioneer in taking the cowboy seriously"; and indeed, it was Roosevelt, Wister, and the artist Frederic Remington— three Eastern contemporaries of "good background"—who in their efforts to catch the "living breathing end" of the frontier produced what in large measure remains the popular vision of the "real West."

For his part, Roosevelt threw a charm over the Badlands in much the way other American writers have over other specific locales. And it was the Badlands cowboy, the rough rider as Roosevelt found him in and around Medora, that he fixed in the public imagination. If he didn't exactly invent Marlboro Country, he brought it into focus as nobody had before him, and ironically enough, a Badlands location not far from Roosevelt's Elkhorn ranch site has on occasion served literally as Marlboro Country. The weathered Badlands rancher who can tell you from personal experience what Roosevelt and the others were up against in their time also knows the going rate for commercial modeling.

To what extent Roosevelt's faith in his ranching ventures was buoyed by the activities of the Marquis, Roosevelt himself never divulged. But by 1884, when Roosevelt had more than doubled his investment, it was all but impossible not to be impressed. Growing by leaps and bounds, Medora had become one of the wildest cow towns anywhere in the West, the sort of place, as Roosevelt said, where vice and pleasure were considered synonymous. The packing plant was in operation; cattle were actually being slaughtered; dressed Badlands beef was rolling east in the Marquis's new refrigerator cars. Most important to a young man like Roosevelt, a man with no business experience and some very hardheaded family advisers to face, the big eastern papers, and the *New York Times* in particular, were now paying respectful attention to the Marquis, the thought being "that the foreigner was not so crazy after all." The Marquis, said the *Times*, ran a "wonderful business."

The château was completed and Madame de Morès took up residence, which to most of Medora was the surpassing event of the summer. In truth, the château was not much more than an overgrown frame farmhouse. There was nothing very fancy about it inside or out. But it was large—

twenty-six rooms—and once the big, square piano arrived from St. Paul and a staff of twenty servants moved in, it became in the minds of the local citizenry as much a château as any on the Loire.

The Madame played Liszt and Verdi on the big piano. She painted in watercolors. Perched sidesaddle on one of the magnificent horses the Marquis had shipped from the East, her face shielded from the fierce Dakota sun by an oversize black sombrero, she looked no bigger than a child. Her features were delicate, and beneath the hat she had a great abundance of lustrous, dark red hair. On a shooting expedition in the Big Horns in Wyoming, the delicate-appearing Madame shot and killed three bears, including a grizzly. The Marquis boasted that she was a better shot than he—the ultimate compliment—and had a special hunting coach built for her, equipped with folding bunks and kitchen.

It would be interesting to know Roosevelt's impressions of her on those occasions when he dined at the château; or when they called on him in New York, for it must also be mentioned here that none of these three, not the Marquis or his Madame or Roosevelt, could ever keep away from New York for more than a few months at a stretch, however fervently or sincerely they espoused life on the frontier. Roosevelt was actually in New York more than half of his famous Badlands years—to be with his infant daughter, Alice, and to keep tabs on the political world he could never willingly abandon, whatever else he felt or said.

Presumably Roosevelt and the Madame found much in common, but he never said so in writing. In the dining room at the château, her patterned Minton china is set out today as though guests are expected momentarily. The little landscapes she painted hang in the parlor. Her books are there; her sheet music is piled on the piano. Years later, Roosevelt's sister Anna would say only that "Theodore did not care for the Marquis, but he was sorry for the wife."

That there should be an underlying tension between two such men was inevitable. Were they figures in fiction, we would know a confrontation had to come. And so it did. But what is so fascinating is the behavior of the Marquis. It was he, not Roosevelt, who played the deciding card, though not in a way that the whole violent pattern of his life would naturally suggest.

It happened this way. The summer of 1885, the Marquis was taken to court still another time on the Luffsey murder charge, and again, after another travesty of a trial, he got off. But from the time the issue was revived and splashed across the newspapers east and west, he saw it as a conspiracy by his business enemies, the beef trust, to destroy him. And in this he appears to have been partly right. Convinced also that Roosevelt had had a secret hand in his troubles—which was nonsense—he wrote a letter to Roosevelt asking him just where he stood, a letter Roosevelt took to be a challenge to a duel. Maybe the Marquis meant it as just that, but the whole tone of it suggests otherwise.

Roosevelt answered that he was emphatically not the Marquis's enemy, but that if the Marquis was threatening him, then he, Roosevelt, stood "ever ready to hold myself accountable." Which made it the Marquis's move.

There was no duel, however, because the Marquis kept his head and let the matter drop. Roosevelt was sure he had called the man's bluff; the Marquis had "backed off," Roosevelt would boast. Others were equally sure the Marquis had done nothing of the kind. Some were so sure, in fact, that they would insist ever after that no such showdown had ever occurred, that the story was a fiction devised by the Roosevelt cult, and one might be tempted to accept that had the actual letters not survived. The Marquis made nothing of Roosevelt's response, it seems reasonable to conclude, because he had never challenged him in the first place.

Had there been a duel—with rifles, pistols, swords (Roosevelt wanted rifles at twelve paces)—almost certainly Roosevelt would have been killed. So if it can be said for the Marquis, as I think it can, that his charismatic presence in the Badlands was partly responsible for Roosevelt's own contin-ued presence—and thus for what was an immensely important experience for Roosevelt—it can also be said that his almost unaccountably cool head in this instance spared Roosevelt for other things.

•　　•　　•

The Marquis's empire began coming apart a year before the tragic winter of 1886–1887. A stagecoach line he had started proved a failure. His sheep turned out to be the wrong breed for the climate, and more than half died. His powerful father-in-law began questioning expenditures, then withdrew his financial support.

Yet none of this seemed to faze the young entrepreneur. Like another celebrated Frenchman of the day, Ferdinand de Lesseps, who was then leading a doomed attempt at a Panama canal, the Marquis talked only of success and dazzled reporters with still more innovative schemes to come. He would open his own retail stores in New York and sell his Badlands beef at three cents a pound under the going price. Good beef at a good price for the working man was his dream. Stock in his National Consumers Meat Company was listed at ten dollars a share. His shareholders, he said, were to be the common working people (just as de Lesseps was counting on the common people of France to pay for his canal). The slogan for his bright red stores, three of which actually opened in New York, was "From Ranch to Table."

But the stock didn't sell. Pressures—from the railroad interests, the Chicago packers, the retail butchers—were too strong. Even had the Marquis been a more adroit businessman, it is very unlikely that he could have survived. It is also true that his range-fed beef simply didn't taste as good as beef fattened in the Chicago yards.

The packing plant was shut down in the fall of 1886. Nobody knows what the venture had cost, and estimates on the Marquis's losses vary from $300,000 to $1.5 million. But it is also quite possible that he lost nothing at all, such was the eventual market value of his landholdings.

He and Madame de Morès were gone before winter came. The château was left exactly as it was, as though they would return any time. Roosevelt, too, had departed by then to run for mayor of New York (unsuccessfully) and to be married again. He was in Italy on his honeymoon when the disaster struck.

Storm on top of storm, blinding snows, relentless, savage winds, the worst winter on record swept the Great Plains. In the Badlands the temperatures went to 40 below. Children were lost and froze to death within a hundred yards of their own doors. Cattle, desperate for shelter, smashed their heads through ranch house windows. The snow drifted so deep in many places that cattle were buried alive. People locked up in their houses could only wait and hope that elsewhere conditions were not so bad. A few who couldn't wait blew their brains out.

The losses, when they were tallied up in March, were beyond anybody's imagining. Not a rancher along the Little Missouri had come through with more than half his herd. The average loss was about 75 percent. Roosevelt, when he finally returned to survey the damage, called it a "perfect smashup." He rode for three days without seeing a live steer.

He kept coming back from year to year but never again in the same spirit, and he seldom stayed more than a week or so. His cowboy time was over. In the mid-nineties, he sold off what little he had left in the Badlands, added up his losses, and arrived at a net figure of $23,556.68, or roughly a quarter of a million dollars in present-day money.

But by every measure other than financial the venture had been a huge success. Roosevelt's physical transformation had been astonishing. He came home "bronzed," "thirty pounds heavier," "rugged," as the newspapers noted. "When he got back to the world again," wrote Bill Sewall, "he was as husky as almost any man I have ever seen . . . clear bone, muscle and grit."

In Medora, Roosevelt had his first direct experience with real democracy, as one Eastern friend observed. In the view of his family he never would have become president had it not been for the Badlands years. They had put him back in shape for life, for politics, for a new marriage and a new family. Out of the experience came the whole Rough Rider idea and, consequently, the TR of San Juan Hill. Of course, some were to find his Wild West enthusiasms just a little tiresome, even questionable in a grown man. On the news that William McKinley was dead, Mark Hanna is said to have exclaimed, "Now look! That damn cowboy is president!"

The subsequent career of the Marquis is appalling. The fact that nobody much likes to talk about that in Medora today is certainly understandable. It is easier to forget that the cowboy getup figured not only in the heroics in Cuba but also in the dreadful anti-Semitic craze that swept France toward the turn of the century.

The Marquis went home to France to proclaim himself the victim of a Jewish plot. The beef trust was now portrayed as the "Jewish beef trust." He, too, turned to politics. He launched his own crusade, a blend of socialism and rabid anti-Semitism, and paraded about Paris at the head of a gang of toughs, all of them dressed in ten-gallon hats and cowboy shirts. With the collapse of the French effort at Panama, he joined with the unsavory Edouard Drumont, a notorious anti-Semite, in an attempt to blame that failure, too, on the Jews. It was this mania that eventually led to the Dreyfus Affair, and the Marquis, before he went storming off to Africa, kept himself in the forefront. His platform rantings set off riots, and in a series of duels with important Jewish army officers he became known as one of the most dangerous duelists in France.

The Marquis was himself murdered in June 1896 by a band of Tuareg tribesmen in North Africa, where he had set off on a lone, harebrained scheme to unite the Muslims under the French flag in an all-out holy war against the Jews and the English. He seems to have been mourned only by his children and by Madame de Morès, who remained his stout defender until her dying day.

A statue of the Marquis stands in a little park in Medora beside Harold Schafer's Chuck Wagon restaurant. The statue and the park were gifts of the de Morès heirs. It was they who turned the château over to the State Historical Society of North Dakota, complete with all its furnishings. And like some of the descendants of Theodore Roosevelt, Antoine de Vallombrosa, grandson of the marquis and present holder of the title Marquis de Morès, is a frequent summer visitor to the town.

I asked him once why he keeps coming back. We were on the road south of town, on our way to see Joe Hild, who owns Roosevelt's old Maltese Cross ranch. Until then we had been talking about his homes in Geneva and Biarritz. Tony, as he likes to be called, picks his words carefully and speaks in perfect American English, without a trace of an accent. "Oh, I like the people here," he said. "Where in my normal life would I meet such wonderful people, so different?" He is circumspect, graying; he wears both a belt and suspenders, a watch on each wrist, a red baseball cap and black basketball sneakers.

I stopped the car to pick up a chunk of scoria from the side of the road, a memento for my writing desk, and he asked me to get one for him also. "Are you interested in geology?" I asked as I got back behind the wheel. "Oh, no," he said softly. "Unless perhaps in connection with oil! I am very interested in oil. Do you know anything about oil?" And we both laughed. Those small oil pumps that look like nodding grasshoppers have become a ubiquitous part of the Badlands landscape, except within the Theodore Roosevelt National Park.

It is the park that remains Roosevelt's Badlands memorial—more than a hundred square miles of natural splendor, camping and picnic areas beside the river, hiking trails, miles of scenic roads. Open year-round, it attracts some 800,000 visitors a year, about 75 percent of them during North Dakota's brief summer.

Antelope, whitetail, and mule deer abound. So do squirrels, beaver, rabbits (eastern and mountain cottontail), skunks, prairie dogs, coyotes, and yes, rattlesnakes. The birdwatcher's checklist issued by the Park Service lists 116 species, but if there is a Badlands bird it is the magpie, with the crow running a close second. Elk, moose, black bear, grizzlies, and the gray wolf have all vanished from the area since Roosevelt's day, but the buffalo herd that roams the park now surpasses any he ever saw.

The great days in Medora lasted all of three years, from 1883 to 1886. Nothing much had ever happened there before and nothing much has happened since, as the world judges these things. Though some ranchers survived the Marquis's collapse and the winter of 1886–1887, Medora did not, and were it not for the château, the park and Harold Schafer's commercial enterprises, the place today would be a ghost town.

In 1919, the year of Roosevelt's death, Sewall set down some of his recollections. Remembering how it had all ended, he wrote, "We were glad to get back home—gladder, I guess, than about anything that had ever happened to us, and yet we were melancholy, for with all the hardships and work it was a very happy life . . . the happiest time that any of us have known."

CHAPTER FIVE

Remington

T HE STORY is that young Fred Remington was standing at the corner of Ninth and Main in Kansas City one summer day in 1885 when he saw a man he knew, a housepainter named Shorty Reeson, coming along in a spring wagon pulled by an ill-kept mare that Remington liked the looks of. Remington was then twenty-four and down on his luck. He had come west to make his fortune and in two years had succeeded in losing a sizeable inheritance, about $9,000, roughly half of what it had taken his late father a lifetime to accumulate. The young man's first Western venture was a sheep ranch in central Kansas. When that failed, he saw his future in "hardware or whiskey—or anything else," as he said. With the money left, he bought into a Kansas City saloon as a silent partner, but within a year it too had failed. In the meantime, his new wife had left him. She was Eva Caten from back home in upstate New York, where they had been married the previous October. After three short months in Kansas City, she packed her things and headed home—once she found that Remington was not a successful iron broker, as he had led her to believe, but the keeper of a low saloon. The one note of promise since her departure was the sale, through a local art dealer, of some Western scenes he had painted.

Was the mare for sale? Remington called to Shorty Reeson, according to an old account in the Kansas City *Star*. She was not, said Reeson (he "being wise in the ways of horse trading"). Was she good under saddle? Remington asked. Best see for himself, Reeson said. So at the busiest intersection in Kansas City, in front of the Grand Junction Hotel, they unhitched the wagon and borrowed a saddle, and Remington swung up to give the horse a try. Satisfied, he agreed to a price of fifty dollars.

And thus the next morning, sometime in August 1885, Remington left Kansas City behind him, heading west.

The scene could hardly be more appropriate—the lone figure of a man on the move, heading into an uncertain, possibly perilous, future in the prime of youth. The background is the Old West, but the man is of greater interest than the background. And of course there is the horse. For Remington there was always the horse. If he could have but one thing written on his tombstone, he once told a drinking companion, it would be "He knew the horse."

Besides, he had an audience for this turning point in his life, a vital element not overlooked in the old account. "They warned him of the perils. He smiled," it says. "They coaxed him, he went." His popularity as a "good fellow" was firmly established. Long afterward, the cashier of a billiard parlor spoke of him lovingly as "One Grand Fred." Recalling the time, Remington said, "Now that I was poor I could gratify my inclination for an artist's career."

He was born on October 1, 1861, in a big frame house that still stands on Court Street in Canton, New York, on the northwest watershed of the Adirondacks, which is about as far north in New York state as it is possible to be without crossing into Canada. His full name was Frederic Sackrider Remington. His father, Seth Pierre Remington, was the proprietor of a local newspaper, a lean, active man, ardent horseman and ardent Republican, who distinguished himself as a Union cavalry officer in the Civil War. His mother was Clara Bascomb Sackrider, whose family had a hardware business in Canton. An only child, little Freddie had the run of the town, his love for which was to be lifelong, as indeed it was for all of New York's North Country. In 1873 the family resettled in nearby Ogdensburg, overlooking Canada on the St. Lawrence River. Seth Remington, "the Colonel," had been made collector of the port at Ogdensburg. He sold his newspaper and for both pleasure and profit began raising and racing trotting horses.

In a photograph taken at Canton shortly before the move, eleven-year-old Freddie, dressed in the visored cap and miniature uniform of a volunteer firefighter, poses with the "heroes" of Engine Company One. Twice in consecutive years Canton's business district—and the Colonel's printing

plant—had been destroyed by fire. The Colonel rallied the town to establish three new fire companies, and Freddie was made an official mascot. On
the Fourth of July he marched with his father and the other men of Engine
Company One at the head of the parade.

Full grown, standing five feet nine and weighing upward of two hundred
pounds, he exuded physical power. A veteran Kansas City saloon keeper
who had seen plenty of rough men in his time described him as "a bull for
size and strength," and said Remington could have been a prizefighter had
he chosen. A Kansas City matron called him a Greek god who fairly
"shone with the light of youth." Even as a schoolboy he cut an impressive
figure. At sixteen, in a letter written from the Highland Military Academy
in Worcester, Massachusetts, he portrayed himself as follows:

> I don't amount to anything in particular. I can spoil an immense amount of
> grub at any time in the day . . . I go a good man on muscle. My hair is short
> and stiff, and I am about five feet eight inches and weigh one hundred and
> eighty pounds. There is nothing poetical about me. . . . They all say I am
> handsome. (I don't think so.)

He had been sent to another military school, the Vermont Episcopal
Institute at Burlington, where he had his first formal art lessons, then to
Highland Academy, where his pen drawings of soldiers and battles were
considered a wonder by his classmates. He had no aspiration to any wealth
or fame that called for excessive effort, he wrote in bantering spirit to one
of his Sackrider uncles. "I mean to study for an artist." More often, he
talked of pursuing a career in journalism like his father, who was now in
failing health and a worry. "Do you miss my 'gab' on martial subjects?" the
boy wrote after a visit to Canton. "Guess if I hadn't come home you would
have died."

At Yale he enrolled in the School of Fine Arts and played football,
making a name for himself as a first-string forward, or rusher, on the Yale
team of 1879—the last of the fifteen-man teams, whose captain was the
famous Walter Camp, the "Father of Football." The program at the School
of Fine Arts was under the direction of John Ferguson Weir, an accomplished, European-trained painter known for his dramatic portrayals of
heavy industry. Instructions in drawing were under John Henry Niemeyer,
"the German," who held to the classic drill of drawing only from plaster
casts and who inscribed on the blackboard a maxim of Ingres's: "Drawing is
the Probity of Art." When asked for guidance by an aspiring young artist
long afterward, Remington said his advice was never to take anyone's

advice, but then added, "Study good pictures and above all draw—draw—draw—and always from nature."

Repeatedly over the years, he would portray himself as self-taught, and in the main this was so. Nevertheless, his Yale training, brief as it was, served him well and in some of his mannerisms—figures of speech, the clothes he wore—he was to remain unmistakably a product of Yale, more Yale than cowboy, ever after. Friends were addressed as "old boy" or "old chap," and words like *bully* became habitual. Traveling to and from the West by train, he was frequently mistaken for an Englishman.

On the death of his father, in 1880, Remington dropped out of Yale after only a year and a half. He tried different jobs in Ogdensburg and Albany, stuck to none, worried about his future, proposed to Eva Caten and was turned down by her father, went west briefly—to Montana Territory, principally for the fun of it—and came home with some sketches and a pale blond mustache. Again he tried a clerk's life in Albany, hating every moment. On coming into his inheritance at twenty-one, he took off for Kansas, the sheep farm, and his string of misadventures.

Neither his mother nor Eva Caten took an interest in his artistic efforts or held any hopes for him in that line. Only one member of the family, William Remington, a favorite uncle who owned a Canton dry-goods store, remained convinced that the boy's future was in art. Had anyone else who knew his story been in Kansas City to see him ride away that summer of 1885, they could not possibly have envisioned all that happened so soon after.

His success was sudden and extraordinary. He became focused as he had never been. His capacity for concentrated effort, his energy and productivity were all at once boundless. In little more than a year, back from his wanderings through New Mexico and Arizona, reunited with Eva, his bank account nicely enhanced by his Uncle Bill, he had established himself as a magazine illustrator in New York. He had an apartment in Brooklyn and an entrée at *Harper's Weekly*, the country's leading magazine, where he made his first call dressed in full cowboy regalia. In short order he was discovered by *St. Nicholas* and *Outing* magazines. In 1887 *Harper's Weekly* alone carried thirty-nine of Remington's drawings and sketches. He received a commission from *Century Illustrated Magazine* to illustrate a new series of articles by young Theodore Roosevelt, articles that would later appear as a book, *Ranch Life and the Hunting Trail*. The next year more than seventy Remington drawings and sketches appeared in *Harper's Weekly*.

His annual income was a princely eight thousand dollars. He was working now in pen and ink, oil, and watercolor. In 1889, the year of his enormous oil *A Dash for the Timber*, he and Eva bought a large house on a hill in suburban New Rochelle, New York, with stables and a sweeping lawn. By 1890, only five years after being down and out in Kansas City, he was one of the best-known artists in America, a full-blown celebrity at age twenty-eight. In 1890 *Harper's Weekly* ran more than a hundred of his illustrations, seven as double-page spreads. Furthermore, he was now writing as well as illustrating. He painted *A Cavalryman's Breakfast on the Plains*, *Cabin in the Woods*, *Aiding a Comrade*, and *The Scout*. He had his first one-man show. Eva described him as working as if he had forty children to support. For a new illustrated edition of Longfellow's *Song of Hiawatha*, the largest commission he had yet received, Remington would produce twenty-two full-page plates and nearly four hundred drawings.

The improvement in his work, meantime, was astonishing. The first drawings for *Harper's Weekly* had, as editor Henry Harper said, "all the ring of new and live material," but they were "very crude" in execution and had to be redrawn by staff artists. An early oil *Signaling the Main Command*, painted in 1886, is so stiff, so awkwardly handled overall, that one wonders how possibly it could have been done by the same artist who painted *Dash for the Timber* just three years later.

In *Signaling the Main Command* everything is at a standstill, everyone rooted to the ground. Horses and men are like cutouts pasted down on a drab backdrop and on each other. There is no air between them, no life in any gesture. By contrast, *A Dash for the Timber* is everything suggested by its inspired title (Remington was good at titles). The massed riders charge pell-mell, nearly head on at the viewer. Their horses are flying—hardly a hoof touches the ground—and the dead weight of the one rider who has been hit makes the action of the others, and of the pursuing Indians, all the more alive. The dust flies, guns blaze away, the wind whips the big hat brims. There is no time for second thoughts. It is big action in big space. The painting is nearly the size of a mural, measuring four by seven feet. It drew immediate attention when accepted for exhibition at the National Academy of Design and remains one of the masterpieces of American painting, let alone Western art.

Some of Remington's subject matter, like *Hiawatha*, had nothing to do with the West. On occasion, the magazines commissioned sporting sketches. *Cabin in the Woods* was a North Country scene, and there were to be more as time went on. It was the West, however, that the editors and his public wanted most, the Wild West—cowboys, horses, soldiers, renegade Indians, and action, lots of action—and at intervals during all the work, he kept going back and forth to the West to gather material. He became known as the expert on the subject. The widespread impression was that Remington's West must be authentic, the *real* West, and this accounted in no small measure for his popularity. The editor of *Century*, the highly cultivated Richard Watson Gilder, is said to have offered Remington a box of cigars and said: "Tell me about the West." "He draws what he knows and he knows what he draws," the readers of *Harper's Weekly* were informed in a biographical essay on the artist.

It was said repeatedly—and usually with Remington's encouragement—that he had been a cowpuncher himself, that he had seen action with the troops, when in truth he had never done either. To be sure, he had experienced a lot of hard riding with the cavalry in New Mexico and Arizona, in Montana and the Dakota Territory. He had known and observed countless cowboys and Mexican vaqueros, Cheyenne, Apache, Sioux, and Crow Indians. He had seen nearly all the West in every season and made friends everywhere he went sketching and painting or simply using his eyes. "Without knowing exactly how to do it, I began to try to record some facts around me," he later explained, "and the more I looked the more the panorama unfolded. Youth is never appalled by the insistent demands of a great profession."

Like so many before him and since, he found the West physically and emotionally invigorating—therapeutic. He loved the air, the clear, dazzling light, the freedom he felt in such "grand, silent country." But it was there also that he had staked his claim professionally—"Cowboys are cash," he told a friend—and rather than trying to dress the part, to play cowboy or soldier, he seems to have gone out of his way to be conspicuously the observer only, to be nobody but Frederic Remington. On a grueling cavalry exercise in the heat and dust of June in Arizona, an expedition that seems to have been designed in part to test his endurance, he measured up well enough to be elected an honorary member of the troop—he was made the mascot again by his uniformed heroes—but he went wearing an English safari helmet.

On another of his forays, in Montana in 1890, he arrived at an Eighth Cavalry encampment on the Tongue River sitting astride a tall horse and wearing a huge brown canvas hunting coat, yellow English riding breeches, and fancy Prussian boots set off by long-shanked English spurs. He was a memorable spectacle. On his head this time was a tiny, soft-brimmed hat, which in combination with the canvas coat made him look bigger even than he was. A man of phenomenal appetite for good food and drink, Remington had become by then "a huge specimen of humanity," weighing perhaps 250 pounds. When he dismounted, it is said, the horse appeared glad to be rid of him.

A young officer who was present on that Montana trip, Lieutenant Alvin H. Sydenham, himself an amateur artist, described Remington as a "big, good-natured, overgrown boy" and left this intriguing account of Remington's working methods in the field:

> I watched this fat artist very closely to see "how he did it." My stock of artistic information was as great when he went away as it was before he arrived. There was no technique, no "shop," about anything he did. No pencils, no notebooks, no "kodak"—nothing, indeed, but his big blue eyes rolling around at everything and into all sorts of queer places. Now and then an orderly would ride by, or a scout dash up in front of the commanding officer's tent. Then I would see him look intently for a moment with his eyes half closed—only a moment, and it gave me the impression that perhaps he was a trifle nearsighted.

One morning before dawn, Sydenham was awakened by a prolonged scratching at the flap of his tent. It was Remington asking for a "cavalryman's breakfast." Sydenham didn't know the expression. "A drink of whiskey and a cigarette," Remington said. The story quickly made the rounds, to the advantage of Remington's already considerable popularity with the men.

To Sydenham, Remington was "a fellow you could not fail to like the first time you saw him," and others would later say much the same. Though never a cowboy or soldier, never a good shot, often bothered by the sight of blood, he relished the comradeship of "hard-sided," plainspoken men, "men with the bark on," who loved the outdoors as he did and welcomed his high spirits and fund of stories. Nothing gave him such pleasure, Remington said, as sitting about with good companions "talking through my hat." He was always just arrived from somewhere afar, always on his way somewhere else interesting. In the words of a lifelong friend, an Adirondack hunter and guide named Has Rasbeck, "Remington never stays put for long in any one place, but there's an awful lot of him while he's around."

He called the soldiers of the Indian-fighting army "my tribe," and they, more even than the cowboys and ranchers, were the "real West," both in what he painted and what he wrote. It was a highly selective reality, to be sure, as he knew perfectly well. The real West of the sod-house homesteader, of crops and families, of small towns and railroads had no appeal for him. He never responded to any of that as did such chroniclers as Willa

Cather or his friend Hamlin Garland, for whom, like Cather, the West was native ground. Remington's Westerner is a horseman, the wild-riding soldier or cowboy, and Remington's West is a place of endless conflict, his horsemen ever battling with the elements or the Indian, another horseman, who to Remington was a true savage and so joined with the elements. Nature in his West is never benign or sustaining. It is remorseless, a killer—and thus antithetical to civilization—to any but the brave and uncomplaining. Indeed, it was the very advance of "the derby hat, the smoking chimneys, the cordless binder" that impelled him, he said. "I knew the wild riders and the vacant land were about to vanish." The whole picturesque way of life of his tribe was as doomed as that of their Indian foe.

While the rest of the country spoke of the advance of the frontier, the "taming" of the West, as a positive force in the building of American civilization, to Remington the frontier was receding and, in the end, a tragic loss. He went west to chase a disappearing past, not to find the future. To him the West was more a place in time than any part of the map or something to own. His paintings and drawings, the things he wrote, had nothing to do with dreams of a home in the West. He bought no land there. He wanted none. He never lived there, never stayed more than a month or two at a time. Some of it he thought ugly and depressing, like the Dakota Badlands that so entranced Theodore Roosevelt. What mattered were those wild riders; they were the "living breathing end" of a time that must not go unrecorded or uncelebrated.

Roosevelt, too, in books and articles, was trying to capture the open-range West before it was gone. So also was their mutual friend Owen Wister, whose stories Remington illustrated. Seeing themselves as joined in common cause, they encouraged, advised, and complimented one another. "It seems to me that you in your line, and Wister in his, are doing the best work in America today," Roosevelt wrote to Remington. He considered Remington the country's greatest living painter and was hardly less enthusiastic about Remington's writing. "Are you aware . . . that aside from what you do with the pencil, you come closer to the real thing with the pen than any other man in the western business?" Roosevelt asked Remington in 1897, by which time Remington had published more than sixty articles. "I don't know how you do it," Roosevelt continued, "anymore than I know how Kipling does it."

Wister was a Philadelphian, a Harvard graduate like Roosevelt, wealthy, citified, a little finicky, anything but a Westerner. Kidding him with advice on how to do a proper Western story, Remington wrote, "Put every person on horseback and let the blood be half a foot deep. Be very profane and have plenty of shooting. No episodes must occur in the dark." Wister privately thought of Remington as a "rollicking animal" and "the most uneven artist I know," as he confided to his mother, but he provided a glowing introduction for a portfolio-sized book of Remington drawings called *Done in the Open.* Remington, he said, was more than an artist, he was a national treasure. It was out of the creative production of Roosevelt, Wister, and Remington—three Easterners—that a heroic vision of the Wild West emerged to claim the popular imagination as the nineteenth century was about to end; and it was in the East, in comfortable surroundings, that their important work was done. Roosevelt wrote his spirited accounts of roundups and bucking horses at a desk at Sagamore Hill, his twenty-two-room house overlooking Long Island Sound at Oyster Bay. Wister "pegged away" at *The Virginian,* the first true Western in American literature, while escaping a Philadelphia winter in Charleston, South Carolina. Remington produced the great body of his work in a studio built to order on his hill at New Rochelle, from where he, too, could catch a glimpse of Long Island Sound.

But of the three, Remington had, as Roosevelt admitted, the greatest talent and the greatest influence. He produced much, much more, in print and on canvas, and with greater feeling. However selective or romanticized his West may be, he loved it with a passion. His work, as he said, was always more a matter of heart than head.

His pleasures were simple. He loved horses, dogs, good cigars, snowstorms, and moonlit nights; fresh vegetables, pancakes, spareribs, pigs' knuckles, salt pork and milk gravy, roast beef—nearly everything ever put on his plate but spinach and Virginia ham, which he thought tasted like stove wood. "How that man would eat," recalled a waitress at an Adirondacks hotel. "My, my, my, how that man would eat!" When he was drinking, which was often, he preferred Scotch or martinis, and apparently he could drink just about anyone under the table. According to his biographers, Peggy and Harold Samuels, Remington could drink a quart of liquor in an evening.

He was a warm friend, by all accounts, a generous host, and a faithful correspondent who enlivened his letters with delightful little drawings, usually as a way of poking fun at himself. His spelling was atrocious. (He spelled *whom* with an *e* on the end, *humor* was *humer.* He even had trouble getting the names of his best friends right.) Dressed for one of his expeditions into New York, he wore a silk hat, kid gloves, patent-leather shoes, and carried a walking stick with an elk-horn handle. Otherwise he was without pretense and considered the best of company by many of the prominent figures of the day. He counted among his friends General Leonard Wood, dramatist Augustus Thomas, architect Cass Gilbert, the painters Childe Hassam and John Twachtman, and his fellow illustrator Howard Pyle.

He and Eva had no children, nor does he seem ever to have shown any interest in children. His life was his work, his travels, his friends, his lunches in town at the Players' Club, an occasional black-tie dinner, and Eva, for whom, it is said, he had an abiding devotion. She was small and dark-haired, with large, wistful eyes. He called her "kid," because she was three years older. In one letter she refers to him as "my massive husband," and in old photographs and drawings of the two together, she looks about one-third his volume.

He named their house at New Rochelle *Endion*, an Algonquin Indian word meaning "the place where I live." At first he worked in the attic, then downstairs in the library. Later, he built his "Czar-sized" studio, twenty-four by forty feet and twenty feet high, with a stone floor, brick fireplace, and a big skylight such as he had never had before. He filled it with his treasured props—old rifles, revolvers, an 1840s cavalry saber, a pair of snowshoes, riding paraphernalia. There was an immense moose head over the fireplace, a human skull on the mantelpiece, Indian rugs on the floor, Indian pots and baskets scattered about—drums, tomahawks, any number of beaded shirts and moccasins hanging on the walls. It was all just as he wanted, the place where he liked most to receive friends or to be photographed. The double doors at one end were high and wide enough for him to bring a mounted horse in and out.

On a typical day he worked from eight in the morning until three in the afternoon, preferably sitting down in a broad, low-slung rocking chair, so that he could tilt back to appraise his progress without getting up. He worked fast, totally absorbed and whistling some tune over and over until it drove anyone else present to distraction. After three, he went for a ride or a long walk, though as time went on and his weight increased, the walks became less appealing. Dinner finished, if there was company he would hold forth in the studio again, "talking half the night." One year he went to Europe on assignment with Poultney Bigelow, a magazine writer and editor whom he had known at Yale. Another year, he made a hurried visit to North Africa, again with Bigelow. Summers, he headed home to the North Country, often to Cranberry Lake, his favorite lake in the Adirondacks, where he would sit in the shade of the hotel porch sketching or trying to hit a loon with his rifle. (He said he shot a ton of lead into the lake and never killed a bird.) With his Adirondack hunting companion, Has

Rasbeck, he made a canoe trip down the Oswegatchie River, from Cranberry Lake to where the Oswegatchie empties into the St. Lawrence, descending 1,100 feet in about fifty-one miles, an adventure he described in his favorite of all the articles he wrote, "Black Water and Shallows." "The zest of the whole thing," he said, "lies in not knowing the difficulties beforehand."

In 1895, one of the most important years of his working life, his first book was published, a collection of fifteen magazine pieces that he called *Pony Tracks.* He painted *The Fall of the Cowboy* and was working now in "mud," as he said, sculpting, and beside himself with pleasure, despite the difficulties of the unfamiliar medium. He had found the recipe for being "Great," he notified Wister.

The result was his first bronze, *The Bronco Buster*, or "Broncho Buster," as he spelled it. "Is there anything that man can't do?" an artist friend exclaimed, on hearing of Remington's latest efforts. Remington was sure his sculpture would make him immortal. "My oils will all get old and watery—that is they will look like *stale molasses* in time—but I am to endure in bronze. . . . I am going to rattle down through all the ages." He had only been fooling away his time until now, he felt certain. "Well—come on, let's go to Florida," he urged Wister, "you don't have to think there. We will fish."

Yet, for all this, the exhilaration of the work, the pleasures of home, friends, the voluminous, convivial style of the man, he was churning with anger and distress, anguish over his weight and his drinking. He was beset with fears of getting old. He abhorred the times he was living in, the "enfeebling" present, as he called it. The country was going to hell. He seethed with indignation over the ineptitude of the "peak-headed, pigeon-brained men in public life." Europe was nothing but a "ten-cent sideshow." Literary critics were "library upholstery."

In one of his stories in *Pony Tracks*, he observed that the cowmen of the West were good friends and virulent haters. Certainly he was too, whether by nature or imitation. When his mother was remarried to a man of whom he did not approve (and for no apparent reason, save possibly that he was a mere hotel-keeper), Remington refused ever to speak to her again.

He despised much of mankind—Italians, Jews, "stinking" Russians, "Polacks," Hungarians—virtually every one of the new Americans pouring into the country. They were the rubbish of Europe, said this most American of American artists. Once he said he liked writing for the magazines because it gave him a chance to use his right, that is, as a boxer does, to hit hardest. In an article called "Chicago Under the Mob," an account of the

Pullman Strike riots of 1894, during which twelve men were killed, he made pointed contrast between the soldiers, his favorite Tenth Cavalry, all "tall, bronzed athletes," and the "malodorous crowd of anarchistic foreign trash" they had to face down. Yet this was mild compared to the outbursts in his private correspondence and some of his diary entries, which went beyond any visceral response to a crisis like the Pullman riots, or the kind of offhand slurs and bigotry common in that day.

"Never will be able to sell a picture to a Jew again," he told Poultney Bigelow; "did sell one once. You can't glorify a Jew . . . nasty humans."

I've got some Winchesters [the letter continued] and and when the massa-cring begins which you speak of, I can get my share of 'em and what's more I will. Jews—injuns—Chinamen—Italians—Huns, the rubbish of the earth I hate.

The country was flooding with trash; it was no longer the America of "our traditions," he remarked in another letter to Bigelow who, as has been said, seemed to bring out the worst in him.

He longed for a war, "a real blood letting." He started harping on it as early as 1891. When revolution broke out in Cuba and it looked as though the United States and Spain might go to war over Cuban freedom, he wrote to Wister as excited as a twelve-year-old. "Say old man there is bound to be a lovely scrap around Havana—a big murdering—sure." It was his ambition, he said, "to see men do the greatest thing which men are called upon to do." His one regret was that so many Americans would have to be killed just "to free a lot of d——— niggers who are better off under the yoke." The only combat Remington had ever experienced firsthand was on the Yale football field.

On assignment from William Randolph Hearst, owner of the New York *Journal*, he and Richard Harding Davis, the era's most glamorous corre-spondent, sailed for Cuba to cover the uprising waged by the rebels, if the rebels could be found. Remington and Davis reached the island in January 1897. Reportedly, Remington soon cabled Hearst: "Everything is quiet. There is no trouble. There will be no war. I wish to return." To which Hearst is supposed to have replied: "Please remain. You furnish the pictures and I'll furnish the war." Hearst later denied the story. In any event, Remington came home empty-handed and sorely disappointed. But when Davis sent a dispatch about an incident in which a refined young Cuban woman, Clemencia Arango, was stripped and searched by Spanish officials on board an American ship in Havana because she was thought to be a courier for the rebels, Remington was called in immediately to do a drawing for the *Journal*. It ran five columns wide, its dramatic effect expertly handled by Remington, who contrasted the pale skin of the naked young woman with three hovering, heavily shadowed Spaniards who have not had the courtesy even to remove their hats. With only the Davis dispatch to go by, he had understandably assumed the Spanish officials were men. It was one of the few times Remington ever rendered the female form. "I don't understand them, I can't paint them," he once said of women. But the drawing caused a sensation. That edition of the *Journal* sold nearly a million copies, a record number. Seeing the story and drawing for the first time, Señorita Arango was mortified. The one Spanish official who had searched her was a woman, she said. The atrocity was a fake.

The war with Cuba, when it came, was the most wrenching, disillusioning experience of Remington's life. It was nothing like what he had expected; it bore no resemblance whatever to the high drama and heroics he had been painting and writing about for so long. There were no horses this time, no grand, silent country for background. Instead, there was smothering heat, mud, rain, yellow fever, dysentery, atrocious food or none at all, the strange jungle closing in all around. He knew he had made a mistake in returning almost from the moment he arrived. "The men were on half-rations, were out of tobacco, and it rained, rained, rained. We were very miserable," he reported in *Harper's Monthly*, writing now with no romantic illusions concerning the glories of war, writing, as it happens, one of the best of all accounts of the brief, ten-week conflict in Cuba.

Nor was he anything but honest about his own behavior under fire: "A ball struck in front of me, and filled my hair and face with sand, some of which I did not get out for days. It jolted my glass [field glasses] and my nerves and I beat a masterly retreat, crawling rapidly backwards, for a reason which I will let you guess." He saw face wounds for the first time and trenches full of Spanish dead. "Their set teeth shone through their parted lips, and they were horrible." It was all horrible. "All the broken spirits, bloody bodies, hopeless, helpless suffering which drags its weary length to the rear, are so much more appalling than anything else in the world that words won't mean anything to one who has not seen it." Worst was the specter of white bodies lying in the moonlight, with dark spots on them. According to Remington, it took him a year to get over Cuba.

Meantime, he painted *Charge of the Rough Riders at San Juan Hill*, which makes the war look more like a football game than what he had written about, and *Missing*, in which he returned to "my war," to give gallantry its due again: a stalwart cavalryman, his arms bound, a rope about his neck, walks stoically to his fate at the hands of his Indian captors, a good soldier to the last.

•   •   •

"I have spread myself out too thin," Remington told Wister as the new century began. He was overworked, "crazy with work." He vowed to do no more writing. After 1905, having published more than a hundred magazine articles and two novels, he abandoned writing altogether. If the fellows who sold groceries could take vacations, he mused, why couldn't he?

He bought a small island, Ingleneuk, in the St. Lawrence River upstream from Ogdensburg, at Chippewa Bay. He and Eva spruced up the house on the property, built a studio and a boathouse and put in a tennis court. Nothing he had ever owned, no place he had ever seen pleased him more. All his life he had needed the outdoors, as a release and a restorative. That had been chief among the attractions of the West. But here he was home in his own part of the world. He could swim, fish, grow vegetables, or, having cautiously eased his immense bulk into place, go paddling off in one of his beautiful cedar canoes built in Canton by his old friend J. Henry Rushton, who is still remembered as the Stradivarius of canoemakers. On moonlit nights he would climb about the rocks along the shore. Some nights were so still and clear he could hear a dog bark over in Canada. It was also an excellent place for him to go on the water wagon, as he said, since Eva allowed no liquor on the island, which in all comprised about five acres.

The best part of it for Remington was that he could work there as nowhere else, "away from publishers' telephones," as he said, "trolleys—fuss that makes life down in the big clearing—which I hate." He was fed up with "progress," now more than ever. In 1885, when he set off for the West on Shorty Reeson's horse, electric trolleys were still a thing of the future in Kansas City, telephones few, long-distance calls made possible only that same summer. The years since had seen the advent of the skyscraper, the automobile, the phonograph, and the adding machine, as well as the discovery of the X ray and the cause of yellow fever—advances in science and technology that brought unprecedented change on all sides and seemed to nearly everyone else entirely welcome, even thrilling. This, after all, was the *twentieth* century. His friend Theodore Roosevelt, now the president of the United States, was building the Panama Canal. Magazine publishing had been revolutionized by the invention of photogravure printing, which for Remington meant his work could now be reproduced in color. He signed an exclusive contract with *Collier's* to do six paintings a year, the subjects entirely of his choosing, for $6,000, and he maintained the rights to the paintings. So because of the new technology he could paint as he pleased, knowing his work would reach an audience of a size never before granted an artist.

Still, he claimed no use or affection for modern times. He was sour on all cities. He refused to own an automobile. To any who thought differently, he said: "Go to your microbes, your statistics, your volts, and your bicycles, and leave me the truth of other days."

His terrible problem was that the adored other days of the West were to be found no more, though he kept trying. "Shall never come west again," he wrote to Eva during one trip. "It is all brick buildings—derby hats and blue overalls—it spoils my early illusions." On a later expedition, a wilderness camping trip near "Buffalo Bill" Cody's ranch in Wyoming, he barely survived a blizzard, too much whiskey, and a "d——— old bed which made pictures all over me." He couldn't wait to get home. "Cowboys! There are no cowboys anymore!" he exclaimed.

In the big studio at New Rochelle in 1905, he had begun his most ambitious project yet, an enormous statue of a cowboy on horseback for Fairmont Park in Philadelphia. It was to absorb him for several years. But at Ingleneuk he concentrated strictly on his painting.

A change had come over his painting. The brushstrokes were looser and the light in his pictures was more diffused. He concentrated more on color than on line. He was painting pure landscapes, with none of the "story" quality obligatory in so much of the illustration he had done since the beginning. He was determined to be accepted as an artist, not "just" an illustrator. Mostly, he was painting to please himself, painting the North Country with a zest.

Evening on a Canadian Lake, among the most evocative of all his works, is of two friends in one of his Rushton canoes. Other paintings from these last summers of his life are *Pete's Shanty, Ingleneuk, Chippewa Bay*, and several oil sketches titled *Pontiac Club, Canada*. They were nearly as much a departure from his previous work as was his first venture in sculpture.

His Western scenes, too, had a different quality. More and more of them were nocturnes like *Night Halt of the Cavalry*. "No episodes must occur in the dark," he had told Wister. Now he was absorbed in painting moonlight.

It was as if he wished to start all over. On Friday, February 8, 1907, he had carried seventy-five of his old Western scenes outside at New Rochelle and burned them. A year later, on January 25, 1908, "a fine winter day," he did it again, building a big bonfire in the snow behind the house. This time he destroyed sixteen, including two of his best-known cowboy paintings, *Bringing Home the New Cook* and *Drifting before the Storm.* "They will never confront me in the future," he noted with satisfaction. His father, too, had once stood and watched his work go up in flames.

Remington at forty-six, the age his father had been when he died, thought about death a great deal. His father, dying of tuberculosis, had wasted away to almost nothing. Remington by 1908 weighed nearly three hundred pounds.

His diary from Ingleneuk, however, is filled with exhilaration in the new work, his unabashed happiness with the life there.

MAY 26　　　. . . am getting on famously with my paintings.

MAY 28　　　Worked to good purpose—made a success of *Pony Herds,* which had got away from me.

MAY 30　　　. . . I am doing great work. A man to work should not have anything else happening.

JUNE 5　　　Beautiful day—worked all morning—have five pictures done . . . am learning to use Prussian [blue] and Ultramarine in proper way.

JUNE 22　　　. . . I have now discovered for the first time how to do the *silver sheen* on moonlight.

JUNE 26　　　. . . made sketch [of] Pete's cabin—a nice impressional use of the vivid greens of summer. . . . Having bully swims these days and feeling fine.

That fall he would write, "I have always wanted to be able to paint running horses so you would feel the details and not *see* them. I am getting so I can stagger at it." He had arrived at an outlook not unlike that described by Delacroix in his journals: "What I require is accuracy for the sake of imagination." Remington was then at work on his *Cavalry Charge on the Southern Plains in 1860,* a painting in concept not unlike *A Dash for the Timber,* but very different in execution. He was progressing with "quite good results," Remington thought, "better tone—looser."

•　　•　　•

With the new work under way, he craved new surroundings. For years he and Eva had talked of building a house of their own design in the country.

They found land in Ridgefield, Connecticut, and began construction. Everything was to be bigger than at New Rochelle. In May 1909 they moved in, and for all there was to do, Remington managed to keep painting. "I am performing miracles," he wrote at the end of a particularly good workday in June. He was bothered by stomach troubles—he thought maybe potatoes were his problem—but in one of the last of the diary entries, on October 9, he writes that he had not been so happy or felt so well in many years. One of his Western nocturnes, *Fired On*, had been purchased for the National Gallery in Washington.

Remington died in the house at Ridgefield on the morning of December 26, 1909. He had complained of intense stomach pains a few days before, when he and Eva were in New York. They made it home that night, but the following day an emergency appendectomy was performed on the kitchen table. It was to no avail. The doctors found that the appendix had ruptured and peritonitis had set in. For about forty-eight hours it seemed to others that the operation had been successful. Christmas Day there was a snowstorm of the kind Remington loved. He seemed to be comfortable through the morning, even optimistic, as the family exchanged presents. But the doctors knew there was no hope, and in the afternoon Remington went into a coma from which he never recovered. He was forty-eight years old.

On the first day of that year, New Year's Day, 1909, the man who in his lifetime had produced more than three thousand works of art wrote in his diary: "Here we go again . . . embarked on the uncertain career of a painter."

III

PIONEERS

CHAPTER SIX

Steam Road to El Dorado

IT WAS not long after the completion of the Panama Railroad in 1855 that Bedford Clapperton Pim declared with perfect composure that of all the world's wonders none could surpass this one as a demonstration of man's capacity to do great things against impossible odds.

"I have seen the greatest engineering works of the day," he wrote, ". . . but I must confess that when passing backwards and forwards on the Panama Railway, standing on the engine to obtain a good view, I have never been more struck than with the evidence, apparent on every side, of the wonderful skill, endurance, and perseverance, which must have been exercised in its construction."

Bedford Clapperton Pim was a British naval officer and of no particular historical significance. He had, however, seen a great deal of the world, he was a recognized authority on Central America, and his opinion was not lightly arrived at.

It should be kept in mind that the first railroads, all very primitive, had been built in Europe and the United States only some twenty years before. France was still virtually without railroads; not a rail had been put down west of the Mississippi as yet. Moreover, such awesome technological strides as the Suez Canal, the Union Pacific, and the Brooklyn Bridge were still well in the future. And so the vision of locomotives highballing through the green half-light of some distant rain forest, of the world's two greatest oceans joined by good English-made rails, could stir the blood to an exceptional degree.

The Panama Railroad—the first steam road to El Dorado—was begun in 1850, at the height of the California gold craze. And by anyone's standards it was a stunning demonstration of man's "wonderful skill, endurance, and perseverance," just as Pim said, even though its full length was only forty-seven and a half miles.

It was, for example, and as almost no one ever acknowledges, the first ocean-to-ocean railroad, its completion predating that of the Union Pacific by fourteen years. Mile for mile it also appears to have cost more in dollars and in human life than any railroad ever built. For fourteen years it was the world's best-paying railroad.

The surveys made by its builders produced important geographic revelations that had a direct bearing on the decision to build a Panama canal along the same route. In addition, the diplomatic agreement upon which the whole venture rested, the so-called Bidlack Treaty of 1846, was the basis of all subsequent involvement of the United States in Panama.

Still, the simple fact that it was built remains the overriding wonder, given the astonishing difficulties that had to be overcome and the means at hand in the 1850s. Present-day engineers who have had experience in jungle construction wonder how in the world it was ever managed. I think in particular of David S. Parker, an eminent army engineer whom I interviewed at the time he was governor of the Canal Zone. Through a great sweep of glass behind him, as we talked, were the distant hills of Panama, no different in appearance than they ever were. It is almost inconceivable, he said, that the railroad survey—just the survey—could have been made by a comparative handful of men who had no proper equipment for topographic reconnaissance (no helicopters, no recourse to aerial photography), no modern medicines, nor the least understanding of the causes of malaria or yellow fever. There was no such thing as an insect repellent, no bulldozers, no chain saws, no canned goods, not one reliable map.

A Panama railroad still crosses from the Atlantic to the Pacific, from Colón to Panama City. The trains run several times daily and on time, and much of the ride—especially if you are in one of the older cars (without air conditioning, windows open wide)—looks and feels as it must have originally. The jungle is still the jungle. The full trip takes one hour and thirty minutes. But except for a few miles at either end, the present line is altogether different from the original. It takes a different route on higher ground. The old road has vanished beneath Gatun Lake, the enormous body of fresh water that comprises most of the canal and that can be seen close by on the right much of the way as you head toward the Pacific.

The original line was a five-foot, or broad, gauge, and it was built as hurriedly and cheaply as circumstances would allow, to take advantage of the bonanza in California traffic. A minimum of grading was bothered with; bridges were all of wood and built none too substantially. The route was always along the line of least resistance. Anything formidable in the way—a hill, a bend in the Chagres River—was bypassed if possible. No tunnels were attempted (there is one on the present line), and the winding right of way chopped through the jungle was just wide enough to let a train pass. Still, this one little stretch of track took nearly five years to build and cost $8 million, which averages out to a little less than ten miles a year and a then unheard-of $168,000 per mile.

Part of the construction problem can be appreciated in a single statistic. In those forty-seven and a half miles it was necessary to build 170 bridges of more than twelve feet each in length.

• • •

Prior to the railroad there had been no regular thoroughfare across the Isthmus of Panama, and this despite the fact that Panama had been a crossroads between the Atlantic and Pacific since the time of the Spanish conquest. Except for a few isolated villages scattered along the Chagres River, the interior was an unbroken wilderness, little changed from the time Panama City was founded in the sixteenth century.

To get from one side of the isthmus to the other, starting from the Atlantic or Caribbean, travelers went up the Chagres by canoe to a point roughly twelve miles from Panama City, then crossed overland on the old Cruces Trail, a narrow, treacherous mule path that in the wet season— nine months of the year—was virtually a river of mud. At best, a crossing from ocean to ocean took four to six days, and for all who survived, it remained one of life's memorable experiences. Letters and diaries are replete with descriptions of insects swarming in great clouds over the river, of encampments swamped by blinding rains, of pack mules sinking to their haunches in putrid muck.

The idea for a railroad to supplant all of that originated in New York in the late 1840s, shortly before the news of California gold reached the East. The founders were three unlikely, dissimilar individuals, none of whom knew anything about building a railroad, even under favorable conditions.

Henry Chauncey was a Wall Street financier. William Henry Aspinwall was a well-known capitalist and member of one of New York's leading mercantile families, long engaged in trading with Latin America. The third man, John Lloyd Stephens, might have been the creation of Jules Verne. A diplomat, lawyer, raconteur, and amateur archaeologist, he was best known as a traveler and travel writer. Indeed he was "The American Traveler," one of the best-selling writers of the time, a red-bearded, good-natured somebody who had been everywhere and seen everything and who cut a great path in New York and Washington social circles.

Aspinwall, with the help of a generous government franchise to carry the mail to California, had established steamship lines to and from Panama on both oceans. So except for the land barrier at Panama he could provide through steamer passage from New York to San Francisco. The railroad, then, was to be the vital land link in the system—in a grand, continent-embracing system that seemed altogether in step with the manifest destiny spirit of the day but to most practical men looked like an extremely speculative affair. On Wall Street the great question was why so "sound" a man as Aspinwall should have become involved.

It was Stephens who, in the initial stages, made the difference, and in human terms his life counted for a heavy part of the price of success—for he was to die of malaria. Alone of the three partners Stephens stayed with the work in the jungle. He was the driving spirit the first two years, the most difficult and disheartening stage of the whole ordeal. He gave up every other interest to see the work succeed, and he had infinitely more to give up. Earlier, in 1841, Stephens and an English architect named Frederick Catherwood had gone into the wilds of the Mexican provinces of Chiapas and Yucatán and discovered, or rather rediscovered, the ancient cities of the Maya. His books on the Mayan ruins, with stunning illustrations by Catherwood, had caused a sensation. But his overriding interest thereafter had been Panama. He envisioned the tremendous, far-reaching impact of a railroad at that singular geographic location, and he threw himself into the task with all the determination and confidence he had shown in everything else he had ever put his hand to.

Stephens was the president of the railroad, which was a wholly American-owned stock company with its main office in the old Tontine Building on Wall Street. The capitalization was a million dollars.

From the legal-diplomatic standpoint the undertaking was made possible by a treaty signed in Bogotá. Panama was still part of Colombia (or New Granada, as it was then known), and for years the government at Bogotá had been urging Great Britain and France to guarantee New

Granada's sovereignty over the isthmus as well as the neutrality of any future isthmian transit, be it railroad or canal. In return the European power was to have the exclusive right to build and operate such a transit. But then all at once, in 1846, the United States chargé d'affaires in Bogotá, a new man named Benjamin Bidlack, acting without instructions, signed just such an agreement, which was eventually sanctioned by the United States Senate. So by binding treaty the United States was to watch over the isthmus, guarantee open transit from ocean to ocean, guarantee Colombian sovereignty over Panama, and build, if it so chose, a railroad or canal. In practice, once the railroad was in operation, it was to mean the more or less permanent stationing of American gunboats in Panamanian waters and the landing of American marines and sailors during a half dozen revolutions or "disturbances," including the disturbance of 1903, the so-called Panama Revolution, which marked the final separation of Panama from Colombia. (The Panama Revolution is another story and a complicated one, but suffice it to say here that the maintenance of open, uninterrupted traffic on the railroad was the pretext by which American military force was used to prevent the transportation of Colombian troops, thereby guaranteeing a bloodless triumph by the local junta and the creation of the new Republic of Panama.)

The first stake marking the Atlantic terminus of the line was driven into some soggy, extremely unpleasant ground in May 1850, at the onset of the rainy season. The site was little Manzanillo Island, less than a square mile in area, which stood at the opening of Limón Bay (the Atlantic entrance to the present canal) and which was separated from the mainland by only a narrow channel. Like all the low-lying shore of the bay, the island was without human habitation and just barely above tide level.

The terrain was such that the work party, some fifty men, had to live on board an old brig anchored near shore. "In the black, slimy mud of its surface," reads an old account, "alligators and other reptiles abounded; while the air was laden with pestilential vapors, and swarming with sand-flies and mosquitoes." All clearing of trees and vines had to be done by hand with machete or axe. Everything that had to be transported clear of the projected line had to be dragged by hand, too, since no draft animals were available. Much of the time the men worked in water up to their waists, their faces covered with gauze to fend off insects, their noon meals stowed inside their hats.

The engineers in charge were Colonel George M. Totten and John Cresson Trautwine, two hard-bitten Americans in their early forties who had recently built the Canal del Dique, joining the Magdalena River to the harbor at Cartagena. Totten was to stay with the railroad through thick and thin, weathering every imaginable kind of hell, including an attack of yellow fever so nearly fatal that his companions built a coffin for him. Totten in fact would remain chief engineer of the line long after it was built, and his word would be close to law on the isthmus for twenty-five years. A small, dark-skinned, dark-haired man with spectacles who wore his whiskers like Abraham Lincoln, he was quiet, self-effacing, and exceedingly tough. Allegedly he also had a sense of humor, though a search through available sources has failed to produce a trace of it.

Trautwine was the one mainly responsible for the surveys and as such probably deserves a good share of the credit. A better survey would be difficult to produce, according to present-day authorities. What Trautwine lacked in the way of equipment he made up for with ability. His *Engineer's Pocket Book* (1871) would make his name famous among a whole generation of bridge builders, railroad men, and canal builders.

Others among this advance guard were Colonel George Hughes, a West Point graduate who had charge of the overall reconnaissance; James L. Baldwin, his assistant; Edward J. Serrell, another assistant who was later to become a builder of important suspension bridges; and a young man known as J. J. Williams, who as an old man would declare that as God was his witness it was he, *not* Trautwine, who drove the first stake.

From Manzanillo Island the line proceeded south, along the eastern shore of Limón Bay; farther inland it picked up the valley of the Chagres River and kept to the valley, crossing the river just once at about midpoint across the isthmus. Still farther, where the landscape turned more mountainous, the route took the path of another river, the Rio Grande, which flows toward the Pacific.

Because of the curious configuration of the isthmus at Panama—with the land barrier running east–west between the oceans—the general direction of the line was north–south, a fact that countless future travelers on the road would never quite comprehend.

The major discovery produced by the survey was a gap in the mountains some thirteen miles from Panama City that was only 275 feet above sea level. This was a good two hundred feet lower than what heretofore had been the lowest known pass at Panama, and, as further explorations and further surveys would verify, it was, except for one at Nicaragua, the lowest pass anywhere along the entire Continental Divide. The gap, the summit of the railroad, was at Culebra, the place where the latter-day canal builders—first the French, then the Americans—would break through the spine of the Cordillera with the great Culebra Cut.

Another important discovery was that sea level on both sides of the isthmus was the same. Until then it had been widely thought that for some mysterious reason the Pacific was as much as twenty feet higher than the Atlantic at Panama. It was a misunderstanding that had appeared frequently in print and still does. But as was found, the difference is in the size of the tides—those on the Atlantic side being barely discernible (little more than a foot), while those on the Pacific, less than fifty miles distant, are from eighteen to twenty feet, or even more. Mean sea level, nonetheless, is the same on both sides—a revelation of extreme value to anyone contemplating a ship canal through Panama.

When actual construction of the road began, progress inland from Manzanillo Island went very, very slowly. Miles of swamp had to be bridged or filled. The effect of the climate on men and materials was devastating. Tools turned bright orange with rust. Lumber rotted. Boots and books grew mold overnight. Men began to sicken and die, mainly of Chagres fever, the common name for a particular variety of malaria. "Having neither a physician nor any comfortable place of rest, their sufferings were severe," wrote a doctor named Fessenden N. Otis, author of the first published history of the road.

While the Gold Rush provided powerful impetus to get the road built, it also greatly compounded the problem of holding on to a labor force, and like every other essential—rails, coal, rolling stock, food, clothing, whiskey, quinine—labor had to be shipped in from somewhere else and at an exorbitant cost. Hundreds of men deserted the work at first chance—thousands as time went on.

Actual construction began in August of 1850 and with high expectations. But by October of 1851, a year and two months after the work had commenced, the line had penetrated only as far as the Chagres, a scant seven miles. The engineers had grossly miscalculated the difficulty of the task, and the company's resources were about gone. The market value of the stock was close to nothing. Things came to a standstill in Panama, and several key people, Trautwine among them, departed to find work elsewhere. Had it not been for an especially violent tropical storm, that might have been the end of the company and the railroad.

The storm struck in November, 1851, and at the height of it two New York steamers, the *Georgia* and the *Philadelphia*, put into Limón Bay for shelter. Until then, the whole time the railroad was being built, the New York boats had been landing as usual at the mouth of the Chagres—at a native village called Chagres—roughly five miles to the west of Limón Bay. There was no proper roadstead at Chagres; landings were by small boat through the surf and at considerable risk. But that was the place where the local boatmen congregated with their canoes, and so it had been Panama's Caribbean port of entry since the Gold Rush began. For some strange reason, no one had considered that the railroad, even if it went a mere seven miles, could be put to use and begin paying its way.

The passengers from the two ships came clamoring ashore, some thousand strong, and demanded transportation up to the Chagres. So after a string of flatcars had been assembled, off everybody went in the driving wind and rain as far as the river, to a village called Gatun, now the site of the great Gatun Locks. From there they continued upstream by canoe.

The pattern was established. Chagres was abandoned as the Atlantic portal. A new town was slapped together on Manzanillo Island with about as much commotion and along much the same lines architecturally as a Western mining town. A tremendous iron lighthouse was built—docks, warehouses, a railroad office ("a respectable fireproof two-story brick building"), hotels, saloons, and a number of other business establishments, one of which, the Maison du Vieux Carré, specialized supposedly in French girls. As time went on the town became justly famous as one of the filthiest, most miserable holes on the Caribbean. Stephens named it Aspinwall, after his partner, but from Bogotá came word that it was to be called Colón—Spanish for *Columbus*—as a tribute to the fact that Columbus had once anchored in Limón Bay.

Any doubts or misgivings there had been on Wall Street concerning the enterprise or the mental stability of its founders now vanished as the money steadily rolled in. By summer of 1852 the tracks were halfway across the isthmus to Barbacoa—twenty-three and a quarter miles inland from Colón—to where the line would cross the Chagres. "Push was the order," recalled one old-time employee, Tracy Robinson, in his little memoir, *Fifty Years at Panama*. "Yet do what they might, strain every nerve, exhaust every resource, the difficulties to be overcome proved almost insurmountable. The climate stood like a dragon in the way. To this day it seems astonishing that any soul survived to tell the tale. . . . The white men withered as cut plants in the sun."

The work force came from all parts of the world—the West Indies, Colombia, Ireland, Wales, France, Italy, China, India, the United States. The best workers were those from Colombia, men who were accustomed both to hard labor and to the climate. The Irish, tough, experienced "navvies" who had built railroads and canals in England, were brought out by Totten specifically to speed things up, at about the time the line reached Barbacoa, but they suffered intensely from the heat and humidity and were highly susceptible to disease. A newly appointed bishop of California, William Ingraham Kip, wrote of the Irish laborers he saw on his way through Panama: "They looked pale and miserable. It is almost certain death to them to be employed here. . . ." The mortality rate was truly appalling. Malaria, the only endemic disease of the isthmus, was the worst killer among all groups of workers, just as it would be later when the canal builders arrived. But men died too of dysentery, sunstroke, cholera, and the dreaded yellow jack.

How many died all told is impossible to say. Though the Panama Railroad Company provided figures later, records of accidents and deaths among white workers were kept haphazardly at best, and virtually never among blacks or other nonwhites. And in the year 1853, as an example, of some 1,590 men on the payroll, 1,200 were black. The consistent management position was that there had been nothing like the death toll commonly spoken of, and that anyone who lived a clean, temperate life on the isthmus was as safe there as he would be anywhere in the tropics or even southern sections of the United States, which was far from true.

The worst year was 1852, the year Stephens died. Cholera swept along the line shortly after the arrival of a boat from New Orleans. That summer alone fifty-one engineers, surveyors, and draftsmen—nearly all of Totten's staff—died of the disease. Among those making the crossing in July was Captain Ulysses S. Grant, who, with several hundred soldiers and their wives and children, was on his way to California for garrison duty. Grant saw more than 150 of his party die at Panama—men, women, and children—and all miserably. In later years he would talk more of the horrors he had seen in Panama than of any battles he had known.

According to the company's records there were at least 6,000 whites employed during the years of construction, and the company put the death toll among these men at 835. But Tracy Robinson, who was no enemy of the railroad, said perhaps 40 percent died, or about 2,500. And no one then even reckoned the number of deaths among the blacks. Perhaps 6,000 men died in all.

Whatever the true figure was, it was an exceedingly high price to pay for forty-seven and a half miles of track, and it was a grim forewarning of the still greater tragedy to follow. When the French attempted their Panama canal thirty years later, under the great hero of Suez, Ferdinand de Lesseps, an estimated 20,000 people died of disease.

More immediately, the sheer number of bodies that had to be disposed of became something of a problem in itself and led to a macabre solution. Since a large percentage of the dead men had no known next of kin, no permanent address, often not even a known last name, it was decided to pickle their bodies in large barrels, then sell them in wholesale lots. The result was a thriving trade with medical schools around the world, the proceeds going to finance a small railroad hospital at Colón.

•   •   •

A huge timber bridge was completed over the Chagres at Barbacoa after enormous effort, then swept away by a flash flood. Heavy rains in the mountains, as the engineers learned, could cause the river to rise forty feet in as little as twenty-four hours. Elsewhere the landscape seemed mainly water, one creek or stream after another, swamps, foul slime-covered pools. In places the roadbed kept sinking steadily and had to be built up again and again, year after year. At the famous Black Swamp, Totten had to probe 185 feet down to find solid bottom.

Pine or spruce ties on earlier sections of the road rotted and had to be replaced with ties of lignum vitae from Cartagena—ties so hard that holes had to be bored before a spike could be driven into them. Then beyond Barbacoa, at Culebra, a substantial cut a mile long had to be dug through blue clay that in the rains turned to a thick, stubborn gum. To get the clay from their shovels the workers had to use scrapers. And here, too, at Culebra, the engineers encountered the terrible slides that were to plague the canal builders.

With all the gold being brought across from California, with so much comparatively well-heeled humanity converging from all directions, gangs of outlaws appeared and began harassing the line. Several brutal murders occurred; workers were beaten and robbed. So when the local government declared itself incapable of policing the line, the company organized its own armed guard, a ragged, barefoot band under the leadership of one Ran Runnels, a Texas Ranger who did not look the part but who did the job with cold-blooded dispatch, inspired, it seems, by profound religious visions. He was subtle; at first he did very little to check the crime wave, but suddenly, early in 1852, he and his so-called Isthmus Guard rounded up thirty-seven suspects, including several well-known Panamanian businessmen, and hanged them all on the inner side of the old Spanish seawall at Panama City. All at once there they were one bright morning. "Silently the citizens survey the appalling spectacle and then go on about their business," wrote one aghast traveler in a letter to his wife in Boston.

To Runnels, who believed himself divinely appointed to cleanse Eden of evil and corruption, it became a holy war, and some six months later, in the fall of 1852, he struck again. This time there were forty-one victims dangling from the seawall. The crime wave abruptly ended.

The terrifying epidemics, the loss of the bridge at Barbacoa, the mud slides at Culebra, and the Ran Runnels scourge were the memorable events, and they figure prominently in most surviving accounts. The smaller, day-to-day difficulties and torments were the less colorful, less picturesque side of the story, and they can be readily imagined: the punishing heat, the torrential Panama rains, the terrible fatigue of physical labor in such a climate, clothes that never got dry, scorpions in boots in the morning, the incessant mosquitoes, sand flies, ticks, the bad food, and nothing—not a blessed thing—to do but work and survive the jungle while throngs of others, thousands upon thousands of people, passed by heading for the new El Dorado.

Severe mental depression became one of the most debilitating of all problems. The Chinese laborers suffered especially. To ease their plight the company resorted to supplying them with daily rations of opium. Of a thousand Chinese laborers brought in probably six to seven hundred died of disease, but among the survivors melancholia became so acute that scores of them committed suicide, some hanging themselves by their own pigtails, others impaling themselves on carefully sharpened sticks or bamboo poles.

In a letter to one of the stockholders Colonel Totten would write: "I am ashamed that so much has been expended in overcoming so little, and take no credit for any engineering science displayed on the work. The difficulties have been of another nature, and do not show themselves on the line."

•   •   •

On November 24, 1853, a locomotive rolled across a new bridge at Barbacoa, this one a bridge of iron, twice the length of the other (625 feet) and built some forty feet above the caramel-colored Chagres. "The Rubicon is passed," announced the Panama *Star*. In another year the line was at Summit Station (Culebra). Five thousand men were at work, with the construction gangs laboring from both ends.

There was no special ceremony when the last rail was put in place. No gold spike was driven, though by all rights, for this railroad especially, there should have been. The last rail went down on the wet night of January 27, 1855. Totten drove the final spike with a nine-pound maul, and at eight-thirty the next morning, a Sunday, he climbed into the cab of a small wood-burning locomotive at Colón and took it and a string of nine cars on the world's first transcontinental run.

Totten called it "as perfect a road as can be found in the United States." A writer for the Aspinwall *Daily Courier* told how the train, "a chariot of fire," came "thundering over the summit, and down the Pacific slope." In truth there were only twenty-eight miles of straight track. The road was so full of curves, the roadbed so tender in places, that the train had to feel its way with extreme caution. The entire first run, ocean to ocean, included twenty-six station stops and took seven hours.

Some weeks later, with the return of the dry season and the arrival of a delegation of stockholders and newspaper people from New York, something like a formal opening was staged. Quantities of champagne were consumed, quantities of roast beef and pickled oysters devoured. The visitors—not an especially distinguished lot, as one of them later conceded—went breezing gaily along through the jungle, exclaiming over the orchids and passion flowers, the multicolored birds that burst into the air, or a chance alligator picked out of the shadows along a riverbank. The ride was so smooth, we are told, that it did not disturb the ash from a cigar.

There were numerous stops en route for water and wood or at little white-frame station houses with green shutters and picket fences that might have been transplanted directly from New England. For the passengers the journey was a surpassing spectacle—as it would be for the hundreds of thousands who were to follow in the coming years, as it would be for anyone who did not have to *build* a railroad through such a landscape.

On we go, dry shod [reads the account of one of the newspapermen] through the forest, which shuts out with its great walls of verdure on either side, the hot sun, and darkens the road with a perpetual shade. The luxuriance of the vegetation is beyond the powers of description. Now we pass impenetrable thickets of mangroves, rising out of deep marshes, and sending from each branch down into the earth, and from each root into the air, offshoots which gather together into a matted growth, where the observer seeks in vain to unravel the mysterious involution of trunk, root, branch, and foliage. Now we come upon gigantic *espaves* and *coratos*, with girths of thirty feet, and statures of a hundred and thirty feet, out of a single trunk. . . .

Again we cross a stream. . . . Then, again, the train coiling its winding way about the base of a hill, and emerging from the forest, the view opens suddenly upon an expanded savanna, where the tropical sun shines down in a flood of light upon a river bending through an undulating park of green verdure, with clumps of trees here and there, with cattle feeding in their shade, and a settlement of native, palm-thatched, bamboo huts, half hid in groves of banana and orange. So we hurry from scene to scene, pushing on through the flood of tropical vegetation, with endless vistas of beauty that come and go like the dreams of a summer's day.

At Summit Station everyone climbed out into the blazing heat to hear the United States plenipotentiary read a speech of which few, including those who were sober, would remember a word. The lasting impressions were of the local oranges on sale (they are green in color, extremely juicy, and delicious) and the gaunt, sallow look of fever in the faces of the railroad employees—like death heads under Panama hats, wrote one man. Such "unwholesomeness," however, was thought to be as much a part of the landscape as the oranges. The revelation that malaria and yellow fever are carried by mosquitoes was not to come for another generation and would not be accepted by the medical profession until after the turn of the century. Swamp gas, emanations from the putrid soil of the jungle floor, "noxious effluvia" hanging in the wet, heavy air—these were thought to be the sources of all fevers and miasmas, and there was nothing anyone could do about it.

The average time for crossing was reduced first to four, then to three hours. Steamship passengers arriving at the isthmus could disembark on one side in the morning and count on being aboard ship on the other side before dark. Business was booming. "My own private opinion is that no speculative investment I have ever known . . . offers such returns," William Aspinwall advised a kinsman. In the next ten years the railroad carried nearly four hundred thousand passengers. Annual receipts during that time, including the panic year of 1857, were never less than $600,000. For five of those years they were in excess of $1 million.

More than $500 million in gold went across the Panama Railroad in this same ten-year period; more than $140 million in silver, $5 million in jewelry, and $19 million in paper money. And the company collected a quarter of one percent of the value of all precious cargo. The variety of freight handled—besides the usual coal, baggage, and mail—was quite exceptional. One traveler who took time to examine the inside of the freight depot at Colón left this description:

Bales of quina bark from the interior were piled many tiers deep, and reached to the iron triangular-braced roof of the edifice. Ceroons of indigo and cochineal from San Salvador and Guatemala; coffee from Costa Rica, and cacao from Ecuador; sarsparilla from Nicaragua, and ivory-nuts from Porto Bello; copper ore from Bolivia; silver bars from Chili; boxes of hard dollars from Mexico, and gold ore from California; hides from the whole range of the North and South Pacific coast; hundreds of bushels of glistening pearl-oyster shells from the fisheries of Panama lay heaped along the floor, flanked by no end of North American beef, pork, flour, bread, and cheese, for the provisioning of the Pacific coast, and English and French goods for the same markets; while in a train of cattlecars that stood on one of the tracks were huddled about a hundred meek-looking lamas [sic] from Peru, on their way to the island of Cuba, among whose mountains they are used for beasts of burden as well as for their wool.

In less than six years after it was finished, having covered all costs (including five years of major improvements from one end of the line to the other—new bridges, improved embankments) the railroad cleared more than $7 million. Stock dividends for nearly twenty years averaged 15 percent and went as high as 44 percent in 1868. Once, with its price per share at $295, the Panama Railroad was the highest listed stock on the New York Exchange. There had never been a railroad to compare with it.

The explanation was obvious enough. The road had a total monopoly on the isthmian transit, and until the completion of the Union Pacific in 1869 it had no competition for the California traffic. Furthermore, the rates set for passengers and freight were, on a cost-per-mile basis, extremely high.

The story is that the original rate card was drawn up purely for fun in Colón and sent on to New York for the further entertainment of the head office. But the head office took it seriously. A one-way ticket was twenty-five dollars in gold (about three hundred dollars in today's money), which came to fifty cents a mile and made it easily the most costly ride on earth. Anyone who objected was of course free to cross in the old manner—up the Chagres, over the Cruces Trail—or, if preferred, to walk across along the path of the railroad. But the old way generally wound up costing fifty dollars or more (for canoes, mules, guides), and just for the privilege of walking on its right of way the railroad charged ten dollars. Since few people ever wished to spend a moment more than necessary en route—because of the terror of disease—almost everyone gladly paid the twenty-five dollars, and the rate stood for years.

"And it must be recorded," wrote Tracy Robinson, "that while there was not the least extravagance in the conduct of affairs, but on the contrary, great simplicity, the officers, clerks, and employees generally were paid generously for their services and the lives of themselves and families made as comfortable as possible under the circumstances."

Food and housing were provided by the railroad. Headquarters was at the railroad's hotel at Colón, the Washington House, a long, galleried frame ark facing the Caribbean. "There the officers gathered for their meals, with the chief [Totten] at the head, in true family style," Robinson recalled. Medical and hospital care were provided free of charge. (Dr. Mañuel Amador, chief surgeon for the railroad for many years, a native of Cartagena, would become the first president of Panama in 1904.) There was a library of sorts, a billiard room, and a stone church, built mostly with railroad money, that still stands.

Many Irish, French, and Italian workers stayed on, as did Jamaicans and other black West Indians, and their descendants are to be found at every level of present-day Panamanian society. A blue-eyed Panamanian with an Irish surname is not uncommon.

The beginning of the end came in 1880, with the arrival on the isthmus of Ferdinand de Lesseps. Totten, by then retired, came down from New York to join the tour. Both men were now in their seventies—two white-haired figures whose respective efforts on two strategic isthmuses had so greatly reduced the size of the world.

As early as 1849 the pioneer oceanographer Matthew Fontaine Maury had declared that the true value of a Panama railroad would be the precedent it would establish: ". . . by showing to the world how immense this business is, men will come from the four quarters to urge with purse and tongue the construction of a ship canal." And such had been the case, except that de Lesseps was the first to arrive with anything approaching a purse (he was then in the process of organizing his Paris-based Compagnie Universelle du Canal Inter-océanique).

Like de Lesseps, Totten thought a through-cut canal along the route of the railroad—that is, a sea-level passage without locks, such as the Suez Canal—was a thoroughly practicable proposition, and, like de Lesseps, Totten was gravely mistaken. The American canal builders, when their turn came, would not only know how to rid the isthmus of malaria and yellow fever, but they would wisely decide not to try a sea-level trench.

Control over the little railroad would be essential to his project, de Lesseps realized, but this was no less apparent to the Wall Street operator who had been busily buying up virtually all of the stock—Trenor W. Park, a tiny sparrow of a man who was practiced in driving extremely hard bargains. Park too readily declared de Lesseps's plan sound and set his price at twice the market value. For about five months after construction got under way de Lesseps continued to hold out, refusing to pay Park's price. His engineers on the isthmus tried to get by as best they could. Meanwhile, the railroad was being run as usual as a separate and very independent

American enterprise. The arrangement was impossible. On June 11, 1881, the road was purchased outright by the Compagnie Universelle du Canal Inter-océanique for $20 million. Park himself cleared about $7 million on the transaction.

Years later, in 1904, when the United States purchased all the holdings of the long-since bankrupt French canal company—its equipment, properties, the unfinished excavations—the railroad was part of the $40 million package. By then the line was in sad shape. Equipment was long out of date and in bad repair; the road itself had to be completely overhauled from end to end and double-tracked. Tonnage carried on the line during excavation of the canal was phenomenal (300 million tons in 1909–1910, for instance) as the endless dirt trains rolled across the isthmus. But it was not really the same Panama Railroad any longer. Track, rolling stock, everything was different. Then, because the roadbed lay in what was to be the canal channel, this line too was taken up—in 1912 after completion of the new Panama Railroad (strictly an adjunct to the canal), or two years before the canal was opened.

Today, in the middle of the Panama Canal—on Lake Gatun—there is an abrupt, lush little island called Barro Colorado, once the summit of a small mountain. For the past fifty years the island has been used by the Smithsonian Institution as a tropical research station. There is a small compound of laboratories and living quarters, and from the screened porch of the main building you can look out over a fair-sized sweep of lake and miles of jungle farther beyond. It is easy to forget that what you are seeing is one of the world's great shipping lanes, for only when a huge tanker appears, its prow emerging suddenly around the distant break in the trees, is there any sign of civilization.

The Panama Railroad passed directly by here. (Traces of it can still be found some sixty or seventy feet beneath the calm, blue lake.) The surrounding wilderness could well be the same as the railroad builders faced, and especially when a rain squall sweeps over the distant jungle, blotting out the view, you try to imagine what manner of men they were, what quality of purpose spurred them on. "Here the bravest might well have faltered and even turned back from so dark a prospect as presented itself to the leaders . . . but they were men whom personal perils and privations could not daunt, whose energy and determination, toil and suffering could not vanquish." Such is the explanation offered in the old history by Dr. Otis; and, as out of fashion as that may sound, it could just be the answer.

CHAPTER SEVEN

The Builders

THEY ARE all gone now—the Roeblings and the assistant engineers Collingwood, Paine, Probasco, Hildenbrand, McNulty, C. C. Martin; and the Brooklyn contractor, plain, blunt William Kingsley, who started things rolling and lined his pockets nowhere near so well as he might have; and "Boss" Tweed and "Brains" Sweeny, who had an "understanding" with Kingsley and might have made a fortune had the ring not collapsed in 1871, only two years after the work was under way; and state Senator Henry Cruse Murphy, the very essence of "Old Brooklyn," and Abram Hewitt and Teddy Roosevelt's black-sheep uncle, Robert Roosevelt, and the bright, scrubbed "Boy Mayor" of Brooklyn, Seth Low, all of whom served on the board; and Thomas Kinsella of the *Eagle*, who stood behind the work from beginning to end; and J. Lloyd Haigh, the shadowy wire manufacturer from South Brooklyn who wound up in Sing Sing.

Some are known more for what they did in later years, like Hewitt, who became mayor of New York; or Dr. Walter Reed, who was then an intern at Brooklyn City Hospital looking after the men brought in with the bends; or an English laborer named Frank Harris, who wrote a famous pornographic book, *My Life and Loves*. But so memorable a figure as E. F. Farrington, the "master mechanic," the one who blew kisses to the crowds as he sailed over the East River the summer of 1876, riding the first wire

105

strung between the towers, fades from the record from the time the work ended. We don't know what became of him. Or of so many others: the stonemasons, carpenters, riggers, machinists, blacksmiths, riveters, and all the ordinary day laborers who went into the terrifying caissons beneath the river for the bonanza wages of two dollars a day.

Only a relative handful even have names now. Mike Lynch remains a known quantity because he is said to have been "the first Irishman" to go into the Brooklyn caisson and the last to come out; and we know of a watchman named Al Smith, because his son and namesake became governor. The other names, the few scraps of personal information available, are mainly from reports on those who were killed.

In all, several thousand people took part over fourteen years, many who were American born, including some blacks, many Germans, some Italians, some English, at least one Chinese, and a great many Irish. They worked a ten-hour day, six days a week, and they were all men—with the sole exception of Emily Roebling.

The last of them died in January 1980, in a home for the elderly in Harlem, at the age of one hundred six. He was Henry Jones; he had been a waterboy during the final part of the work in 1882 or 1883, which would have made him eight or nine at the time.

Even the spectators are gone now. Governor Al Smith, who grew up on South Street, "in the shadow of the New York tower," loved to describe the spectacle of workers scrambling high up among the cables. When he was eight or nine, his father took him across the temporary catwalk, while his mother stayed home, sitting in her chair, saying her rosary over and over the whole time they were gone. It was his mother who told him of the horrifying work in the caissons. "Perhaps had they known," she would say, "they never would have built it."

But build it they did, calling it a variety of names—the East River Bridge, the New York Bridge, the Brooklyn Bridge, the Roebling Bridge, the Great Bridge, or merely the Bridge—and to anyone who knows what they went through, it can never be thought of as just an engineering marvel, or an architectural masterpiece, or the perfect expression of nineteenth-century industrialism, or a turning point in urban American history, or a nice way to go over the river. It is, besides all that, their story.

•   •   •

It was conceived in winter, in the mind of John Augustus Roebling, the illustrious pioneer builder of suspension bridges and wealthy wire manufacturer of Trenton, New Jersey. According to the accepted account, he was caught in the ice on a Brooklyn ferry and "then and there," scanning the distance between shores, envisioned his crowning work. His oldest son, Washington, age fifteen, happened to be with him at the time.

This was in 1852, thirty years before the fact. It was not until after the Civil War and after the opening of the celebrated Roebling Bridge at Cincinnati that William Kingsley went to Trenton to talk about building one at Brooklyn. Kingsley had no specific kind of bridge in mind. No one in Brooklyn did, apparently. It was the man they wanted, not a particular plan—which is fascinating, since the man was exactly what they were not to have.

John A. Roebling's brilliance was well established. His abiding confidence in science, as all of science and technology were known, was in perfect harmony with the very Jules Verne outlook of the times. "It will no longer suit the spirit of the present age to pronounce an undertaking impracticable," Roebling had written. A German by birth, he had been trained at the Polytechnic Institute in Berlin. He was the first to manufacture wire rope, or cable, in America; the first to perfect a suspension, or wire-hung, bridge that could carry a railroad (at Niagara Falls); the first to dare anything even approaching the size and weight of the bridge at Cincinnati. He was a technical virtuoso, designer, mathematician, inventor, industrial entrepreneur, a success at everything he put his mind to.

Further, his bridges were thrilling to see, as his Brooklyn clients found for themselves on the tour he led cross-country to Cincinnati and Niagara Falls in the spring of 1869. They could count on a triumph of art no less than advanced engineering, he assured them, and to judge by his photograph, the look in the pale, intense eyes must have been something.

In appearance, in manner, he was above the crowd and all business. Once, on a call to Washington, D.C., during the Civil War, he scrawled a note on the back of his card and sent it in to General John Charles Frémont: "Sir. You are keeping me waiting. John Roebling has not the leisure to wait on any man."

There is more, however, and it, too, bears on the story. We don't know everything, which is a shame, since we can never know enough about genius, but in unpublished family correspondence and his own journals, he emerges as a figure of strange, sometimes violent, lights and shadows. He was cold, vain, and suspicious, a man tormented by insomnia, bad digestion, and spells of terrible self-recrimination. He plunged into spiritualism, became a fanatic—there is no other word for it—on hydropathy, the water cure. His children, for whom he had little time, were terrified of him. *Brutal* is a word Washington Roebling used to describe him.

An unforgettable vignette has come down through the family. John A. Roebling stands outside the Trenton mill where a number of donkeys are used to drag heavy strands of wire through long beds of sand, as part of the finishing process. One of the animals dallies or strays from the prescribed path, and John A. Roebling walks up, takes it by the head, and breaks its neck.

When the youngest of his children, Edmund, misbehaved in some unknown fashion, Roebling nearly beat him to death. The boy ran off, disappeared, and was later found in a Philadelphia jail where, according to his brother Washington, he had had himself entered as a common vagrant "and . . . was enjoying life for the first time."

"The hero is admired and proclaimed a public benefaction," Roebling himself wrote in private. ". . . But nobody knows. . . . Who can hide me from myself?"

The heaviest blow he inflicted on Washington was his own untimely, hideous death just as the real work at Brooklyn was about to commence. There was a foolish accident. Roebling was standing beside the ferry slip, helping with the surveys with such concentration that when the boat docked he neglected to get out of the way. The boat jammed against a stringpiece, which caught and crushed his foot. Washington was with him when it happened, and later, when he had several of his toes amputated, without anesthetic at his wish, and later still through the final, gruesome, agonies of lockjaw. Roebling had dismissed the doctors, insisting that water, poured steadily on the open wound, was the only cure.

The bridge he had projected on paper was to surpass any on earth in size and "audacity." Two stupendous gothic towers, larger than anything on either skyline, were to reach 270 feet in the air, while four great cables would carry the roadway, or deck, more than a hundred feet above the river, high enough so all but the largest of the clipper ships could pass below without trimming their top gallants. An unprecedented $7 million was at stake, Roebling had estimated, not to mention the reputations of his clients. But as of the morning of July 22, 1869, he was dead, and, Washington being the only one around who knew enough to carry on, the others—Kingsley and Murphy—saw no choice but to put him in charge at once.

The Colonel, as they called him, was then all of thirty-two years old. He had only the most preliminary plans at hand, as he later acknowledged, no working drawings, "nothing fixed or decided." All he really had to go by were his wits, experience, and "vitality," a favorite Roebling word. He was married and the father of one child, little John A. Roebling II. His salary was handsome, $10,000 a year, but his expenses would run beyond that, so financially the bridge was to mean no profit for him, not a dollar in fourteen years.

It was the understanding since boyhood that he must follow in his father's path, he being the oldest son. He had been sent to the Rensselaer Polytechnic Institute at Troy, New York, in 1854, then, four years later, to Pittsburgh to begin his apprenticeship working on a bridge of his father's over the Allegheny River. After the war, he was dispatched to Cincinnati to become his father's first assistant. With the Cincinnati Bridge completed, he was off to Europe with his bride for nearly a year to study the use of pneumatic caissons in advance of the work at Brooklyn. Other, younger sons were kept at home, meantime, consigned to the prospering family wire business.

Washington never reported to anyone but his father; he was forever being judged by his father. The war was the single interruption, but even then it was his father who, one highly unpleasant evening at the dinner table, ordered him out of the house and into the army. The father despised slavery, so the son must march with Mr. Lincoln's army.

In some ways they were alike. The elder man played the flute and piano, the younger man the violin. Washington could "make a violin talk," we read in a letter from a friend. He had his father's extraordinary physical stamina, his father's steadfastness in the face of adversity. He had been raised on an unyielding Germanic pride in one's work, on duty and cold baths in the morning. But Washington also had a lovely, wry sense of humor. He was soft-spoken, informal, modest to a fault, some thought. He deplored vanity as the most costly of human follies. History, he had decided, favored the vain, and he had little faith in history. He was drawn to astronomy and botany, was particularly strong in geology, and had begun what would become one of the finest mineral collections in the country, if not the world. He adored Goethe (in the original German), chess, opera, roses, a good cigar, the absolute dark of night out of doors, and architecture, which, he came to believe, was the "noblest" art. He drew beautifully. His mind was not the creative engine his father's had been, still he was exceptionally observant and retentive, and could improvise with amazing speed and ingenuity, a gift prized among American engineers of his generation.

The biggest experience of his life until Brooklyn was the war—and in many ways it is the key to the man and what he did at Brooklyn. He had been through "any quantity of hard fighting," from Manassas Junction to Antietam to Gettysburg to the Wilderness to the siege of Petersburg. Miraculously he survived—at Antietam a cannonball came so close it sucked the air out of his lungs—and he came out a brevet colonel, having enlisted as a private the day after his father ordered him from the house. Also during the war, he built several successful bridges of his own, not his father's, design; fell very much in love; and, from watching some of the Union Army's most celebrated figures at close range—Hooker, Meade, Grant—formed decided views on what qualities counted most in a leader. Courage was essential. So was a level head and a reserve of strength for emergencies. So was "the intuitive faculty of being at the vital spot at the right time."

Many people were struck by what seemed an air of imperturbable calm about him. A fellow officer observing him during the siege of Petersburg described him as "a light-haired, blue-eyed man with a countenance as if all the world were an empty show." Washington himself said his eyes were green and confided to his future wife, Emily Warren, sister of his commanding officer, General G. K. Warren, that in truth he worried about almost everything.

•   •   •

He took charge at Brooklyn without hesitation, knowing as did nobody else how much his father had left unresolved, and knowing that unlike his father he had no one standing by should anything happen to him.

The able and, as it turned out, exceedingly loyal staff he assembled were nearly all younger even than he. Not the least of the arresting facts about the Brooklyn Bridge is that the average age of the engineers who undertook to build it was about thirty-one. All the magnificent drawings were executed under his direction—developed, more often than not, from his preliminary sketches, and subject always to his final approval. He ordered materials, wrote specifications. His lengthy annual reports to the trustees remain models of thoroughness and clarity, for, along with everything else, he wrote very well.

The two giant pneumatic caissons were his supreme contribution, however, and a test of everything that was in him. They were the foundations upon which the towers would stand, or to put it another way, they were the part of the bridge nobody would ever see and the part upon which everything depended. And they are still there, beneath the towers, beneath the river, exactly where he calculated they ought to be.

Readers of such publications as *Harper's Weekly* or *Scientific American* were asked to imagine a colossal, bottomless wooden box filled with compressed air, to keep the river out, and held in position on the riverbed by the tower being built on top. Inside the box were a hundred men or more digging away with picks and shovels. As their work progressed (around the clock), and as the tremendous weight of the tower increased steadily, the box was being forced ever so slowly deeper and deeper in the riverbed until finally it would rest on bedrock. The box was equipped with air locks, iron chambers with trap doors, so the men could come and go without loss of air pressure, and a system of water shafts, the ingenious means devised by Washington Roebling for the removal of excavation. The dimensions of the Brooklyn caisson, the first to go down, were 102 by 168 feet.

Nothing came easily. Boulders jammed beneath the outer or cutting edge. The river came in. As the caisson sank deeper and air pressure within had to be increased, men started experiencing a strange ringing in the ears. Their voices had a thin, eerie sound, and the heat and humidity of the compressed air became almost intolerable. Work in such an atmosphere was exhausting beyond anyone's experience. And scary. The only illumination was candlelight or limelight. When fire broke out in December 1870, it burned into the huge overhead timbers with such intensity, because of the compressed air, that it seemed impossible to put out. Newspapers carried headlines of "The Terrible Conflagration." Roebling was in the caisson, directing the fight, for more than twenty hours, knowing the whole time that the fire could eat into the roof like a cancer and weaken it to the point where the tremendous weight of the tower would come crashing through.

"Colonel W. A. Roebling has given the work his unremitting attention at all times," William Kingsley reported to the trustees, "but especially at all the critical points is he conspicuous for his presence and exertions. During the fire . . . when the destruction of the caisson was imminent, he remained in the caisson all night, putting forth almost superhuman efforts to extinguish it, and only came out when he supposed that the fire was extinguished, and when he felt the symptoms of paralysis . . ."

What he felt was the onset of the bends, or caisson disease, then still a mystery. In his determination to be always where he was needed, he customarily went in and out of the caisson more often in a day than anyone, and he was invariably, as we now know, coming out—out of the compressed air—far too rapidly. He was carried to his home on Brooklyn Heights and rubbed all over with a solution of salt and whiskey. Then, only an hour or two later, when a message arrived saying the fire had broken out again, he dressed and went back. His decision this time was to flood the caisson, something he dreaded doing. As it was, the tedious repairs of the fire set everything back three months.

They hit bedrock on the Brooklyn side at forty-four feet, six inches. On the New York side it was a different story, and the suffering from the bends there became alarming. Every two feet that the caisson descended meant another pound of pressure added to the air inside. As Roebling wrote, hardly anyone escaped without experiencing pain of the most intense kind—"like the thrust of a knife," said one worker. In April 1872, with the caisson at a depth of seventy-odd feet and still no bedrock, two men died. The strain for Roebling was nearly unbearable, as his wife later said. On May 18, a third man died, and that same day Roebling made the most difficult and courageous decision of the project.

Staking everything—the success of the bridge, his reputation, his career—he ordered a halt. The New York tower, he had concluded, could stand where it was, at a depth of seventy-eight feet, six inches, not on bedrock, but on "hardpack"—sand. From examinations of the strata he had determined to his own satisfaction that no movement had occurred at that level since the time of deposit millions of years in the geologic past; so, he reasoned, it was "good enough to found upon." To have driven the caisson to bedrock, he estimated, might have taken another year, and cost possibly a hundred lives.

Sometime later, while seeing to the final details inside the caisson, before it was filled in with concrete, Roebling suffered another collapse, this one far more serious, and from that point on he was to be seen no more. He became as the years passed the famous, mysterious "man in the window," hidden away from everyone, unseen, but supposedly seeing all and running it all from his upstairs room.

Nowhere in the history of such great undertakings is there anything comparable. He directed every step of what was then the largest, most difficult engineering project ever attempted, with all its risks and complications, entirely in absentia. Nobody could see him except his doctors, a few chosen trustees, a few chosen subordinates, and his wife, and never more than one or two at a time. He was never known to go near the bridge or to set foot on it in all the ten more years that the work continued. Only when the bridge was finished would he reemerge, inconspicuously, his health then, he acknowledged, much improved.

For about a year he was not even in Brooklyn, as supposed. He was running things from a sickroom in his father's house in Trenton. But in 1873 he returned to the house in Brooklyn, 110 Columbia Heights, with its sweeping river panorama, and from then on the popular picture of the lone figure at his window, telescope or field glasses at hand, the bridge in the distance, is accurate.

What was the matter with him? Why did he never come out of hiding? The common explanation was that he suffered complications resulting from his time in the caissons—from the bends, in other words. It was also rumored that he was out of his mind, and that if the truth were known his wife was in charge.

Those who did know never said much in explanation, but, interestingly, they also never referred to the bends or caisson disease by name. In a letter to his son years later, Roebling would recall being in such a state that he had to be fed. He was unable even to lift his arms, which may well have been a consequence of the bends. He also complained of failing vision, a symptom not associated with the disease, and for a considerable time was incapable of reading or writing anything.

Farrington, the master mechanic, a notably forthright, direct individual, said Roebling had become "a confirmed invalid . . . owing to exposure, overwork, and anxiety"—which is practically a textbook definition of what in that day was called neurasthenia, or nervous prostration. "He is not so sick as people imagine," Emily Roebling would explain when, in the final days of the work, a single reporter was permitted into the house. His problem, she said, was an inability to endure people or their talk. Talk especially had a "very debilitating effect."

From his own later correspondence, now in a collection at Rutgers University, we know that a "course of electricity," or early, primitive electrical shock treatments, were tried, and they could only have been extremely painful. "Often the doctors said I could not live from day to day," he would write. For the rest of his life he would remember a summer heat wave in Brooklyn when he was "in bed" and the thermometer registered a hundred degrees or worse. He suffered unendingly, that much is certain. Recalling almost anything to do with the bridge or Brooklyn, he would speak of "that fearful time," "that terrible burden," "the tortures I endured." "When I think of what I endured at Brooklyn, my heart sinks within me," he would write to his son.

It is also conceivable that he had become addicted to drugs, and this too may have had something to do with his self-imposed seclusion. We know he was given morphine during the worst agonies of the bends and that morphine addiction as a consequence of just such situations was common. We know also that in later years, suffering from a variety of ills and pains, he relied rather heavily on laudanum, the most common narcotic of the day, and so there is little reason to suppose he did not do the same at Brooklyn. The one reporter who was allowed in at the end was struck by two things when taken in to see Roebling: the first was how well he looked, the other was the "imposing array of medicine phials" on a side table. This could mean nothing at all or it could be that it was the reporter's way of raising suspicions in the minds of readers who were far more conversant with drugs and problems of addiction than many present-day readers appreciate.

Roebling's own explanation of his plight, expressed in a letter to one of his staff, was that he had pushed himself too far. Our imprecise contemporary term would be a nervous breakdown. The remedy for "nervous diseases," he said, was to sit and keep quiet. Relief, if it came at all, could, he found, come "only through mental rest of all the faculties and especially the emotions." And while it is impossible to know just what he meant by the "emotions," it is also impossible not to wonder how much of his problem was psychosomatic in nature. He had made himself a prisoner in much the way his brother Edmund had, and perhaps for him too it meant freedom of a kind, perhaps the same freedom from his father, who could only have been an overpowering presence so long as the bridge remained unfinished and his own duty to the great man's vision continued unfulfilled. Only in isolation could he hold on, keep his head. "I can only do my work by maintaining my independence," he insisted to the trustees at one point.

Whatever the nature of his troubles, however mystifying his situation, his intellectual faculties seem to have suffered not at all. That he could keep everything in his head as he did is astonishing, like someone playing six games of chess at once blindfolded and winning them all. Nothing was done except as he specified. His was the single commanding intellect throughout, as his assistants were the first to acknowledge.

Also, most important, he had, as he put it, "a strong tower to lean upon, my wife, a woman of infinite tact and wisest counsel." She was tall, "strikingly English in style," with brown eyes and a cheerful, mobile expression. He wrote of how gracefully she moved, how entertaining she could be in conversation. "I think we will be a pair of lovers all our lifetime," he had written to her during the war, and from every indication we have, they were.

She became his private secretary, his nurse, and constant companion, his means of contact with the trustees. She could talk to them, he said, as could no one else and with a conviction that carried great weight. When he was first stricken she had gone to Henry Cruse Murphy to explain the situation and was told things could continue as they were, with her husband in charge. She had expected his troubles would last only a short time.

She organized correspondence, kept his daily journal, and assisted in drafting specifications—mountainous tasks all in longhand. If the workers were his troops and he the commander on the hill, she was the trusted aide-de-camp, much as he had been for her brother in the war. If he was indispensable to the bridge, she was indispensable to him. She went to the bridge with his orders, or to be his "eyes," often several times a day and in all kinds of weather. By the final stages she was meeting with manufacturers to explain how certain parts had to be fabricated.

In the files of the Roebling Collection at the Rensselaer Polytechnic Institute there is a copy of a speech given by a graduate, a contemporary of Washington Roebling's, at a dinner in New York in 1882, the year before the bridge was completed. Emily, we read, was a "woman of unusual executive ability. . . . She is firm and decided, with opinions on almost every subject which opinions she expresses with great frankness. To her natural talents for organizing are found tact, energy, unselfishness and good nature . . ."

Progress on the bridge all the while had come steadily, but slowly, in the face of one problem or frustration after another. Work was stalled by bad weather, financial crises, and labor troubles. Trustees complained of the delays. Spinning the cables was supposed to have been the smoothest part of the process, since the system had been perfected on earlier Roebling bridges, but then, in 1878, up popped J. Lloyd Haigh, the wire manufacturer, with his neat bit of deception. Had Roebling been on the job in person, it might never have happened. As it was he had warned the trustees in writing that Haigh was nobody to do business with and, further, if they did some checking they would find that Haigh was financially beholden to Abram Hewitt, the very member of the board who was doing the most to see that Haigh, not the Roebling company, got the contract.

The deception, once discovered, was painfully simple. Some of Roebling's own people had been stationed at the Haigh mill to inspect and certify each wagonload of wire before it went to the bridge, but between mill and bridge a switch was made. Wagon and driver pulled into a building, the approved wire was replaced with an equal quantity of rejected wire, then wagon and driver went on to the bridge, while the good wire was returned to the mill to be run past the inspectors all over again. By the time Haigh was found out a lot of bad wire had gone into the cables, a realization that raised desperate cries from the trustees.

Roebling figured that Haigh had taken them for roughly $300,000. But the bad wire could stay in the cables, he announced, since, in his original calculations, he had included the possibility of some such problem arising and had made the cables more than strong enough to compensate. Yet the thought that such corruption was literally woven into the bridge could never be forgotten, and least of all by Roebling himself.

As a consequence of "The Great Wire Fraud," the Roebling company, from which he had severed connections, was awarded the contract, as it should have been in the first place. That Roebling wire was the finest on the market and fairly priced had never been disputed. But Hewitt, who held the mortgage on Haigh's mill, had convinced the board that use of Roebling wire on a Roebling bridge represented a gross conflict of interest.

In the large scrapbook she kept of the newspaper coverage given all things pertaining to the bridge and her husband, Emily Roebling later inserted a small item reporting that J. Lloyd Haigh was breaking rocks at Sing Sing.

She was her husband's representative at such lavish, publicized affairs as the 1880 dinner at Delmonico's for Ferdinand de Lesseps, the hero of the Suez Canal, which had opened the year work on the bridge was begun. She was her husband's staunch defender when, in the very last part of the work, some newly appointed trustees led by Seth Low tried to fire Roebling from his job—in a "spirit of reform"—and almost succeeded. Finally, it was she, at his request, who was first to ride over the bridge by carriage, in advance of the official opening. She went in an open Victoria, carrying a rooster as a symbol of victory.

•   •   •

The grand opening took place on May 24, 1883, and was cause for the biggest celebration ever seen in Brooklyn or New York. The President of the United States, Chester A. Arthur, a New Yorker, led the parade over the bridge to Brooklyn, accompanied by a future President, Governor Grover Cleveland. The work had taken nearly three times as long as the five years John A. Roebling had estimated, and the cost had come to nearly $16 million, or more than twice his original figure.

The cost must also include the life of John A. Roebling and the others who followed. John French, a rigger, John McGarrity, a laborer, and Thomas Douglass, a stonemason, were killed when a derrick fell. Henry Supple, another rigger and "one of the best men upon the bridge," had the top of his head taken off when a strand of wire snapped. Thomas Blake was killed in the same accident. Ross Harris died in a fall. August Denning died in a fall. Hensen, Read, Delaney, Collins, Noone, McCann, Elliot, Higgens, and two men named Murphy died in falls. McLaughlin, a machinist, was "killed instantly" by a falling stone. Dougherty was crushed to death by a falling derrick. So was Enright. Mullin was crushed by a stone being swung into place. Cope, a rigger, had the job of guiding a wire rope onto a hoisting drum. When he saw the rope was not running as it should, he kicked at it. His foot slipped and his leg was wound around the drum, crushing it so badly he died "almost instantly." Brown lingered on in the hospital before he died. His back had been broken when a coal bucket fell on him.

Those known to have died of the bends include John Myer, Patrick McKay, and an Englishman named Reardon, who began work on the New York caisson on May 17, 1872, and died May 18, the day Roebling ordered the halt.

According to an interview in the *Eagle* with C. C. Martin of Roebling's staff, two others named Deneiss and Gardiner also died—though Martin could not recall how—which brings the rough total to twenty-seven.

The grief and hardship experienced are of course immeasurable. In an official report of the trustees, as an example, it is recorded that the widow of Henry Supple received as compensation for her loss $250. Because the family of John McGarran, who was permanently disabled by a fall, found themselves "entirely destitute," he was awarded $100. To what degree other victims of the bends suffered as Roebling did, or died an early death because of the ordeal, we can only imagine.

Roebling himself, incredibly, outlasted all the others on his staff. Emily, who later earned a law degree and became known for her efforts in behalf of women's suffrage, died in 1903. He was the last leaf on the tree, as he said, absorbed in his books, his greenhouse, his minerals, the wire business, feuds with his brothers, and in writing long letters to his adored son. The few times he is known to have gone out on the bridge, with Emily and later by himself, he did so with no fanfare. Confusion over whether he or his father built the bridge dogged him until the end. "Most people think I died in 1869," he wrote.

He died in Trenton in his own bed at age eighty-nine on July 21, 1926, almost fifty-seven years to the day after his father's death in Brooklyn.

Interestingly, those who worked on the bridge had little or nothing to say about it once it was finished. All the speeches and poetry, the long essays, the editorials extolling its beauty and significance were provided by others. Roebling, too, said almost nothing on the subject. He—they all—seemed to prefer to let their work speak for itself.

CHAPTER EIGHT

The Treasure from the Carpentry Shop

Early in 1969, because a bit of hardware on the Brooklyn Bridge had begun to show signs of wear after nearly ninety years, a young civil engineer working for the City of New York's Department of Transportation was delegated to hunt up the original drawings of the item. The "trunnion," as it is called, is a steel joint assembly, or gudgeon, about eighty of which are used to connect the vertical cables of the Brooklyn Bridge to the roadway out at the center of the river span where the greatest movement occurs. It is not an especially complicated or interesting device and it need concern us no longer, but like every other part and piece of the bridge, it had been custom-made to begin with and so could be replaced only by remaking it from scratch. Hence the need for the drawings.

Francis P. Valentine, the man sent for the drawings, was then twenty-nine years old, large and bearded, a native New Yorker and resident of Brooklyn who has been rightly described by his friend David Hupert as "an absolutely dedicated public servant." His instructions were to go to the department's carpentry shop at 352 Kent Avenue, a small, nondescript brick building beneath the Brooklyn end of the Williamsburg Bridge, and to look through the files that were in storage there.

Valentine was advised to wear old clothes, but he had no idea what to expect.

What he found, what he saw the morning he first walked into the shop, was one of the most remarkable treasures in the whole history of the building art, a collection totaling some ten thousand original blueprints and drawings, and what is so amazing is that for all the bewildering disorder they were in, the layers of dust and filth, he sensed almost at once the extent of their value. And in this he was the rare exception, for the drawings had been known to others in the department for years. Kept mainly for possible reference needs, for just such emergencies as the trunnion problem, they had been gone through, in part, by perhaps as many as twenty or thirty people at one time or another. Yet the idea that they might be worth something, that many were, in their way, magnificent works of art, not to mention historic documents of great consequence, had thus far failed to dawn on anyone of authority. In fact, one official, the engineer in charge of all East River bridges, previously had ordered that the drawings be thrown out because they were taking up too much space, and this would have been their fate had it not been for the carpenters who worked in the shop—William Jeblick and Joseph Vecchio, among others—who decided it might be best if they simply ignored the order. As Jeblick remarks, "It would have been a shame to see such things go to the dump, when they should have been in a museum."

Most of the drawings were packed into huge wooden file drawers, giant chests as old as the bridge itself, but hundreds of others were piled in rolls on top of these chests, and on shelves, tables, every which way, wherever there was space. The light was poor and the dirt and dust were "unbelievable," as Valentine remembers.

> Every time I pulled open a drawer a cloud of dust came out in my face. None of it looked like much at first, mostly blueprints, what you'd expect. Then after maybe four or five drawers, I began finding wonderful hand drawings, some of them enormous. I noticed many of these had WAR written on the bottom and I couldn't for the life of me understand why anyone would want to write "war" on the bottom of a drawing. I saw the drawings were dated—I realized they were a *hundred years old*—and I thought, "My God, what am I looking at here?"
>
> Then it struck me, WAR, that's Washington A. Roebling, the engineer who built the Brooklyn Bridge—these were Roebling's own signed drawings!

After going through approximately seventy drawers, he found the trunnion drawings he had been sent for, but in the weeks following he kept insisting to his superiors that he had found—rediscovered—something of far greater importance and that steps must be taken to preserve the collection. "The people who had seen the drawings before never seemed to realize that they included Roebling originals," he explains. "They had no idea of the extent of the collection, never knew, for instance, that it included a profile of the bridge, a *drawing* mind you, measuring 30 feet."

But presently Valentine was told by his immediate boss, the late Edward Backus ("a wonderful, wonderful man"), that if the drawings meant that much to him then he might take a day or so a month to keep going through them, to determine what all was there.

This was still in 1969, the year of the landing on the moon, when a technological achievement like the Brooklyn Bridge seemed just a little quaint, a relic from a different world, let alone a different age, as I know from personal experience. For I, too, at that time, was digging my way through another long-neglected Roebling collection—letters, memoranda, personal diaries, scrapbooks, and the like, all pertaining to the bridge—that had been in storage for years, unsorted, uncatalogued, at the Rensselaer Polytechnic Institute, in Troy, New York. Still, the more Valentine worked with the drawings the more fascinated he became—and determined to get them out of the carpentry shop and into safekeeping. He called the Long Island Historical Society to see if anyone there could advise him what to do. He called the New York Historical Society and the Museum of Modern Art. He described what he had found. "Nobody seemed interested. Nobody felt it was important. They'd ask me how many drawings there were and when I said I thought maybe ten thousand, they'd right away say that was more than they could ever handle. I couldn't get anybody even to come see what I was talking about. And back at the office a lot of people gave me the impression that I was out of my mind."

He tried several newspapers, and at length, in 1973, the Trenton *Times* sent somebody over to the carpentry shop and ran an article. Still, nothing happened, not until a year or so later when Valentine discovered that David Hupert worked at the Whitney Museum of Modern Art.

Until then Hupert had been only another of Valentine's neighbors in the Park Slope section of Brooklyn, a nice, friendly fellow who played on the same softball team. For some reason he can't explain, Valentine had never known what Hupert did for a living, but once he found out, things began to happen. Hupert not only came to the carpentry shop—"I just stood there in utter amazement," he remembers—but with Valentine's help selected sixty-five of what he regarded as the most aesthetically striking drawings of the lot, then rounded up the necessary funds to have these

properly cleaned and mounted for an exhibition at the Whitney's downtown gallery. Most of the work on the larger drawings was done by the head
"paper conservator" at the Metropolitan Museum of Art, Merritt Safford.
A century of accumulated dirt had to be removed—mold, mildew, and
thousands upon thousands of tiny, dark specks, roach feces, every one of
which had to be picked off painstakingly by hand. The cost of preparing
the sixty-five drawings was $15,000.

The show, when it opened in May 1976—the first public display of
the drawings—was a huge success. The longer it was up, the greater the
attendance, which is the reverse of the usual pattern. Remembering the
response, Hupert says, "No show we ever did had such an outpouring of
affection, all for that bridge." Still, there was not money enough to do a
catalogue—only a poster was published, a reproduction of the original
thirteen-foot "presentation" profile—and the drawings on display represented but a tiny fraction of the whole, too tiny even to qualify as the tip of
the iceberg.

Interest in the rest of the collection, all still at the carpentry shop, had
meantime become most intense. The Municipal Archives and the
Brooklyn Museum had gotten wind long since of what Hupert was up to
and were highly displeased about it. Each commenced to lay claim to the
collection. The drawings belonged to the city, insisted the Municipal
Archives, and so therefore the drawings belonged in the Municipal Archives. The Brooklyn Museum argued that it was better equipped to give
the drawings proper care and housing, and to put them on public view, and
that after all it was *Brooklyn's* bridge. More important, the Brooklyn
Museum also sent an associate curator, Barbara Millstein, to appraise the
situation at the carpentry shop, and if there is a point in the story at which
one might say that the drawings were at last "saved," this is it. For
Millstein's commitment to the collection was to be unrelenting. Over the
next several years, assisted by a volunteer coworker, Gail Guillet, she did a
thorough inventory of the entire collection, complete with descriptive data
on every item, a simply staggering task. While ultimately, in 1976, her
museum lost out to the Municipal Archives as the rightful proprietor of
the collection, no one, not Frank Valentine or David Hupert or anyone at
the Municipal Archives, would ever contest her hard-earned standing as
the authority on the drawings, and it was the Brooklyn Museum that put on
a mammoth exhibit of three to four hundred of them in 1983, in honor of
the bridge's one hundredth anniversary.

The Municipal Archives now has physical possession of the treasure.
The drawings were finally removed from the carpentry shop in 1976, seven

years after Valentine first found them. But what of the drawings themselves after all? What, finally, is the real value of this extraordinary mountain of paper?

Of particular importance, to begin with, is the fact that it is a *complete* record, and a complete record of almost any engineering feat of that day would be a major find. But this is the complete record of the Brooklyn Bridge, once the largest, most celebrated bridge on earth, "The Great Bridge," the unprecedented, pioneering work that captured the heart of an entire era. It is essential to understand what a complete record in this instance actually means. Since every component was custom-made, and very often a first of its kind, there is a drawing for every component, sometimes several, from the masonry of the towers down to a manhole cover.

The bridge in the plans is infinitely more than the bridge you see. Among the most magnificent drawings in the collection, for example, are those of the giant wooden caissons. Then there are drawings by the hundreds of machines large and small, various kinds of hoisting apparatus, compressed-air pumps, cable-making equipment, every last device needed to do the work, again most of it custom-built and virtually all of it long since vanished. The huge Victorian train terminals that once stood at either end of the bridge, as well as the bridge trains that for years shunted commuters to and fro between Brooklyn and Manhattan—these also are to be found in the collection, every detail beautifully delineated.

The drawings are signed, and not by Roebling only. A grand total of sixty-four different draftsmen and assistant engineers are represented, and the names that figure most prominently are men about whom we happen to know quite a lot. These are not anonymous works in other words; nor are Wilhelm Hildenbrand or George W. McNulty, William Paine, Francis Collingwood, or C. C. Martin, to mention only a few, names without faces, personality, stories of their own, as we know from the written record. Some were among the very best in their profession, and each played a specific, identifiable part in the fourteen-year-long ordeal of building the bridge.

Wilhelm Hildenbrand, who did the major pictorial renderings, will serve as an example. Born in Germany, he was still in his twenties when work on the plans commenced in 1867, which made him one of the youngest of Washington Roebling's amazingly young staff. Hildenbrand, who had been hired initially by old John A. Roebling, was powerfully built, clean shaven, and an intimate of the Roeblings, never people to take friendships lightly. He had even taken part in some of John A.'s spiritualist seances in the big house at Trenton. Before joining the Roeblings, Hildenbrand had designed—at all of twenty-two years of age—the great arched roof of the train shed for Cornelius Vanderbilt's new Grand Central Depot. In the course of his first several years under Washington Roebling, he did all the detailed masonry plans, as well as the architectural designs for the New York Approach, that is, the long span leading to the New York tower. As time went on, he was responsible for most of the mathematical calculations; he worked out the details for the superstructure of the roadway. He wrote a book on cable making. In all he gave more than sixteen years of his life to the creation of the bridge, as much nearly as Washington Roebling, and in his subsequent career he built the Pike's Peak Railway and a large suspension bridge of his own design at Mapimi, Mexico.

The drawings by Washington Roebling, the commanding intellect, number some five hundred.

But then, in the last analysis, one comes to something in these drawings impossible to catalog, that has little or nothing to do with however much biographical or technical background one might compile. It is the incredible care and concentration you feel in even the least of the drawings, the pride, the obvious love—love for materials, love for elegance in design, love of mathematics, of line, of light and shadow, of majestic scale, and, yes, love of drawing—this passion in combination with an overriding insistence on order, on quality, that we of this very different century must inevitably stand in awe before. You feel what these people felt for their work and you can't help but be drawn to them.

Present-day engineering or architectural renderings look very little like these. If in a modern drawing, for example, rivets need be shown, a few suffice, the rest are indicated with a small *x*, and a marginal note specifies the number required. In these from the last century, as Frank Valentine likes to point out, "If there were 140 rivets in a connection, every rivet was drawn, and every one showing how the light would strike it." In drawings such as those of the caissons, each bolt and brace is shown; even the grain of the wood is rendered meticulously in watercolors. In part, but only in part, this can be explained by the fact that many who worked on the bridge were illiterate, or at least so far as reading plans, but as superb craftsmen they could build just about anything if it were pictured exactly as it was meant to look, exactly as it was supposed to be put together.

They who made these drawings were a different breed from our present-day technicians, that certainly is unmistakable, and possibly the most significant difference can be seen in their regard for the total setting in which the bridge was to stand. In these drawings the bridge is never viewed as an isolated entity, the sole focus of interest. It is not the bridge alone that is portrayed in exquisite detail: it is the geological strata through which the foundations must be dug; it is all the little streetscapes over which the bridge will rise, each building done with careful attention to its actual size and character, not merely "suggested" with a perfunctory pencil flourish. One drawing is devoted solely to the mast height of the different sailing ships that will be passing beneath the bridge.

For a long time historians have looked upon the Brooklyn Bridge as a kind of grand but solitary redemptive symbol rising out of the Tweed years, the Grant years, standing alone and above it all, literally and figuratively. Now they must look also at the drawings. The easy, hackneyed labels for post–Civil War America, talk only of Gilded Age greed and frippery, won't do in the face of such work. Had the bridge succumbed to the wrecking ball by now, and were we left with only the drawings to go by, we would still have to conclude that that was no ordinary era.

"When the perfected East River bridge shall permanently and uninterruptedly connect the two cities," wrote the editor of the Brooklyn *Eagle*, Thomas Kinsella, in the spring of 1872, "the daily thousands who cross it will consider it a sort of natural and inevitable phenomenon, such as the rising and setting of the sun, and they will consciously overlook the preliminary difficulties surmounted before the structure spanned the stream, and will perhaps undervalue the indomitable courage, the absolute faith, the consumate genius which assured the engineer's triumph." With the rediscovery of the drawings of the builders, our appreciation for their "consumate genius," for the pains they took in everything, is greater now than ever.

CHAPTER NINE

Long-Distance Vision

In the mid-1920s, in several parts of the world, a number of brave, skilled young men and women began taking to the air at the controls of a variety of aircraft, most of which, by today's standards, were unenviably small, fragile, and poorly equipped. They saw themselves as a new breed of pilot, as pioneers in a new age of aviation. All in their twenties—roughly the same age as the century—they were flying in one of the new airmail services, or surveying possible routes and landing sites for commercial air travel, "seeking footholds on the future," as one of them said.

In a brief heyday of about a dozen years, they set records for distance and speed, crossed oceans and uncharted mountain ranges, explored entire continents, flying in every kind of weather and more by instinct than by instruments. It was exciting, difficult, often dangerous work. Many of them were killed. Six were lost trying to fly the Atlantic Ocean before Charles A. Lindbergh Jr., the finest pilot of the era, flew the 3,610-mile stretch from New York to Paris nonstop and alone, without radio or sextant, in a single-engine plane of only 223 horsepower. He was twenty-five years old, and the historic date was May 21, 1927.

These were no amateur pilots. They were intensely professional, intensely serious about the craft of flying and about their own role in history. They were also, on the whole, extremely good-looking, which added greatly to their glamour. Amelia Earhart, Beryl Markham, and the idolized Lindbergh were as handsome as screen stars. If an exception like Antoine de Saint-Exupéry looked, as somebody remarked, more like a tall, tonsured monk, he could draw amusing pictures and do card tricks on the level of a professional magician.

But most remarkable is how many of them proved to be writers of exceptional grace and vision, authors of more than a score of books. Lindbergh wrote seven, beginning with *We*, a hugely popular account of his early life and the Paris flight, which was rushed into print that same year. Anne Morrow Lindbergh, her husband's copilot and radio operator on later expeditions, was a diarist and poet who hardly ever stopped writing. Her first published work, *North to the Orient*, described the unprecedented survey flight the couple made in 1931 in a small seaplane from New York to China by the great circle route over northern Canada and Alaska, touching down in eastern Siberia and Japan. Sinclair Lewis called it "one of the most beautiful and great-hearted books that has ever been written."

Like Lindbergh, the Frenchman Antoine de Saint-Exupéry began as a mail pilot, flying the Sahara and the Andes, and is known worldwide for the novel *Night Flight*, for his now-classic children's fable *The Little Prince* and for the autobiographical *Wind, Sand and Stars*, which was a best seller and winner of the National Book Award in 1939. His *Wartime Writings 1939–1944*, a collection of his letters and articles, was published here in 1986.

Beryl Markham of Kenya, who looked a little like Greta Garbo, was the first woman to fly the Atlantic from east to west (in 1936). She wrote a high-spirited, often poetic "remembrance" called *West with the Night* that was only rediscovered and reissued a few years ago.

Others included Nevil Norway, an English pilot and aeronautical engineer who wrote novels on aviation under the name of Nevil Shute; John Grierson, another Englishman and a veteran long-distance flyer, who wrote a half dozen books about his adventures, and Amelia Earhart, the first woman to fly the Atlantic alone, who wrote three books, including *Last Flight*, which was compiled after her death by her husband, the publisher George Palmer Putnam.

Though of different nationalities and differing abilities as pilots, these aviator authors were alike in their love of the freedom of the profession, their love for the still unspoiled, distant corners of the Earth and their affection for their fellow pilots. "The dignity of the craft is that it creates a fellowship," said Saint-Exupéry.

Further, aviation was their common cause. With the advance of the airplane, they were sure, the old barriers of time and distance would give way, bringing humanity closer together. That they would share a common crisis in such faith is also part of their story. Ironically, it would be Lindbergh who later renounced with the greatest fervor the whole idea of progress through technology of any kind.

•   •   •

They made of their pioneering time and its aftermath a body of literature like none other. Everything seemed fresh in that time of "early morning horizons," as Anne Lindbergh remembered.

This is how Beryl Markham in *West with the Night* describes her first flying lessons:

> We began at the first hour of morning. We began when the sky was clean and ready for the sun and you could see your breath and smell traces of the night. We began every morning at that same hour, using what we were pleased to call the Nairobi Aerodrome, climbing away from it with derisive clamour, while the burghers of the town twitched in their beds and dreamed perhaps of all unpleasant things that drone—of wings and stings, and corridors of Bedlam.

Why should these pilots have written so much and so well? The early days of railroading produced no literary works of distinction. We have had no literary stars among race-car drivers, or among astronauts as yet. So why these aviators? And why works of such beauty and power that speak to us still after so long a time?

Part of the answer, I believe, is in their feeling for the earth and its beauties. They flew *with* the land, as Lindbergh described in the striking first paragraph of his Pulitzer Prize–winning *The Spirit of St. Louis*, a larger, more detailed and contemplative account than *We* of the Paris flight. It was September 1926, when he was flying the mails:

> Night already shadows the eastern sky. To my left, low on the horizon, a thin line of cloud is drawing on its evening sheath of black. A moment ago, it was burning red and gold. I look down over the side of my cockpit at the farm lands of central Illinois. Wheat shocks are gone from the fields. Close, parallel lines of the seeder, across a harrowed strip, show where winter planting has begun. A threshing crew on the farm below is quitting work for the day. Several men look up and wave as my mail plane roars overhead. Trees

and buildings and stacks of grain stand shadowless in the diffused light of evening. In a few minutes it will be dark, and I'm still south of Peoria.

Lindbergh is removed from the ground like a young god, his vantage point the gift of a machine, a De Havilland biplane with a 12-cylinder, 400-horsepower Liberty engine. With night coming on, he feels the earth's curve and turning. He has the wind in his face as he looks down from his open cockpit. He is close enough to the farmland to pick out details. He marks the cycle of crops, the signs of seeding and harvest. He is in touch with the earth, and he is in touch with his fellow men who, importantly, are harvesters. He sees them; they see him and wave.

It was their practical need to fly with the land that, more than anything, distinguished these pilots from those who would follow. The sky was their frontier, their element. Something about the sky stirred them to their souls, as Melville and Conrad had been stirred by the sea. But they were never detached from the land in mind or spirit. It was of necessity, to keep their bearings, that they flew with rivers and kept eye contact with mountains and plains. Lindbergh, in his vivid, carefully composed paragraph, fixes our attention on the good earth of Illinois before saying a thing about the adventure of flight. Our true bearings, he tells us, are south of Peoria.

There is often a nearly sensual feeling for airplanes as well. The aviator writers prided themselves, found the most realistic kind of reassurance, in knowing their airplanes.

"So he had found his world again," Saint-Exupéry wrote of his valorous pilot Fabien as he takes off in the novel *Night Flight*.

. . . A few digs of his elbow, and he was quite at home. He tapped the dashboard, touched the contacts one by one, shifting his limbs a little, and, settling himself more solidly, felt for the best position whence to gauge the faintest lurch of his five tons of metal, jostled by the heaving darkness. Groping with his fingers, he plugged in his emergency lamp, let go of it, felt for it again, made sure it held; then lightly touched each switch, to be certain of finding it later, training his hands to function in a blind man's world. Now that his hands had learnt their role by heart, he ventured to turn on a lamp, making the cockpit bright with polished fittings and then, as on a submarine about to dive, watched his passage into night upon the dials only. Nothing shook or rattled, neither gyroscope nor altimeter flickered in the least, the engine was running smoothly; so now he relaxed his limbs a little, let his neck sink back into the leather padding and fell into the deeply meditative mood of flight, mellow with inexplicable hopes.

The airplane offered a spiritual pilgrimage in ways other machines never had. These aviators wrote of being lifted out of themselves by the very act of flight, of becoming part of something infinitely larger than themselves. This was the discovery of all discoveries in their farflung ventures that mattered foremost. He was never so aware of all existence, never less aware of himself, Lindbergh said, than when flying. The miracle of the airplane, wrote Saint-Exupéry, is that it plunges us "into the heart of the mystery." For Anne Lindbergh, the sensation of flight was more like that of great music and art, or the brilliant, clear passages of a book. Beryl Markham used the word *religion* and wrote of seeing things for the first time in proper proportion: "I saw the alchemy of perspective reduce my world, and all my other life, to grains in a cup."

The only daughter of an Englishman who settled in Kenya's Great Rift Valley to raise racehorses after the turn of the century, Markham took up aviation as a means of earning a living. From 1931 to 1936, she flew mail and supplies and occasional passengers to the distant reaches of Kenya, the Sudan, Tanganyika, and Rhodesia. Encouraged by Baron Bror von Blixen, husband of the author Isak Dinesen, she started a business spotting big game from the air, working closely with Blixen and Denys Finch-Hatton, the classics-quoting white hunter portrayed by Robert Redford in the film of Dinesen's *Out of Africa.*

Whether, as has been said, Markham was Dinesen's rival for the attentions of Finch-Hatton, I don't know. But he and Blixen figure prominently in *West with the Night,* while Dinesen receives no mention. Indeed, Finch-Hatton is described as the most charming of companions, "a great man who never achieved arrogance." Markham and he flew often in the new plane, a bright yellow Gypsy Moth, that he had brought by boat from England. In one of the book's memorable scenes, her old flying instructor, Tom Black, for reasons he can't explain, tells her not to accompany Finch-Hatton on the flying expedition in which he was ultimately killed.

Because of her glamorous looks and several unsuccessful marriages, Markham was a popular topic of conversation in Nairobi society. When her book appeared in 1942, the gossip was that she hadn't written it. The real author, supposedly, was her third husband, who was not a flyer but a hard-drinking American ghost-writer named Raoul Schumacher. The charge, which she denied, seems unfair and unlikely, though Schumacher's encouragement and editorial help were undoubtedly important, as she acknowledged on the flyleaf.

For all the pilot writers, the prospect of death was something to be faced with every takeoff. "I was in sheer physical terror the whole time," Anne Lindbergh wrote privately after one long, grueling flight with her husband. John Grierson crashed three times flying the Arctic route to Canada. Saint-Exupéry—"Saint-Ex" to his friends—crashed in the Egyptian desert en route from Paris to Saigon, and for three days he and his mechanic survived on a pint of coffee, a little white wine, a few grapes and an orange, until found by passing Bedouins. But then, Anne Lindbergh noted in her diary, Saint-Ex was always crashing. He was too much the artist to be a proper pilot, she thought, and he would be killed if he kept flying.

•   •   •

Were they aviators who wrote or writers who took up flying? That is difficult to say, though I suspect that Saint-Exupéry and Anne Lindbergh would have written under any circumstances. The appeal of aviation as they knew it and the appeal of writing were much akin. There was a corresponding chance for independence and individuality, the exhilaration of risk, the appeal of the inevitable solitude demanded in both lines of work. On the practical side, they knew their notoriety meant a public.

They knew, too, that whether they as individuals survived the next flight, or the next, the pioneering age they were part of was certain to be short-lived, that with the steady advance of aircraft and instruments, their kind of flying would soon be a thing of the past—which only intensified both the experience and their need to record it.

"After this era of great pilots is gone," observed Beryl Markham, "as the era of great sea captains has gone . . . it will be found, I think, that all the science of flying has been captured in the breadth of an instrument board, but not the religion of it. . . . And the days of clipper ships will be recalled again—and people will wonder if clipper means ancients of the sea or ancients of the air."

In the introduction to his wife's book *Listen! The Wind*, Charles Lindbergh foresaw the day when passengers flying the Atlantic would have no more contact with the elements or the water below or any of the beauties of the earth's surface than if they were riding a train through a tunnel. For the feeling of real flying, he said, future travelers would have to turn to books like *Listen! The Wind*, an account of ten days during the most ambitious flight of the Lindberghs' career together—a 30,000-mile circumnavigation of the Atlantic made in 1933, the year after the kidnapping and murder of their infant son.

What began in the mid-1920s was pretty much over by the late thirties.

The end of their era should be marked in 1937, the year Hitler's Luftwaffe practiced mass bombing on the Spanish city of Guernica, and Amelia Earhart, attempting to fly around the world, was lost in the Pacific near the Marianas. By August 1939, over supper on trays in a summer house on Long Island, Lindbergh and Saint-Exupéry were comparing notes on "that thrilling period of aviation that is past," as if it were already ancient history. "But I never know," said Saint-Exupéry with a laugh, "whether it is not my own youth I am regretting." He would soon be facing the Luftwaffe over France.

Lindbergh by this time had made a widely publicized trip to Germany, where he was given the red-carpet treatment by the Nazi high command. He toured their aircraft factories, flew their latest fighter planes. His visit had the secret blessing of the American military, as a means to determine German strength. But when, at a dinner at the American Embassy in Berlin, Air Marshal Hermann Goering surprised Lindbergh with a medal, the shock and outrage at home were not to be forgotten.

On his return to New York, furthermore, Lindbergh joined the isolationist America First Committee. Believing another conflict so soon after the First World War would mean the end of Western civilization, he was convinced the United States should stay out of it. He grew increasingly strident in his public statements to the point where many thought him a traitor. Later, after Pearl Harbor, he flew combat missions in the Pacific.

In *Flight to Arras*, a book that had great effect in the United States, Saint-Exupéry portrayed the valor of his comrades in the French air service as they tried—with terrible losses—to hold back the Germans. When Saint-Exupéry was reported missing after a reconnaissance mission over the Mediterranean in 1944, Anne Lindbergh, grieving over the news, wrote that there was something especially terrible about the word "lost."

"It has a special agony of its own," she wrote, "quite distinct from death . . ."

The airplane made it a war such as was never dreamed of, as Saint-Exupéry noted in 1940. Lindbergh, seeing the devastation of Europe after the German surrender, felt only revulsion for the whole of science and technology, especially aviation. The man who had been its greatest hero longed now to renounce his profession and live with nature. This was in the spring of 1945, before Hiroshima.

Beryl Markham gave up flying and went back to her father's trade of raising horses. She never wrote anything more. Nevil Shute left England for Australia and wrote *On the Beach*, the most haunting evocation we have of a world dying of radiation after an atomic war.

"What frightens me more than the war is the world of tomorrow," Saint-Exupéry told his mother in 1940. Central to all he wrote was the theme of responsibility. In *The Little Prince,* it is the fox, finally, that tells the Little Prince what really matters in life, by reminding him of the flower, the single rose, he had cared for at home on his own small planet. "Men have forgotten this truth," says the fox. "But you must not forget it. You become responsible, forever, for what you have tamed. You are responsible for your rose."

Writing of his friend Guillaumet, an intrepid mail pilot, in *Wind, Sand and Stars,* Saint-Exupéry said that moral greatness derives more from a sense of responsibility than from courage or honesty. "To be a man is, precisely, to be responsible."

When he was eleven, Lindbergh traveled to Panama with his father to see the canal in its final stages of construction. In his lifetime the senior Lindbergh had seen the abolition of slavery, the advent of the telephone, and now the canal. "Great changes are coming," he told the boy. Probably the change he would have least expected—or understood—was the view his son had arrived at by the time he reached his father's age.

The evil of technology was not in technology itself, Lindbergh came to see after the war, not in airplanes or the myriad contrivances of modern technical ingenuity, but in the extent to which they can distance us from our better moral nature, our sense of personal accountability.

In the last book he wrote, his *Autobiography of Values,* published posthumously in 1976, he described a bombing run over the Japanese-occupied city of Rabaul in New Guinea during World War II:

When I pressed the red button on my stick, it was hard to believe I had released a high-explosive bomb. But there it was, deadly and irretrievable, apparently floating in the air. I saw it clearly for a moment as I climbed, and within seconds a pinhead puff of smoke appeared behind me in the city of Rabaul, a puff so small and far away that I could not connect it to the button on my stick, or realize the writhing hell it covered on the ground. I had carried out my mission, and felt little responsibility for what I had done.

In Africa, Beryl Markham was drawn to kinship with life's elemental forces that she saw in the Masai people, the same people, interestingly, that Lindbergh was drawn to in the final phase of his life. "Africa is less a wilderness than a repository of primary and fundamental values," Markham wrote.

Lindbergh was told by a Masai warrior that civilization is not progress.

"We have known freedom far greater than yours," he told Lindbergh, and Lindbergh never forgot the moment. "The primitive," he wrote in *Autobiography of Values*, "teaches that life itself, unforced life, is progress, a fact our civilization tends more and more to overlook." He became obsessed with the essence of life and concluded that we all must for the sake of the survival of humanity. He had called his first book *We*, because he saw the Paris flight as a victory of man and the machine. Later he wrote of the "vicious circle" of technology. He no longer trusted rationality. Quite the contrary: "I have found that the irrational gives man insight he cannot otherwise attain."

He had come a very long distance indeed.

The most fascinating thing about the Lindbergh story is not the Paris flight, not the planes he flew or the fanfare he ignited, but Lindbergh himself. "As our civilization advances," he said in a speech in Minnesota in 1972, "if our follies permit it to advance, I feel sure we will realize that progress can be measured only by the quality of life—all life, not human life alone."

What he saw then, at the close of his life, was the imperative need for balance between man and nature. This was his long-distance vision.

Beryl Markham, who spent her last years in Kenya, died in 1986. Anne Morrow Lindbergh, a widow since 1974, lives in Connecticut in the small house she and her husband built after their children were grown. The last of the pioneer pilots, she is still writing.

IV

FIGURES IN A LANDSCAPE

CHAPTER TEN

Cross the Blue Mountain

THE FICTION of Conrad Richter stands alone. His frontier stories, set East and West, have an authenticity, an unerring ring of truth that is extraordinary, and many, like *The Sea of Grass*, are still in print after more than a generation. Others include *The Lady*, *The Light in the Forest*, and *A Country of Strangers*. His great Ohio trilogy—*The Trees*, *The Fields*, and *The Town*—is an American masterpiece, as vivid and as moving an account as we have of pioneer life. The central character, Sayward Luckett, an illiterate Pennsylvania girl who crosses with her family into the Ohio wilderness after the Revolution and there makes her life, is among the memorable figures in American fiction. The portrayal of the primordial forest of the time is unforgettable.

But Conrad Richter was my friend, and this is a personal reminiscence, not a review or literary appraisal. It is one man's homage to an authentic and exceedingly modest American artist about whom too little has been said.

We met for the first time in July 1963, at his home in Pine Grove, an old crossroads and market town on Swatara Creek in eastern Pennsylvania. At seventy-two, he was then working on what was to be his last published novel, *The Aristocrat*. I had come because I wanted to do an article about him. The article never materialized, but the friendship did, despite the considerable difference in our ages and much else.

137

"No doubt you will be driving over on Route 22," he had written in advance. "If so, after you pass the junction to Route 183 and a little later the Midway Diner, you will see ahead an overpass before which there is a turnoff to Route 501 on which you cross the Blue Mountain. In town after crossing the railroad, turn right, then left, and our house will be on your right. One o'clock will be fine, a little before or after."

The house, a white stucco on Maple Street, was the largest I had seen while driving into the town. There was a neat front walk, a small front porch with columns, a larger screened porch over to one side. Everything—house, walk, me—was bathed in cool green light under the shade trees. "The perfect house for the town doctor" was my thought, and then, when he greeted me at the door, he could have been the doctor himself.

He seemed older than in his photographs, and more impressive-looking, a straight, spare, clean-shaven man with thin white hair and fine features and marvelous crystal-blue eyes. He was about my own height, five feet eleven, and he was in his shirt sleeves, but he wore a necktie and the white shirt was spotless. Later, when we were in the dining room—his work area—I saw that he had tiny squares of adhesive tape, each very clean and clinical-looking, fixed to the tips of the fingers of his left hand. He would bite his nails otherwise, he explained. Children in town often asked about it, he said. He told them he was a bank robber.

We covered a good deal of ground before evening, and though years have passed and he is dead and buried there in Pine Grove, the memory of all he said is very clear, even without the notes I kept. The next spring I returned, and then again with my wife the year following. A correspondence began that lasted until his death.

He told me about his boyhood before the turn of the century. We went to see the brick house in Pine Grove where he was born. He spoke of his father, a Lutheran preacher who began as a storekeeper and whose life story is the subject of A Simple Honorable Man. He talked of the growing season on that side of the mountain, of the Amish and the Pennsylvania Dutch, of going to work when he was fifteen, of a job in the mines, of driving a team, of working as a timberman, farm hand, bank teller, of his first newspaper job on the old Johnstown Journal and of the hard-boiled city editor who had told him without a trace of rancor, "Boy, you'll go far!"

When he smiled I was often struck by how much he resembled General Eisenhower, who was exactly the same age—only a day's difference—and whose people all came from Elizabethville, only about twenty-five miles from Pine Grove.

He described the farm he had bought in a high valley in central Pennsylvania soon after he and Mrs. Richter—Harvena Achenbach of Pine Grove—were married, and he talked of their sudden, desperate move to New Mexico in 1928 when the doctors said she had tuberculosis and would not last the year. The care and attention he gave her—year in, year out—I learned of from her and from their daughter. He mentioned only the struggle to survive on his writing and, with a light in his eye, talked of the very different, raw sort of place Albuquerque had been in those days. In 1950 they had returned to Pine Grove, she still bedridden much of every day.

He had no heroes, he said, at least not historical heroes. He had been to Monticello once and was disturbed by what he saw. "He didn't think Jefferson's democratic principles quite matched his aristocratic way of life," I read now in my notes. "He mentioned the long distance his slaves had to carry the food to the master's table and the place where he chose to be buried, enclosed in a spiked iron fence, removed from the rest of mankind."

I once asked him whose fiction he admired. He thought a moment, then said, "Turgenev." And that seemed to be that.

Often and with great passion in his voice, he talked of the despoiling of the American land, the despoiling of the American Indian, and on one or two occasions he talked, though guardedly, of his lifelong interest in the occult, an interest he believed most writers shared. "But you have to be so careful about what you say," he would add, meaning he might be taken for a crackpot. Once, when I went to get a drink of water from the kitchen tap, he stopped me short, warning that the water came through copper pipes. Copper poisons the water, he insisted, which at the time impressed me as extremely silly. The remark led to further talk of his belief in natural foods, his enthusiasm for organic gardening. I learned of his friendship with Louis Bromfield and his long interest in the theories and publishing enterprise of J. I. Rodale, a name I had not heard before.

One evening he put on his hat and we walked uptown to visit an aged cousin who had spent most of her life abroad and whom the townspeople called the aristocrat. His novel then in progress was her story and he was exceptionally fond of her, a painfully frail person of amazing spirit living in dim Victorian splendor on Tulpehocken Street. Her comments on life and the passing scene pleased him no end—comments such as these, from his manuscript, which, on another occasion when my wife was with me, he read aloud:

> These days you're not supposed to get mad. They say it's murder on your blood vessels. I don't only get mad but I kick the swinging door as I go through. It's such a handy place to take it out on.
>
> I hear that townspeople say I'm common. They don't use the word like we do. They mean I don't care what old clothes I go around in and like Mother, I speak to everybody.
>
> Princess Vershaliv said to me, "Yes, I knew Alfred Noyes on the Isle of Wight. In fact I lived with him for three years. I suppose that isn't exactly a nice thing to say." "No," I told her. "It's a perfectly terrible thing to say. But how interesting."

During the Depression years in New Mexico, continually in debt, he survived on short fiction—stories for *The Saturday Evening Post* in the main—but writing, as one critic has noted, "with typical care and integrity." The first of the novels—and his fi st financial success—was *The Sea of Grass*, which did not appear until 1937, when he was approaching fifty. Being a late bloomer, as he said, weighed on him and had much to do, I believe, with his remarkable productivity. His writing was "slow and painful, something to be avoided." Still, there were days "when the typewriter keys are pure velvet." He worked every day, beginning in the early morning. Altogether, in thirty-odd years he wrote fifteen published novels, a collection of short stories, and a novel for children, in addition to keeping a daily journal (unpublished) and compiling a shelf of notes on early rural life and speech, of which more in a moment.

His shyness could be monumental. I don't think I ever knew a more private man or one half so modest—by nature, not by design. He had no public side, no act. The man known by his comparatively few friends was the man. Beyond his small family, those who knew him best and longest were Alfred A. Knopf, his publisher, and Paul R. Reynolds, his literary agent. A writer living in Pine Grove, Richard Wheeler, was somebody he saw often. So were a Pine Grove banker and his wife, Mr. and Mrs. Charles Hikes, who lived in a beautiful old stone farmhouse outside of town.

No one was allowed to make a fuss over him. When *The Town*, the concluding volume of the Ohio trilogy, won the Pulitzer Prize in 1951 and Mrs. Hikes and others in Pine Grove wanted to celebrate with a dinner in his honor, he would have none of it. In New York to receive the prize, he stayed in an out-of-the-way hotel and registered under an assumed name. He made no television appearances to promote his books. He made virtually no public appearances of any kind: he didn't like it; he wouldn't do it. In 1961, when he won the National Book Award for *The Waters of Kronos*, he refused to mount the platform at the ceremonies, refused to make a speech, something no author had done in the history of the awards. His brief acceptance was given instead in writing, and was read aloud by Alfred Knopf.

Yet for all that he liked to work, he could *only* work, he said, with life stirring about him—hence the desk in the dining room, in full view of the street and anyone coming up the front walk, with double doors open to the front hall and an intolerable (to me) German cuckoo clock declaring every hour.

Troubled by restlessness, he would pack the current work in a suitcase, lock the house, and drive with his wife to the west coast of Florida, if it was winter, or, in summer, to Pawcatuck, Connecticut, or Mount Desert Island, Maine, where they would take a small house for several weeks. But if while away he saw a car with Pennsylvania plates on the street, he would at once strike up a conversation with the driver, enjoying himself as though he had discovered one of the world's most interesting people. On the highway in his big cream-colored, secondhand Cadillac, he drove fast and extremely well. His vision was phenomenal. He would pick out a caterpillar crossing the road up ahead, then swerve just enough to miss it.

The problems of his craft, he said, were chiefly "problems of compression." He labored for clarity and order and for power through simplicity. I don't think anyone ever worked harder to make it all seem so effortless, as if the story were being told in the only way it could be told, easy, natural, not a word more or less. Some of the later work (I think in particular of *A Country of Strangers*, a brief, haunting account of a white girl raised by Indians) has an almost mythic simplicity, as if generations of telling have worn away everything extraneous, leaving only pure story.

The hard work ought never to show, he felt, never intrude. Nor should the research. Historical details—those descriptions of period costume, furniture, social customs and the like that lesser writers play on so heavily for "color"—were used but sparingly. Recognizable historical figures or events are seldom mentioned in his books. In truth, I don't believe he much cared for history in the conventional sense. As some people are born with perfect pitch, he had a perfect sense of time past. Isaac Bashevis Singer remarked that it was as if he had actually been there and came back—a transmigrated soul—to tell his stories.

His love was for the great mainstream of early life in America, for "obscure, unremarkable men," for "men and women whose names never figured in the history books but whose influence on their land and times was that of the people itself." You could say, I suppose, that he was a patriot, in the largest, best meaning of the word.

•   •   •

There is great tenderness in his stories, much that is raw and earthy, much that is funny, and not a little cold-blooded violence. The land is never merely the setting; it is elemental to the story, vast and full of power and mystery. His characters do not merely move across a landscape; it is part of them and they are part of it. In the New Mexican books, of which *The Lady* is my favorite, it is the immense open grassland, "the land running on and on." In the trilogy it is the ancient trees, "a race of giants," that shut out the light.

> There they stood [Sayward Luckett reflects] with their feet deep in the guts of the old earth and their heads in the sky, never even looking at you or letting on you were there. This was their country. Here they had lived and died since back in heathen times. Even the Lord, it seemed, couldn't do much with them. For every one He blew down, a hundred tried to grow up in its place.

The first intimations of the Ohio story came to him in the 1930s while living in a log cabin among the big pines, up seven thousand feet in the Sandia Mountains east of Albuquerque. Years of careful research followed in various parts of the country. He was never happier, I once heard him say, than when he was working in a good library, with a table spread with old books and rare old maps and personal journals. His search was for the "endless small authenticities, without which life would not be life."

The spoken language of the frontier was particularly important to him and he took great pains to track it down, combing through court records, letters, interviewing old-timers in New Mexico, in rural Pennsylvania and Ohio, not just for their yarns but for their vocabulary. He compiled his own thesaurus, a collection unlike any I have ever seen, to get as close as he could to what he called "the great mother tongue of early America," which, as he appreciated, was a very different kind of speech from the formal written language of the time. The words and expressions filled a heavy looseleaf notebook—*dominie* (for preacher), *plunder* (meaning one's earthly possessions), *on tenterhooks* (uneasy), *painter* (panther), *By the tarnal!* (which was about equivalent to "Well, I'll be damned!"), *chimly* for chimney, *crick* for creek, *middle* for stomach, *bury hole* for grave. The Great Lakes were *the English seas*; the devil, *Old Harry*.

The names for his characters were also drawn, in part or whole, from original sources—Sayward, Achsa, Solie (for Ursula), Jake Tench, Judah MacWhirter, Azariah Penny, Mathias Cottle, Buckman Tull, Will Beagle.

Interestingly, his favorite character, or at least the one he took the most obvious pleasure in, was not one of his homespun figures, but a young Massachusetts lawyer, Portius Wheeler, a very misplaced soul in Ohio by all appearances. All but useless with a rifle, "a slight, almost delicate figure," Portius has fled from civilization because of some youthful misdeed that is never explained. It is he who marries Sayward Luckett and who becomes a leading figure, a judge ultimately, in the new civilization in Ohio—in New England transplanted. Conrad Richter in his youth had wanted repeatedly to escape from civilization. He was a "free thinker," as is Portius. Much about Sayward, he told me, was patterned after his wife, Harvey, as he called her. So it would be easy enough to leap to a number of conclusions, which I will not, except to say that the sense of humor Portius brings to the story and that of Conrad Richter are one and the same:

> "I want to ask you a very personal question, Mathias," he said, and his face was grave as a gravestone. "Is it true you had ancestors?"
>
> "It's a lie!" Mathias called out, bristling. "I never did, nor my boy either. His head's clean as yourn."
>
> "Well, they say that you slumber in your sleep," Portius plagued him.
>
> "It's false as a gypsy!" Mathias shouted. "I never once did! Not since I was little, anyway."
>
> —*The Fields*

The underlying values expressed in the trilogy, in all the novels, are the old-fashioned primary values—courage, respect for one's fellow man, self-reliance, courtesy, devotion to the truth, a loathing of hypocrisy, the power in simple goodness. He called them "the old verities" and he was sure they were vanishing from American life. He had no patience with such expressions as "the Puritan ethic." He thought most of those who used that expression never bothered to understand what the Puritans were about.

His work was widely praised. In 1966, when the trilogy was reissued by Knopf as one volume under the title *The Awakening Land*, a critic in *The New York Times* hailed him as a "modest giant" among American writers. His following was an impassioned one; readers had—have—a devotion to his books of a kind rarely known. *The Trees* went through fourteen editions in hardcover, as well as sixty translations in some twenty languages. Yet none of his books was ever a best seller; there was no overnight fortune, no fortune anywhere along the line. He was never fashionable.

He went his own way, hard as it was, heedless of literary trends, seldom reading reviews of his own work, for example, and everything he wrote is in essence a celebration of a proud, stubborn individualistic spirit. He believed in gain from hardship, as is also implicit in his stories, what Shakespeare called "benefit of ill," an expression he liked to quote. Human energies—love, art, perseverance, wisdom—are born of difficulty, he would say in his quiet manner, his eyes never straying from your own.

One September he came to Martha's Vineyard, where I live. It was a beautiful cold gray day with the wind out of the north and long horizontal rain clouds hanging low over a rough dark-green sea. He was standing on the front porch when I returned from a walk with my two small sons. He had simply appeared, unannounced, not wishing, as he said, to cause us any bother. He and Mrs. Richter had already found accommodations in one of the hotels that were still open. He wanted to see the children, he said, to see where we live. But in less than a day he grew terribly concerned over the fact that the ferryboats were not running on schedule because of the weather. He had no appointments to keep on the mainland and there was so much that we wanted him to see on the island. But in another day he was gone. Perhaps he had accomplished what he had come for; perhaps his uneasiness had to do with being separated from the mainland, the literal land mass of the continent. He had never gone to Europe, I know, because he felt it would hamper him, hurt him as a writer. Mexico was all right because Mexico was part of the same land mass.

I saw him last in Pine Grove three months before his death. He had been bothered by heart trouble but looked fine. He was born on October 13, 1890, and 13 was a number he liked. The number he did not like was 30, which in newspaper work is used to mark the end of a story. He died of heart failure in 1968, on October 30.

CHAPTER ELEVEN

The Lonely War of a Good Angry Man

As far as anyone knows, the first white man to settle in Letcher County, Kentucky, was a North Carolinian by the name of James Caudill, who came over Pine Mountain in 1792, raised a cabin near the headwaters of the Kentucky River, and became, as a state historical marker near the site proclaims, "progenitor of a large, widespread mountain family."

Immense changes have come to eastern Kentucky in the time since, but in Letcher County, and particularly in Whitesburg, the county seat, Caudills still abound. Their names figure regularly in the columns of Whitesburg's weekly *Mountain Eagle* ("It Screams!") and take up most of one page in the phone book; they own lumberyards, run for judge, mine coal, win scholarships, get killed on the highways, get married (to one another, on occasion), bear and rear more of their line; and if they happen to be born with more than ordinary ability or ambition, chances are excellent that they will one day pack up and leave Letcher County, thereby carrying the Caudill blood ever farther afield. The reasons so many leave are plain enough to see: poverty of the kind that has become synonymous with the word Appalachia, inadequate education, few jobs, and the grim prospect that the one thing left of any real value or beauty—the land—is being rapidly ripped to shreds by what is euphemistically known as surface mining.

But there is one very able and talented Caudill—a great-great-great-grandson of the original James—who has not only elected to stay on in Letcher County but has for years been fighting to save what remains of that Cumberland Mountains domain of his forebears and to bring to national attention the plight of the people who live there. He is Harry Monroe Caudill (KAW-dle, it is pronounced), a Whitesburg man. He has taken on the strip miners, the loggers, the government dam builders, politicians, bureaucrats, the T.V.A., and several major U.S. corporations. He has written books, newspaper and magazine articles, and countless letters. He has spent hour upon hour of his own time attending local meetings, arguing before judges, appearing on television, lobbying in Washington, guiding interested visitors from "the outside" on tours of his home country, all in a single-minded and deeply felt one-man campaign to stop what he sees as the senseless mutilation of the place he knows and loves better than any other.

Testifying before a Senate committee in 1968, Caudill expressed the view that there are two great crises in America. One is a crisis of people, white and black, who are impoverished and embittered and who, in their frustration and hatred, threaten to burn everything down. The other is of the American land. And as he is quick to point out, in his part of America the two crises exist side by side and are directly related to one another.

Wendell Berry, a Kentucky author and poet and a great admirer of Caudill, says, "Harry's interest in conservation really begins with people. He doesn't think of conservation, or any issue, as an abstraction, the way so many do. He sees his country being destroyed every day and he sees what that does to human beings. The other thing about Harry, maybe the most important thing, is that he *lives* with the evil he is fighting, and that makes him a rather unique kind of crusader. He doesn't have to read about environmental troubles in the newspapers, he just looks up at the hillsides."

The troubles Caudill sees are gaping yellow wounds slashed sideways along the steep wooded slopes of the mountains that crowd around Whitesburg. One such cut can be seen from Caudill's own backyard. About half a mile up the mountainside, it is an old cut, a relatively small one, and like numerous others to be seen from the roads that wind through eastern Kentucky, it does not look terribly bad from below. The trees cover much of it half the year. It might be something as commonplace as a highway cut, unless you know better. But up on the strip mines themselves the view is very different. There is a place, for example, known as Pigeon Roost, near

Hazard, a town in neighboring Perry County. There the land looks as if it might have been the set for *All Quiet on the Western Front*. The devastation covers hundreds of acres, all of them wild and unspoiled only a few years back. Huge gashes have been ripped out of the mountainsides and lie raw and exposed, with no green cover. To judge by the vast unrelieved stretches of yellow clay, baked iron-hard by the sun and speckled with greasy dark splotches where poisonous acid has seeped through, nothing will ever grow there again.

From the edge of the cut, enormous eroded slides of still more clay, rock, and debris spill down the mountain slope, and out of these protrude the blackened remains of great trees that have been knocked askew by the enormous weight of the slides. It is as though the entire landscape, as far as the eye can see, had gone through a hideous convulsion or been ravaged by some crazed monster. But then far below, a mile or more, in a trough of untouched green, sits a cabin with a few wrecked cars scattered about it like toys; and because the strip miners have long since gone, there is total quiet except for the sound of radio music and, now and then, a faint voice or two. Someone lives down there, you realize.

I grew up in Pennsylvania, where I lived near strip mining much of my life, but I have never seen anything like the strip mining in eastern Kentucky. It is beyond belief, and sickening.

•   •   •

Until the late 1950s little strip mining had been tried in Kentucky. Now the bulldozers, the scoops, the diesel shovels, the mammoth coal augers are churning away day and night. In steady procession gigantic Mack trucks creep off the mountains, their brakes crying against the weight of upward of twenty-five tons of coal each. When they roar through Whitesburg, the ground trembles. Of the one hundred million tons of coal being mined annually in Kentucky, half comes from strip mines, and in years to come that percentage is certain to increase. Moreover, much of the strip mining is done on land owned by corporations located outside Kentucky, and the major customer for the coal is the Tennessee Valley Authority, long portrayed as a model of enlightened land use.

Most of the strip mining is carried on by small, independent "operators," nearly all of whom are also lessees of the big coal-land companies. These include such well-known giants as Occidental Petroleum, National Steel, U.S. Steel, Bethlehem Steel, and International Harvester, all of which are based outside Kentucky and all of which own, or own other companies that own, vast tracts of the state's mineral resources. The big corporations, then, rarely do the actual strip mining themselves (a point their public relations people stress emphatically); that part of the process is left to the local operators. And thus it has been for some time, with the result that mountain people, rightly or not, believe the hidden hand of absentee corporations is behind virtually every move by the strip miners. Mountaineers have an old festering hatred of big corporations and big-city money; and increasingly among some of the young there is the more modern attitude that the "system" is rotten and ought to be destroyed.

Yet the fact remains that strip mining is the quickest, easiest, and cheapest method thus far devised to get coal; and, for the operator, it is an exceedingly profitable business. Thus not only in Kentucky but in a dozen other states strip mining continues at a brutal pace.

Further, with the nation's need for fossil fuels increasing steadily, and with innumerable new electrical power plants buying and burning even the lowest quality coal, there seems every likelihood that things will get worse. Where once coal was a seasonal commodity, it is now in demand year-round, due in good part to the electrical power required for air conditioning. "We can sell anything that's black," says one operator. In the northern corner of Letcher County, the Beth-Elkhorn coal company, which has its headquarters in Pennsylvania and is owned by Bethlehem Steel, has announced plans to tear up a thousand acres of choice woodland to "recover" some seven million tons of coal. According to statements made by one company official, the strip mine cuts on the land will run a total distance of somewhere between 120 and 150 miles. (Numerous Kentuckians find a kind of gallows humor in the fact that Bethlehem is currently running a costly advertising campaign—a series of what are called "conscience ads" in the trade—to tell the American public how much it is doing in behalf of the environment.) The biggest independent operator in Perry County, Bill Sturgill, boss of a number of strip-mining companies, now has a fifteen-year contract to supply T.V.A. with two million tons of strip-mined coal per year, all for just one power plant.

•   •   •

For Harry Caudill the seriousness of all this goes beyond the pitiful ugliness, or the bitter irony that those who live with the ravaged land get virtually no share of the coal or the money made from it. The ecological consequences of even one small strip mine are extraordinarily varied, complex, and damaging.

In eastern Kentucky, where the mountains are as steep as any in Appalachia, strip mines are contoured around the mountainsides like gigantic snakes. The cuts are L-shaped, with the "highwall" (the vertical side) exposing raw rock to heights of thirty to fifty feet. In many cases these immense man-made cliffs completely isolate entire mountaintops.

The coal is stripped from the flat shelf, or "bench," of the cut, and since there is no convenient place to pile the "overburden," the topsoil, rock, and clay that cover the coal seam, it simply gets shoved over the brow of the bench, smashing or smothering every tree, or anything else, that happens to stand below. ("Spoil bank" is the strip miner's term for the huge heap that builds up.) As a result, about three acres of mountain are "disturbed" for every acre actually mined. Then roads are needed to get at the coal, and building them tears up another eight acres or so for every mile. And since there are generally two or three seams at different elevations, little of the average mountainside is spared.

Using the conventional equipment, a crew of seven can keep a strip mine advancing along the face of a Kentucky mountain at a rate of about one hundred yards a week. The coal market being what it is, most cuts are worked by two twelve-hour shifts. At dark the big headlights go on, the violence continues.

But the real shattering of the ecology of a mountain begins after the strip miners have come and gone. The resulting troubles continue for years and at a cost no one studying the problem is as yet able to estimate. Even before the rains hit them, the spoil banks begin to move. Full of churned-up slate and mangled trees, spoil banks are highly unstable and slowly succumb to the pull of gravity with a dry, sliding sound one can actually hear. When the inevitable mountain storms strike, rushing water slices into them like a knife. Frequently, like the giant slag heap at Aberfan, in Wales, a spoil bank will let go altogether and thunder down on whatever lies below, which in several instances has been somebody's house. Landslides block streams and highways, and in the words of a government report, "economic and esthetic values [are] seriously impaired."

Even ordinary erosion will cause extraordinary damage in little time. Water races off the mountain loaded with silt, gravel, and the deadly sulfuric acid that drains out of exposed coal or its overlying strata. Creeks that a boy could jump over only a few years ago are now as broad as two-lane roads, blasted out in a way reminiscent of the hydraulic mines of the Old West. Other creeks are so clogged with sludge they have to be cleaned out two or three times a year at considerable cost to the state. Studies indicate that the annual sediment yield from strip-mined lands in

Kentucky is as much as one thousand times that of undisturbed mountain areas.

Slimy with mustard-colored coal silt and poisoned by mine acid, thousands of Kentucky creeks and streams are quite literally "dead." Nothing lives in them. The putrid water is good for nothing, and it stains and poisons just about anything it comes in contact with.

Every spring, farms a hundred miles or more from the mountains are flooded by rivers thick with silt from such tributaries. On the Kentucky River, on the other side of the state, annual floods have been part of its cycle for as long as anyone can recall. But fifty years ago the spring floods were rejuvenating. Like the Nile, the Kentucky bestowed on every acre it touched a fine, thin layer of silt rich with organic matter, very fertile and very welcome. Now, because of bad farming, logging, and strip mining on the upland slopes, the same river leaves a fine, thin film of yellow clay that hardens to the consistency of concrete and is, as one farmer says, about as fertile.

Less obvious but equally serious are the profound scars left on the spirits of the mountain people, who see their country, one of the most beautiful regions in America, being dismembered before their eyes. Farms that have been in the same families for generations are made worthless. Fine timber is destroyed as though it had no value. Public roads, long believed to be the salvation of so-called backward sections, are ruined by the punishing weight and wear of immense coal trucks. Surrounded by ugly abuse of the land, many people become ever more slovenly. Abandoned strip pits are used as dumping grounds for garbage and wrecked cars. Spoil heaps catch fire, often from burning rubbish, and smoulder for months, even years, casting an evil-looking, vile-smelling haze over the landscape.

As might be expected, those who suffer most from such tragic by-products of strip mining are the poorest, least educated, least articulate, and least able to comprehend why things are happening as they are, or what, if anything, can be done about it. More than anyone, Harry Caudill speaks for them.

In 1965 he helped found the Appalachian Group to Save the Land and People, the region's first serious effort to organize public protest. He also deserves a major part of the credit for Kentucky's various strip-mining laws, which he fought for long and hard back at a time when taking such stands in eastern Kentucky was a lonely and dangerous business. In 1954, when the state's first attempt at a strip-mining law was up before the legislature in Frankfort, Caudill was the only representative from eastern Kentucky to vote for it. A law passed in 1966 was said to be the best in the country, though Caudill himself thinks it is nowhere near tough enough. Highly skeptical about how well it is being enforced, he likes to quote a friend who says it is a little like legalizing rape, so long as the rapist first agrees to restore his victim to her original condition. Caudill also emphasizes that nothing is being done about land strip-mined prior to 1966, which means about 100,000 acres.

• • •

The law has been revised and improved some. Among other things it prohibits strip mining on slopes steeper than 28 degrees; it requires that the operator grade back spoil banks to about the slope of the mountain and seed the mined area before moving on; and it empowers the Division of Reclamation in Frankfort to suspend an operator's permit or fine him one thousand dollars for each day that he fails to abide by these and other regulations.

A colorful brochure issued by the state shows strip-mine benches in Letcher and adjoining counties where fruit trees have been planted and appear to be surviving, where a nitrogen-building green cover, a legume known as *Sericea lespedeza*, grows waist deep, and a highwall has been so effectively back-graded and replanted as to be unnoticeable. Such places do exist in eastern Kentucky and are indicative of what can be done. But they are few and far between and greatly outnumbered by places where reclamation has failed. As the reclamation people themselves readily admit, many strip mines and particularly those along Kentucky's so-called "hot" seams (in which the acid content is extremely high) cannot be restored no matter what is done to them, short of trucking in new topsoil, which no operator is about to try and might not work anyway. Even where conditions are ideal for the prescribed reseeding program (a solution of seed, water, and fertilizer is sprayed over the exposed spoil), there is, as one reclamation official says, no hiding a strip mine.

Still less progress has been made in checking erosion and acid drainage, or in preventing spoil-bank slides. Small dams thrown up to catch silt have proved pathetically ineffective. Though the chief reclamation objective— to get a quick green cover down—is the best solution to the overall erosion problem, only a small percentage of the cover ever amounts to anything, or at least in time enough to do the job. A walk along most "reclaimed" mines is a discouraging experience. Where tiny trees have been planted, twenty are dead stubs for every one that is green. To judge by the stony, water-gullied clay all about, the heaps of rock and pools of foul water, the future for that one green survivor will be most precarious. About the best the reclamation people can say in defense of their efforts is that things are being handled better than before.

The handsome brochure, on the other hand, closes by stating, "Land is being restored to a desirable contour, water pollution is being minimized, successful planting of affected areas is being accomplished, and the strip-mining industry is enjoying a far better public image."

The kind of reclaimed mines pictured in the brochure are known by critics of the program as "Grim's Garden Spots," after Elmore Grim, director of the reclamation program; the severest critics, including Caudill, say that the objective of a better image for strip miners is really what the program is about. Talking privately, Caudill takes a bleak, fatalistic view of the future in store for Kentucky, or any portion of the American land beneath which coal can be found. Indeed, he takes a dark view of the drift of American life in general and what, if anything, can be done about it.

Others, however, point to him as a shining example of just how much one man can do, and for all his private moments of despair, he "sallies forth," as he would say, all the same, a sort of Kentucky-style combination of John Muir, Mark Twain, and Don Quixote, doing battle in his own way, on his own terms, and he is hands down the most eloquent and effective voice for conservation in all Appalachia.

Like most mountaineers, Caudill tends to be independent, obstinate, and at heart a fighter. Though a member of such conservation organizations as the Sierra Club and the National Audubon Society, he never presents himself as, say, "a Sierra Club man." He prefers to be his own man. Often he has no other choice, for the "conservation issues" he gets involved with in Kentucky are seldom disputed in quite the way they would be in other parts of the country. As he remarks, "It should be remembered that we have in this section a decided inclination to settle our differences with dynamite."

Caudill makes his living as an attorney in Whitesburg (population eighteen hundred). His offices are on the ground floor of the Daniel Boone Hotel on Main Street. He is forty-seven years old, married, and the father of three children, one of whom, another James Caudill, has already made his own mark in the community by being the first boy from Letcher County ever to go to Harvard University.

Caudill himself attended the University of Kentucky on the GI Bill and received his law degree there. He is president of the Letcher County Bar Association, a former state legislator, a Democrat with grandfathers who fought on opposite sides during the Civil War. He is a tall, spare, bookish, long-legged man who dresses neatly, talks with a deep, musical mountain accent, walks with a limp caused by a German bullet in Italy, and goes about with a rather long look on his long face except when he is telling stories. Except for his time at college and the war years, he has spent his whole life in Letcher County ("dear old Letcherous County," he calls it). His father, Cro Carr Caudill, was a coal miner who lost an arm in a mining accident and was later elected clerk of the court in Whitesburg. "Cro Caudill? Sure I remember him," says an elderly mountaineer. "He only had the one arm, but he'd give you a good big hug with it—especially when he was lookin' for a vote."

Much of Harry's boyhood was spent in and about the courthouse listening to stories told by the "eminent citizens who congregated there." The high importance placed on the storytelling art in eastern Kentucky Caudill explains with a story (naturally) about an old friend, Judge L. Hayes, who had no regular Christian name, only the letter "L," and who used to say, " 'Bout all we have got to do down here is chew 'baccer, drink liquor, and tell lies."

•   •   •

Caudill has collected stories of his mountain country for as long as he can remember, and he tells them magnificently, lovingly, in the rolling, rhetorical style of Kentucky's old-time country lawyers. Many of his stories come from "old characters" he has "hunted up". ("You know, those old people just love to talk," he says, at the conclusion of a yarn he may have taken fifteen minutes to tell.) And many were included in his first book, *Night Comes to the Cumberlands*, widely recognized as one of the finest studies of Appalachia and its history ever written. Published in 1963, it had a profound effect on the long-standing, popular impression of life in "hillbilly" country, and particularly in Washington during the Kennedy administration. Secretary of the Interior Stewart Udall compared it to John Steinbeck's *The Grapes of Wrath* as a call to the American conscience. Soon after the book appeared visitors from Washington and New York—reporters, magazine photographers, government officials, representatives of the large foundations—began arriving in Whitesburg to meet Caudill and set off on what his wife, Anne, calls "Harry's horror tours." Some visitors were astonished to discover that whenever Caudill spoke it was in the same cadences as the book, as though he were speaking from a prepared script. But the reverse was the case: Caudill had dictated the entire book. "He had been out walking in the woods one afternoon," his wife says, "and when he came in he told me he had been thinking about where all these people [in and around Whitesburg] came from originally and about what had happened to their country; so I began taking down what he was saying, and when we were finished we had just this big pile of typed pages, no chapters or anything, and we weren't at all sure anyone would want to publish it."

Another book, *Dark Hills to Westward*, was published in 1969. Part fiction, part history, it is a spine-chilling tale about a young woman named Jennie Wiley, who was carried off by Indians in 1789, saw her children murdered, and later made an epic escape through the Kentucky mountains. But there are still other stories, full of hilarious episodes and characters, and it is these he tells with the greatest zest, often slapping his knee with one big hand, and at the finish tilting back his head and muttering, "Oh my, oh my!"

Caudill's stories nearly all deal with the same themes—the harsh, uncertain life of the mountaineer from pioneer times to the present, the kind of courage engendered by such a life, and the particular variety of politician that Kentucky has home-grown down the years. In one way or another, all the stories are related to the land. For it would be hard for Caudill, as for most people from his section of Kentucky, to imagine the course of human affairs disassociated from rivers, creeks, draws, mountains, hollows, bottomlands, and all that grows or lives in, on, or near them, or that may lie buried beneath them. And it is this kind of vision, this attitude toward the place where he lives, that gives Caudill's kind of conservation a special significance. He is not simply dedicated to saving scenery. For him the scenic wonders, the ecology, the people and their stories, are all part of the land and in total represent a heritage only a vandal would degrade or destroy. And so it is that he finds the desecration of his small portion of America an unconscionable, unacceptable outrage.

Caudill's part of Kentucky is neither the gracious bluegrass-and-blooded-horses Kentucky of legend nor the bustling, modern, industrial Kentucky of the state's western half. He lives in the other Kentucky, set in the rugged Cumberland uplands to the east, where steep, wrinkled mountains, lush in spring and summer, extravagantly colorful in the fall, bleak as can be in winter, cover some ten thousand square miles and are sliced into a bewildering tangle of narrow, twisting valleys that shelter something like half a million people and what appear to be at least ten thousand hulks of abandoned automobiles. "The old cars from Cincinnati and Dayton all come down here to die," one man told me.

•   •   •

Until the latter part of the nineteenth century it was country that had changed little since pioneer times. Then timber buyers began arriving with what seemed fancy offers for the immense stands of trees, most of them hardwoods, to be found nearly everywhere they looked.

> The eyes of the "furrin" timber hunters must have popped with amazement [Caudill writes in *Night Comes to the Cumberlands*]. The great poplars and white oaks grew, for the most part, near the base of the hills and in the coves, while the lesser oaks and chestnuts predominated on the sharper points and near the hilltops. Countless walnuts dotted the forest, thousands of them without blemish and a yard or more in diameter. The Goliaths were the superb, pencil-straight poplars, some of them towering 175 feet and achieving a diameter of seven or eight feet.

There were enormous hickories, maples, beeches, ashes, black gums, pines, and hemlocks, an abundance and variety of trees such as could be found in few places on earth by then. The buyer was offering cash money in amounts seldom dreamed of in the mountains; the seller usually thought he was getting the better of the bargain. The going price was fifty to seventy-five cents a tree, and from about 1870 on, thousands of mountaineers were busy with cross-cut saws. By the 1930s nearly all the virgin timber was gone; another supreme natural treasure had been destroyed.

Today the hardwoods are only beginning to come back. In all Kentucky there is but one sizable stand of virgin woodland, some 550 acres in Letcher County known as Lilly's Wood. The late Lilly Cornett, former owner of the property, loved trees and turned down all offers from the timber buyers. (Along Line Fork Creek he is remembered as "the most peculiar man you ever saw . . . carried his money in an old Buffalo tobacco bag and dressed all raggedy.") For the past few years, it has appeared that Lilly's Wood, too, was headed for the sawmill. But Caudill and others, including the Louisville *Courier-Journal*, mounted such a concerted drive to rescue the trees that the state, with the help of the U.S. Bureau of Outdoor Recreation and the Nature Conservancy, finally stepped in and bought the property. The last remnant of the immense forest that once covered the whole of eastern Kentucky has been saved.

But the destruction of Kentucky's trees was a minor tragedy beside what happened after the railroads came in and made it possible to take coal out. Coal was known to exist in the mountains by the earliest white explorers. Yet it was not until the end of the nineteenth century that the railroads began penetrating the Kentucky highlands and thereby put an end to the way of life that had existed so long undisturbed. Even by the turn of the century, Whitesburg had no telegraph, no telephone. Its only connection with the rest of the world was a narrow road twenty miles over the mountains. But with the arrival of the Louisville & Nashville Railroad, Lexington became a "daylight ride" from Whitesburg. A Seth Thomas clock was installed in the courthouse cupola and set to standard time. Things began to change rapidly. As a little history of the town written at the time states proudly, "The Romance of these hills—heart of these noble old Mountains should be Dig, Dig, Dig—The Open Door—The Open Sesame, To Old Midas' Mints. Here all one has to do is to tickle the sides of Old Mount with a pick and an avalanche of 'gold' rushes down."

Into Kentucky, close on the heels of the timber buyers, came the mineral buyers, affable, storytelling agents representing northern bankers and businessmen. Their purpose was not to purchase land, only the rights to whatever minerals lay beneath it, and they found the pickings better even than had the timber buyers. Thousands of mountain landowners put their X to the so-called broad-form deed, the now infamous legal document that not only gave the coal companies title to whatever "mineral and metallic substances" might lie beneath the soil, but authorized the grantees to do whatever was "convenient or necessary" to extract those same substances. To insure against further troubles with the owner of the property, a final clause absolved the coal company of all liability for any damages resulting from its mining operations.

The price generally paid for such rights was fifty cents an acre. On the average, over the years, an acre would yield a minimum of five thousand tons of coal, worth today about twenty thousand dollars. But the truly tragic consequences of all this would not be felt for another generation or more. No one back then had any reason to imagine anything like strip mining.

By 1912 or so the railroads had been built, and, as Caudill has written, the vast, backward Cumberland Plateau was tied inseparably to "the colossal industrial complex centering in Pittsburgh, and a dynamic new phase in the region's history had begun." The coal companies put up houses, whole towns; doctors, teachers, coal miners, and their bosses began moving in. The coal began rolling out in endless carloads. A ten-hour day in the mines was routine. Men died of "black damp" (methane gas), cave-ins, explosions; or, like Caudill's father and his older brother, they were crippled for life. Still, wages were good by standards of the day, extraordinary by Kentucky standards, and nobody complained much until the Depression struck. Then followed years of suffering in the coal towns. The dole and the first chronic despair made themselves known in the moun-tains, and as Caudill likes to remind people, it was then, too, that the mountaineer, traditionally clean in his personal habits, began making garbage dumps of his streams, many of which had already been ruined by silt and sulfuric acid draining out of the mines.

With the Depression also came John L. Lewis and his United Mine Workers, a massive W. P. A. program, and in time, the war. Coal became a cash crop again and stayed that way until 1947 and 1948, when coal production hit its peak in Appalachia. In the 1950s came automation, more hard times in the mountains, and the start of one of the most important migrations in American history. Between 1950 and 1960 something on the order of one and a quarter million people left the mountains to find work in the cities, to become part of what would be labeled "the urban poor."

•   •   •

It was at this same time that strip mining began. If anyone objected, out came the old mineral deeds. A property owner would one day be informed that the bulldozers were about to arrive to rip open the land, and there was not a thing anyone could do to stop it. The owner's father or grandfather or someone years before had put his or her mark to a broad-form deed. When such cases were taken to court, the courts decided in favor of the coal companies.

The issue was litigated anew in 1968 in the Kentucky Court of Appeals, the state's highest court, with the judgment going again in favor of the coal industry. Until then the strip mining proceeded unchecked, quickly becoming an intensely emotional, dangerous issue, with no shortage of abusive language on either side. With feelings mounting, the bulldozers soon became targets for more than just invective. Snipers began firing from nearby wooded hills—sometimes using armor-piercing bullets. ("Where those bullets hit the steel," Caudill says, "it looks just like somebody dragged his fingers across the butter.") Operators and sheriffs returned the fire, and at least one man, Tom Fuson of Pineville, was killed. Then, one night in the fall of 1968, a watchman for the Round Mountain Coal

Company in Cowfork was captured by four unidentified men who proceeded to blow up (with the company's own store of explosives) nearly $750,000 worth of equipment. A giant Number 9 "dozer," the biggest made by Caterpillar, was destroyed, as well as a truck, a jeep, a coal auger, three rubber-tired high-lifts, three generators, and a giant diesel shovel. In another such after-dark strike a bulldozer was blown completely in two, a feat that left a lasting impression on everyone who saw it, since such work, it is said in tones of great respect, could only have been handled by an expert. No one was arrested.

"And just suppose we did make an arrest," a state police detective told Tom Bethell, a reporter for the *Mountain Eagle*. "Try getting a Knott County jury to convict the guy. They never would."

With so much going against them, why, one might wonder, do the strip miners keep gouging away? The answer, aside from money, is that there are significant attractions to strip mining that must not be overlooked or underestimated if one is to understand the problem.

Importantly, with strip mining it is possible to work with much bigger equipment than with ordinary underground mining. In simplest terms, this means fewer workers can mine more coal faster. A strip miner can produce about thirty tons a day, more than twice the output of a miner below ground. In an auger strip mine, where huge boring machines with steel bits sometimes seven feet in diameter are used, production is greater still.

Strip mining is also much safer. Men do get killed in strip mines—from falling rock or overturned equipment—but the risks involved on the job are nowhere near as serious as in a conventional mine. There are no slate falls to contend with; no deadly gas; no silicosis or "black lung" caused by inhaling coal dust. Nor is there any of the psychological fear of going underground.

Perhaps the most important appeal of the whole business of strip mining is that it is so simple. One need not even be a miner to run a strip mine, a fact that scornful "true" coal miners are quick to emphasize. An ability to handle heavy earth-moving equipment is about the only expertise required. With the proper machinery—bulldozers, chiefly—the operator simply scrapes off the topsoil, then the subsoil (which generally includes a lot of rock and requires blasting) down to the coal seam. He then scoops up the coal and dumps it into trucks, which haul it away to a coal tipple. There the coal is transferred to railroad cars, which carry it out of the mountains.

And added to all that, the strip miners still have the law on their side. In June of 1968 a broad-form deed was contested before the Kentucky Court of Appeals, and the court upheld the deed. The case involved LeRoy Martin and his wife, who owned a ten-acre parcel of land in Knott County, the mineral rights for which were held by the Kentucky River Coal Corporation under a broad-form deed. It was a historic test case. No other state in the union still honored broad-form deeds for strip mining. The decision was a tremendous blow for the small landowners, for conservationists, and for Harry Caudill, who was the Martins' counsel.

Caudill, however, hopes to contest the broad-form deed again. He would like to take it to a federal court. All that is needed, he says, is a client who is willing, and financially able, to stick with the case all the way to the Supreme Court, if necessary. In the meantime, court fights of other kinds continue.

There is, for example, the illustrative case of Vernon Barnett. Seven years ago Barnett bought a house on an acre of ground on Yellow Creek in Knott County. He had spent thirty-six years down in the mines, lived always in a company house, knew nothing but mining, and was now disabled by black lung. But for once he had a place of his own. In the time since, the mountainside behind his house has been strip-mined, and now a huge spoil bank hangs over his head like a volcano. At one point two men from the mine came down to advise him, "unofficially" they said, not to sleep in any room facing the mountainside. There was no telling what might let go and come crashing through his windows.

After one rainstorm the water surged through the creek beside his house with such fury that it moved a giant boulder sixty feet. His own water supply began to give out, until only a trickle came from the kitchen faucet. "Not enough even to do dishes," his wife says. When Barnett went to see the operator, he was told the coal company would "make good" on any damages. But as Barnett says, "When you are trying to go to sleep at night and you know that spoil bank is hanging up there, you don't think much about who will be paying for 'damages.' You think about getting buried alive." Friends have urged him to move out. Barnett has decided to take his case to court and has asked Caudill to represent him. He says he "can trust Harry," as do numerous others who have tried to fight the strip miners.

As one might suspect, Harry Caudill is not universally popular in eastern Kentucky. The state reclamation people give him ample credit for getting the law on the books in the first place. "He served his purpose," says Elmore Grim, the tall, businesslike director of the program. But Grim and those who work for him suggest that Caudill gets the operators so furious that it sometimes seems they make trouble out of spite.

Grim insists that the best way to make progress is to work with the operators, to get them to "see the light." His inspectors look over every strip mine in Kentucky on an average of once every two weeks, he claims. He has closed down several for failure to conform to the law, but, as he admits, he has still to enforce it to the hilt. "Why, we've got enough law on the books now to shut down every strip in this state. That is, if we were to nitpick. But we can't do that. We've got to find out how these things can best be handled, reasonably and intelligently.

"Hell, I could be a dictator. But the federal government doesn't even know what to do. Take acid mine drainage. Nobody knows what to do. Stop it up on one side of a mountain and it will start coming out the other side, where the streams are good. Plug it? The plug will blow, and what a mess that is. . . . I don't know the answer. This isn't like geology or agronomy, where you can go and look up the answer in a library. We're writing the book as we go along."

Grim, a professional forester most of his life, talks with impressive passion. "If there isn't an answer to strip mining," he says, his voice rising, "then I'll be the first to say stop it." Then he adds, "What we need is time, time to experiment."

To which Harry Caudill says, "Oh, I suppose they will be experimenting all over these poor benighted hills for years and years to come."

•   •   •

About the worst Grim and those in his camp have to say about Caudill is that he is "overemotional," a term used frequently against conservationists. Others say Caudill is careless with facts. Even Anne Caudill allows that "research has never been our line." But Loyal Jones, who is the executive director of the Council of the Southern Mountains at Berea, Kentucky, and who knows Appalachia and its problems as well as anyone, says, "To criticize Harry Caudill on accuracy is about like saying that Thomas Wolfe's portrait of his mother was not precisely accurate. Harry speaks to sway people and to get at a kind of truth that is beyond facts and figures."

Not surprisingly, it is the coal operators who have the strongest language for Caudill, whom they see as a self-serving spouter of pieties and slander. The *Mountain Eagle* quoted one man as saying, "When he [Caudill] gets up in the morning, he stands in front of the mirror and smiles at himself and wonders who he's going to slander today. It must be a nice life." When a *Life* writer, David Nevin, was gathering material for a strip-mining story, a coal operator told him, "I went to college with Harry Caudill. He was a sonofabitch then and he's a sonofabitch now." When Nevin related this to Caudill afterward, Caudill only smiled and replied softly, "Strip mining has become a very big business."

It is not uncommon for some coal operators to suggest that Caudill, or anyone else who speaks out against them, is somehow in league with the Communists. But this seems in keeping with other public pronouncements made by some of the industry's leaders in other parts of the country. At a convention of the American Mining Congress in Pittsburgh, James D. Reilly, vice president of the giant Consolidation Coal Company (which is owned by the Continental Oil Company), said that conservationists who demand that strip miners do a better job of restoring what they tear up are "stupid idiots, socialists, and Commies who don't know what they're talking about. I think it is our bounden duty to knock them down and subject them to the ridicule they deserve."

One of Caudill's staunchest allies is the *Mountain Eagle*. Tom Bethell, a Bostonian and former editor with the Houghton Mifflin Company who writes for the *Eagle*, came to Whitesburg largely as a result of reading Caudill's first book, and with Tom Gish, the paper's editor, he has been doing some exceedingly tough, crusading coverage of eastern Kentucky's many problems. Scarcely a week goes by that Gish and Bethell are not after the strip miners in one way or other, often by running an open letter or article by Harry Caudill. "Although we do all our own editorials on the subject," Gish says, "a lot of people say Harry really wrote them." As a result, all the traditional devices for "bringing pressure to bear" have been used on the paper: advertising has been withheld by local tradesmen who sell products or services to the coal companies, and open support has been given to an opposition paper, *The Community Press*, published at nearby Cromona. At one point emotions got so strong that an arsonist was reportedly hired to burn down the cabin Bethell was living in, and three antipoverty workers (Appalachian Volunteers) who had been sympathetic with the anti–strip-mine faction were arrested on sedition charges and put in jail. Although tempers eventually quieted down, hatreds over the issue persist below the surface. One afternoon, as I was taking a photograph of Gish and Bethell in front of the paper's office on Main Street, a burly strip-mine operator who happened to be standing nearby became so infuriated that he did all he could to ruin the picture, standing directly in the way and shouting in my face, "We don't want any more of you goddamn outsiders coming around here giving this county a bad name." The idea that strip mining itself might give the county a bad name, or that most strip miners are themselves "outsiders," had apparently not crossed his mind.

To a large degree his feelings are understandable, since Letcher County has been the subject of numerous articles and television reports, including one by the BBC, and a film for the Houston Hemisfair, during the making of which the leader of the film crew was shot and killed by an elderly local man who did not want his property photographed for such purposes.

Why so much attention has been focused on Letcher County—when there are dozens of other places in Appalachia where the same or similar problems are just as dramatically on display—is readily explained: Harry Caudill. His own magazine articles and books have been read in New York and Washington by those who make editorial or policy decisions, and from what they read it appears that in Whitesburg there is a unique man, someone who can talk intelligently about the problems, someone who belongs there and must know whereof he speaks; and so to Whitesburg they come. In July 1969, when CBS was looking for places to show what America was doing as the first men landed on the moon, one of the communities picked was Whitesburg, because a CBS producer, Bernard Birnbaum, had read Caudill's book, and had later met Caudill and listened to him talk.

To many in Whitesburg, including its business people, drawing such attention is a grave mistake. A coal operator like Bill Sturgill, who has known Caudill since college days, cannot understand why Harry behaves as he does. When Caudill was campaigning for strip-mine legislation it was Sturgill who led the attack against him, claiming that if the law were passed it would put every strip miner out of business. Sturgill stressed the importance of strip mining to the local economy. His 287 employees were earning from $7,500 to $12,000 a year, he said. He himself was making annual purchases from some 104 different companies and individuals amounting to more than six million dollars—all this in contrast to Harry Caudill. "It is still a matter of record," Sturgill wrote in a letter to the *Courier-Journal*, "that Mr. Caudill does not support the economy or provide job opportunity, but rather has made much personal gain from advertising worldwide the ills and misfortunes of his friends and neighbors."

•   •   •

For Sturgill and other operators the idea that there may be something fundamentally wrong with strip mining seems almost impossible to grasp. As they see it, they are helping to serve the nation's energy needs; they are providing jobs, making dollars move in their communities, making other-wise valueless land pay. Coal is Kentucky's great cash crop, a point they take pride in.

To Wendell Berry such men are blinded by the jargon of free enter-prise—"as if," he says, "the freedom of free enterprise implied freedom from moral responsibility." Loyal Jones believes the problem rests on the pernicious notion that people and the land are there to be exploited, used up, and consumed, and that the roots of such beliefs can be traced to frontier times. Harry Caudill sees strip mining as symbolic of something more serious. "I think it tells us more than anything except war about the darker side of our nature. I remember coming home from the war on a hospital ship and worrying about that. I began to think that perhaps that darker side would prevail. This devastation of the earth is a manifestation of that tragic, base side, the side that in the Bible is represented by Satan and his works."

Caudill's conviction is that strip mining ought to be the subject of a national policy, that federal laws must be enacted as soon as possible and strictly enforced. "The current Kentucky law and the way it is being handled is a little like attacking a crocodile with a cornstalk," he says. He wants strip mining outlawed anywhere that the slope of a mountainside exceeds twenty degrees, and authorized only where *total* reclamation can be carried on promptly and effectively. He supports the system used in several European countries—in England, Germany, and Czechoslovakia, among other places—where the topsoil is carefully put aside and the subsoil and rock kept separate. Then, once the coal has been removed, rock, subsoil, and topsoil go back in their original order, the layers being compacted during the process. "There's no reason why we can't do that if they do."

To pay for this, coal prices will have to be raised. "The way it is now, coal is undercutting the price of other fuels at a hidden cost to tremendous stretches of the American land."

More must be done to enlist the interest and energies of the great corporations. In Caudill's view the nation's industrial centers are being fuelled by Appalachia, with coal and with low-paid workers, and Appala-chia is getting little in return. "I don't think the men at the top of those enormous corporations are wicked men. But you know there's not a one of them that has ever been down here to see things with his own eyes, to see what is going on here. Not a one! And yet, the decisions they make have everything to do with how we live here. So we just can't help but think they have no interest in people, or in the land. They're just interested in coal and profits."

Indeed, Caudill sees a prevailing lack of interest in Appalachia, despite all that he and others have had to say. "The millionaires and the celebrated politicians like to come to the Kentucky Derby, of course, and they always make a great big show of that, but just try to get them to come over here!"

What Caudill keeps calling for is an informed understanding of the Appalachian land. "This is always thought of as a bleak, poor, broken-down, God-forsaken place here. But the truth is, this mountain island has tremendous natural resources, not the least of which is its people, and if we can make changes in the ways the land is utilized, then we can become the premier part of the United States. We have plenty of green country, an abundance of water, a superb climate, minerals, strategic location, extraordinary beauty. And as the shortage of open land in this nation grows more and more serious, all this magnificent country is going to have a value far surpassing anything like coal. And we just can't afford to sit back and watch all that be destroyed so a few people can get rich now. One of these days the dear old federal government is going to have to come in and spend billions of dollars just to repair the damage that's already been done. And guess who will have the machines and the workmen to do the job? The same coal operators who made the mess in the first place will be hired to fix it back, and the taxpayers will bear the costs."

The larger, desperate need, Caudill believes, is for a whole new land ethic. "Unless we change our attitudes toward the good earth of this planet, I doubt that life will last a great deal longer. Look how short a time it took us to destroy Lake Erie. And there is absolutely no evidence that the human race is learning the dire need for restoration. If you read history, you see that this has happened many times before on a smaller scale.

"Just imagine this," he says. "If those three men who went to the moon had started to befoul their aircraft, if they had begun to tear it apart and fill it with all manner of filth, we would say they had gone mad. But here we are on this planet, this huge spaceship, befouling it, ripping it asunder, and nobody seems to say very much about that. Nobody seems to care."

Such imagery can have a profound impact when Caudill appears before a Senate committee, or when he is writing for national publications. One article, in *Audubon*, did much, for example, to generate interest in saving Kentucky's spectacular Red River Gorge from a dam to be built by the Army Corps of Engineers. The campaigning against the dam was led chiefly by the Louisville *Courier-Journal* and later received national publicity when Justice William O. Douglas arrived to lead a hike through the area in jeopardy. The gorge was saved.

And for every person who is against Harry Caudill, there appear to be many more who are wholeheartedly for him. "He is the one man who can speak for every one of those people who know instinctively that strip mining is wrong and that it is the ruination of their homeland," says Wendell Berry, while another Kentucky writer, Mrs. Siller Brown, a coal miner's widow who does a regular column in the *Mountain Eagle* about things her neighbors tell her over the phone, says flatly, "Harry Caudill is a good man."

When I asked Caudill why he stays on in Letcher County, he first smiled at his wife, then told a story about one of his favorite characters, Old Claib Jones, who took part in numerous mountain feuds after the Civil War, killed twenty men, later repented his sins, and lived to a ripe old age. At one point, during the "Holbrook and Underwood War," Claib and five other men were pinned down in a cabin, surrounded by a large Underwood force and some policemen who had been called in to help finish Claib off. The attack began before dawn and kept up until midmorning, when suddenly the shooting stopped and Alvis Underwood's wife was sent in to ask Claib to surrender. It is at this point in the story that Harry Caudill's eyes begin to light up.

"So you know the message Claib sent back? 'No,' Claib said. He said, 'We want to fight on a while longer anyway.' Now wasn't that wonderful? And I guess that's the way Anne and I feel: we want to fight on a while longer anyway."

CHAPTER TWELVE

Miriam Rothschild

Mᴵʀᴵᴀᴍ Rᴏᴛʜsᴄʜᴵʟᴅ knows all about butterflies and fleas, birds, fish and poisons, ladybugs ("my real first love"), medieval meadow grasses, Shetland sheep dogs, photography, farming, Clark Gable, and the wild flowers of Israel. She designs her own clothes. She has an art gallery devoted to paintings by schizophrenics. She owns a pub. She has raised six children and she is one of *the* Rothschilds.

Of her eccentric Uncle Walter, her favorite Rothschild, who was an outstanding British naturalist, she has written a lively biography, *Dear Lord Rothschild*. About fleas, her specialty, she has written possibly a quarter of a million words in books and learned papers. A single cupboard at Ashton Wold, her country estate, contains sixty thousand microscopic preparations of fleas. But this, she insists, is nothing much at all compared with Uncle Walter's operations.

"Imagine," she says, "two and a quarter million butterflies, thirty thousand bird skins, three hundred thousand beetles, and one hundred forty-four giant tortoises!" Imagine, indeed.

In a framed photograph on her bookcase Uncle Walter, in top hat and high-button shoes, sits astride a live giant tortoise, urging it forward with a bit of lettuce on the end of his walking stick. "That," she explains, "was Rotumah, the famous giant tortoise that died of sexual overexcitation.

Walter found that tortoise in the garden of a lunatic asylum in Sydney." Rotumah was 150 years old, the oldest, largest tortoise in the world, so Walter brought it to England. "And he got the doctor from the asylum to travel with it. That's the best thing of all!"

She sometimes acts as though she is having too much fun with too many interests ever to be taken seriously. But she is a scientist of the first rank. Her work on fleas, her butterfly studies, and her encouragement of other scientists have brought her all sorts of awards and honors. In the citation for an honorary degree from Oxford (1968), she was lauded for contributions to anatomy, chemistry, entomology, pharmacology, neurophysiology, and zoology. "It is unusual too [the citation continued] that in natural science anyone, still less a woman, should receive an honorary degree without any degree already from any university." In 1985, she was made a Fellow of the Royal Society, the highest honor in British science. Yet Miriam Rothschild had little academic training of any kind—her family believed it would stifle the joy of learning.

"Brilliant is not an inappropriate word for her," says Robert Traub, a professor of microbiology at the University of Maryland Medical School, with whom she has collaborated on two books and several papers. "People talk about genius and use the term loosely, but this is really it."

•   •   •

Her latest project is with wildflowers, and seen surveying one of her experimental meadows, she makes a memorable figure. Short, sturdy, rather heavyset, she goes clomping along in large green rubber boots, gray hair tied back in a blue scarf, trailed nearly always by one or more of seven Shetland sheepdogs. Her uniform is a comfortable, loose-fitting dress and matching jacket she contrived herself and had made up in several colors. It is all she ever wears. "I've got a very great deal that I have to do," she will tell you. "It's important to cut out the trivialities."

She needs no more than four hours' sleep a night. She keeps a suitcase packed at all times, to avoid the fuss of packing for her frequent trips, and she has forsworn city life. "I appreciate museums. I have to go to libraries in London, but in the city it takes such a lot of energy to cut out the things you *don't* want to hear and you *don't* want to see." Besides, she contends, all the "big dramas" happen in the country.

She lives year-round at Ashton Wold, in strange, overgrown English country splendor, a two hours' drive north of London in North-amptonshire. Deep woods enclose much of the property. Overhanging trees and shrubs brush the sides of your car as you approach. Weeds grow nearly knee-high in the gravel courtyard. The grass goes uncut. Vines and creepers run wild over half the house, a big, sprawling, gray stone affair built by her father in 1900. It is where she was born in 1908 and it looks abandoned, or as though the Rothschilds have fallen on hard times, if such a thing can be imagined—a look exactly to her taste. "Very attractive," she says with a smile, as if nothing more need be explained.

Her father, Charles Rothschild, was a gifted amateur entomologist who, on a trip to Egypt before she was born, discovered the rat flea, the one that carries bubonic plague. At the time the rat flea was a new species and he named it *Xenopsylla cheopis*. Charles and his older brother Walter were the sons of Nathan Mayer, or "Natty" Rothschild, head of the great merchant banking firm of N. M. Rothschild & Sons and the first Lord Rothschild. An earlier Nathan Mayer, Miriam's great-great-grandfather, the first of the English Rothschilds, had arrived from Frankfurt-am-Main in the middle of the eighteenth century and established himself as a cloth merchant in Manchester. Nathan Mayer, as he said, was all business. In fifteen years, having switched to banking in London, he was helping finance Wellington's armies.

After Nathan came Lionel Rothschild, a great friend of Disraeli, who made history by financing Britain's purchase of the Suez Canal in 1875. But it is Lionel's son, Natty (1840–1915), described by Miriam as gruff, sentimental, and dapper, who ranks as one of the most brilliant financiers of all time. In the popular press he was considered the real ruler of England, and was the first Jew to take a seat in the House of Lords.

Though Natty's two sons, Walter and Charles, each conscientiously took part at N. M. Rothschild & Sons, neither cared a thing for banking. At the ripe age of seven, Walter announced he was going "to make a museum" and spent the better part of his life pursuing that ambition. In time his collection exceeded that of any private individual anywhere, ever. Housed in the Rothschild estate called Tring, it is now part of the British Museum.

Charles, though a far better banker, preferred science to finance, specializing in fleas and butterflies. It was on a butterfly hunt as a student that he first fancied a portion of wild countryside near the village of Ashton, where the house now stands, and concluded he must have it. On inquiry he learned that it already belonged to his own father.

Miriam's memory of Charles is limited. He was ill through much of her childhood, and in 1923, when she was fifteen, he took his own life. It was thus that Uncle Walter, the second Lord Rothschild, who had no children, became such a large part of her world.

Walter is assured a place in history because he is the Lord Rothschild to whom Arthur James Balfour, the British Foreign Secretary, addressed the famous Balfour Declaration of 1917, saying His Majesty's Government viewed with favor the establishment of a national home for the Jews in Palestine. It was written in the form of a letter beginning "Dear Lord Rothschild," the title Miriam chose for her book.

Two things distinguished Walter as a naturalist, she says—unbounded enthusiasm about every conceivable kind of living creature, and near total recall of everything he ever saw, heard, read, or wrote. "He remembered every letter he'd ever written. Never kept copies of them." To be sure, he also had financial resources beyond most people's imagining. Still, Walter's reach often exceeded even the Rothschild grasp. He was constantly short of money or in debt. At times he had four hundred people on his payroll collecting specimens all around the world.

Walter's eccentricities were legendary. As an M.P. he once caused a sensation in the House of Commons by showing up in a white top hat. On other occasions, he drove down to Hyde Park with his coach drawn by a team of zebras. Because of a lifelong speech impediment—an almost crippling lack of breath control—he found normal conversation impossible. "You never knew what was going to happen," she remembers. "Either the words came out in a bellow, which absolutely raised the rafters, or else it was a whisper. He was always embarrassed, and you were always embarrassed, and then silence fell."

But Walter was a born naturalist, and naturalists, she is sure, are born, not made. She herself began breeding ladybugs at the age of four and remembers taking a tame quail to bed with her. "I just always loved animals and I was passionately fond of flowers. That's the sort of thread that's gone through my whole life." She learned from her parents, from Walter, and from years of living at Tring with Walter's collections.

"Collections are basic to zoology," she stresses, recalling drawer after drawer of his butterflies. Walter had made butterflies his entomological passion beginning in 1895, having said good-bye to beetles, as she writes in her biography. The way other wealthy Victorians collected Chinese porcelains or rare gems, Walter amassed butterflies, and the rarer the better. The result was surpassing, perhaps the most valuable butterfly collection in existence. It was possible to open drawers and see spread before you an entire order in all its variety and from every quarter of the globe. "The mind just took off," she remembers.

Her own earliest, serious work, starting in her twenties, was in marine biology. After her marriage, she concentrated on flea studies, partly because it was work she could carry on at home. With children to raise, her microscope became her escape, her marijuana, as she says.

"I had six children, so it was quite, you know, a full-time job. But at about eight o'clock in the evening, when they had all gone to bed, I used to settle down to the microscope, and there was nothing more delightful— when the evening would get quieter and quieter and even the sort of clink of cups vanished, and you could settle down and look at these marvelous colors. You could forget the world, and in fact, I used to be brought back to Earth by falling into the microscope with sleep at about one o'clock."

She catalogued her father's flea collection, from which she published a five-volume study. In time she became the world's leading authority on bird fleas. With the appearance of *Fleas, Flukes & Cuckoos*, her sprightly book for the lay reader published in 1952, she became known as the "Queen of the Fleas." What fascinated her especially was the acute dependence displayed by fleas and parasites, and the degree to which they gave evidence of their evolution. Her style was altogether her own.

"A parasite's life is an impressive gamble," begins one chapter. "Indeed it is difficult to envisage insecurity on such a scale. The chances of a grouse roundworm finding a grouse are far less than the reader's chances of becoming the parent of quads, or a cabinet minister."

• • •

With her son-in-law as photographer, she was the first to record the flea's leap, one of the miracles of nature. ("If you were a flea," she informed me, "you could jump to the height of Rockefeller Center and you could do that about thirty thousand times without stopping.") Her most important research, however, concerned the rabbit flea, carrier of a viral disease fatal to rabbits called myxomatosis. She discovered that, unlike any other insect parasite, the rabbit flea has a reproductive cycle dependent on the hormonal state of its host. The female rabbit flea can produce offspring only while living on a pregnant female rabbit, the flea drawing on the rabbit's estrogen supply. The flea larvae are also then in place to feed on debris in the rabbit nest.

In addition to fleas, she worked on mites and ticks (which are large mites), and a large, brown, gull-like bird called a skua, which spends most of its life at sea and gets most of its food by piracy, attacking other seabirds until they drop their catch. Research on butterflies and moths led to discoveries about the relationships between insects and plants, and particularly on the use of plant poisons by insects as a defense mechanism.

Working with Tadeus Reichstein, who with two others won a Nobel Prize for his isolation of the hormone cortisone, she reported how the monarch butterfly protects itself by storing within itself poisons drawn from the milkweed plant—poisons to which the monarch has evolved an immunity—making it quite unpalatable to birds and spiders.

More recently she discovered that her beloved ladybugs—or ladybirds, as she calls them—are also extremely poisonous. A single ladybug egg, she found, can kill a cat if injected into the bloodstream. "Just one egg!" she says, her face filled with wonder.

At present she is working with caterpillars, allowing them to feed on castor-oil plants and other euphorbias with extraordinarily toxic seeds, which the caterpillars use as protection from bird predators. She grows about a half dozen such plants in the old, rather worse-for-wear greenhouses of the estate. There are worktables covered with plastic sandwich bags filled with seeds so poisonous they can't be touched. There are tables filled with seedling wildflower plants, a cage with a veteran white rabbit from her days of rabbit-flea work, a pet magpie that she has raised by hand safe from exposure to hornets, in preparation for the day when a hornet with its stinger removed could be put into the cage.

The idea was to determine how much of a bird's fear of hornets is inherited, how much learned from experience. If the bird were to eat the hornet, then obviously the fear was learned, which is what Miriam expected and what did not happen. She was flabbergasted, she admits, when the bird refused to go near the hornet.

She has just completed a book on insect tissues and with entomologist Traub she is producing still another flea study, this on the discovery in Utah of a flea of Latin American origin called a chigoe that burrows into the ear of a mouse and grows to the size of a pea. Until recently none was known in North America.

Wildflowers, however, are her main preoccupation, her experimental gardens and meadows her greatest pleasure. In the eyes of any conventional farmer she is busy growing weeds—wild poppies, cowslip, cornflowers, corn marigolds, harebell, wild violets—and harvesting their seeds as a cash crop, an enterprise local farmers once took to mean she was "absolutely crackers."

Wildflowers are rapidly disappearing from the countryside, she stresses, and the loss is not just one of beauty. "You're losing the gene pool and that's something that, once gone, you can never get back. That's millions of years of evolution down the drain." Creating nature reserves as a means of protection, the scheme favored by her father, is no longer enough. Instead, she wants to reintroduce wildflowers everywhere possible—along highways, rivers, in parks, backyards, vacant city lots. She had been told that to recreate a medieval meadow—a wild hayfield with approximately the variety of grasses and flowers common to medieval England—would take about seven years. She has done it in three, recreating a meadow containing one hundred species.

"I think the flowering meadows are going to come back. They're finished now. We just have these terrible monotonous crops of dull green grass. I mean it, it is so boring. I don't know how the horses can stand the stuff."

While machines can be used for harvesting some of her wildflower crop, most of it must be done by hand. It is slow, unusually tedious work, and consequently many of the seeds are extremely expensive. Two pounds of harebell seed, as an example, sell for nine hundred English pounds. But her work has stimulated enormous public interest, and harebell, as it happens, is the seed second in demand after cowslip. In time, she hopes to market more varieties, including wildflowers mentioned in the Bible.

•   •   •

Beyond her gardens and experimental meadows and the encroaching woods she loves as her father did, the estate opens out into broad wheatfields, rich, flat land almost like prairie that seems to go on indefinitely. The one interruption is the tiny village of Ashton, which includes the pub and art gallery. The thatched-roof pub is the Checkered Skipper, named for a rare butterfly. By her direction, the decor is all natural history exhibits, making it a pub like none other in England. The gallery includes only paintings by schizophrenics—strange, intense works, many of amazing skill and nearly all dominated by images of large, threatening eyes. The paintings are part of a collection she had assembled with an art therapist, Edward Adamson. None of it is for sale, nor is there another collection comparable to it. (Schizophrenia is an "old interest." To help understand and treat schizophrenics, she and her family founded the Schizophrenia Research Fund in London.)

At one time, during the Second World War, there were six thousand Americans billeted in and about Ashton, and every year there are some who come back for a visit. They were part of the Eighth Air Force. The Rothschild wheatfields were once Polebrook Field. Miriam's house was the base hospital. She remembers well the intense excitement when the American B-17 Flying Fortress bombers first arrived from the United States. No one had seen planes that flew so high or that left vapor trails.

Of the American airmen, she says, "I thought they were absolutely tremendous . . . they won the war for us, no doubt about it." One of those she got to know best was Clark Gable, then an Air Force major, whom she delights in talking about, telling what a crack shot he was (they often went shooting together in the evenings, he at rooks, she at targets), and how he had almost no sense of humor.

More than three hundred missions over Germany were flown from her now tranquil fields. One colossal hangar still standing is used to store potatoes.

"You know I was the first person to install seat belts in a motorcar," she told me as we drove out to see the site of the old airfield. "It was in 1940, when the first American aviators arrived in civilian clothes, even before you got into the war. I saw the safety belts they had in their training planes and I said we ought to have those in motorcars." Using a girth from an old sidesaddle, she made up seat belts for her car and tried without success to have the idea patented.

It was during the war that she met and married a British commando and war hero named George Lane, a marriage that was dissolved in 1957 though he is still a good friend. To many of her scientific colleagues it also seemed that she did remarkably little with her mind all that time, little at all of consequence, which was puzzling largely because it was so out of character. Nor did she offer an explanation. Only long afterward did it become known that she had been involved with the famous Enigma project, working with the top-secret group at Bletchley Park, trying to crack the German code. Scientists from many fields were enlisted and marine biologists were known to be particularly good at such work. She got a medal from the British government for her part, yet still won't say anything about what she did.

"I never hated anything as much as I hated the war," she told me, recalling the airmen who did not come back. "It's impossible to describe it. You know, for years afterward when I woke up in the morning, my first thought was, 'Well, thank God the war's over.' "

Her conventional farming enterprises are large-scale and serious business. "I *am* a farmer," she says emphatically. Farming has supported her and all her scientific researches year after year. But farming, as she points out, is "an old story" in the family. Grandfather Natty was an avid breeder of shire horses, president of the Jersey Cattle Society, and active in developing new agricultural practices. The farms at Tring, where she spent so much of her youth, were showplaces and a favorite stop for visitors from all over the world.

Though Walter Rothschild found talk difficult, Miriam, in addition to everything else, is one of God's great talkers and never more so than when she reflects on the changes that have come to our relations with the natural world.

"Somehow people have lost the sense of being in a landscape. There are no more figures in a landscape like there used to be. I tell my children they're like Sputniks spinning in space with a sort of speedy background swooshing by. You just see the figure, the landscape is gone."

I asked her if her recipe for life is different from what it was twenty-five years ago.

"No, not at all. If I had to wish one wish for my children, I would wish that they were interested in natural history, because I think there you get a spiritual well-being that you can get no other way, and what is more, life can never be long enough. . . . I think all naturalists retain a sort of keen interest in what's going on in life. It's all part of natural history. I mean Karl Jordan, curator at the Tring Museum, was ninety-six and he was just as enthusiastic as he was at nineteen and I always remember him sitting at the microscope saying, 'I shall know it all in the next world, I shall know it all in the next world!' "

She was settled on the couch in her study, one of her dogs curled up beside her, the picture of Uncle Walter on the tortoise displayed directly behind her.

"I must say," she said, "I find everything interesting."

CHAPTER THIRTEEN

South of Kankakee: A Day with David Plowden

"**I** THINK THAT in many cases—as I was just saying a minute ago—I ask perhaps too much of my audience. I'm asking them to really take the time to look. . . . To me everything that I see is very important in those pictures, even down to the last blade of grass. And so I demand an enormous amount of myself and I'm demanding an enormous amount, I think, of my audience, maybe too much. . . . I gave an assignment to my students: I said, 'Go out and photograph something that's boring. Go out and photograph the state of being bored—to see if it's possible.' Some of them did it beautifully."

"What did they photograph?"

"Almost all of them photographed something that was very still. A great many of them photographed the classrooms—which I felt made a point. And one of them photographed *me!*"

It is an overcast, extremely humid morning in August, and David Plowden and I are in his gray Datsun station wagon heading out of Chicago, southbound on the Dan Ryan Expressway. Traffic is heavy in every lane, the air foul with exhaust fumes. Plowden knows the road and drives fast, talking rapidly all the while.

"Every time I go to one of these places it's as if no one else has ever been there before to photograph it. I really don't give a damn whether anybody was there ten minutes before. . . . I want to discover it and work with it and explore it myself. People are always saying to me, 'Well, where do you think you belong?' I had an exhibition in Chicago last year. And lots of people came. And one man said, 'Ah—do you think your work has become more formal because you've come to the Institute of Design?' And I said, 'Well, if it has, I'm not aware of it, and, moreover, I don't want to be aware of it; I don't want to become self-conscious.' I suppose I always feel that to be concerned with oneself is not really an important thing. I don't feel that photography is a means of self-analysis. You start analyzing your work and you start asking your students to get themselves on the line all the time about what they're doing, and where do you lose the magic? And it's so easy because you become so self-conscious and so intellectual and so analytical about it in the long run that you lose that wonderful sort of ego that you have that says, 'Oh, goddamn it, I don't care; I love it anyway; I'm going to do it!' "

South Side Chicago, so painfully different from the splendors of the lakeshore, so removed from suburban Winnetka, where Plowden lives, stretches on endlessly. We pass the Illinois Institute of Technology, where he teaches. It is the famous campus by Mies van der Rohe, and in the dim, colorless light it looks dreadful to me, barely distinguishable from the drab surroundings.

We are off for a day to see "real country," as Plowden says, "south of Kankakee." His voice is deep and melodious. He is the son of an English actor and he sounds a little like one himself. "South of Kankakee," he says now again, happily, theatrically, giving it a ring like a refrain from Kipling.

An hour later, approximately ten miles south of Kankakee on Interstate 57, he turns off at a place called Chebanse, a drab little town on the Illinois Central Gulf Railroad. He is driving very slowly now, looking at everything. Halfway along what must be the main street, parallel to the railroad tracks, he pulls into a parking lot beside a grain elevator and lumberyard. The lot is empty except for a dump truck. He gets out and walks slowly back and forth, looking at the elevator and its attendant buildings. He stops, stands still, and, hands in pockets, studies a car parked at the curb beside the elevator, and says he wishes it weren't there.

He is of less than medium height, about five feet seven, and a little on the stout side. He is wearing khaki work pants and a blue-checked shirt. The pants are about an inch too long and scuff the ground. The whole back of his shirt is dark with perspiration.

He is still studying the scene when the noon siren goes off at the firehouse. A man comes out of the lumberyard office—a tall, angular man in bib overalls who looks Plowden over before taking his lunch pail from the front seat of the dump truck. He and Plowden nod hello, and the man walks back into the office.

There is a nice breeze blowing now out of the north, but the sky is still overcast. "A good day for details," Plowden assures me. He is setting up a tripod and to this mounts the Hasselblad 500-C, which is his favorite camera. "You know, the hardest thing is to get started. You can rationalize away the whole day and never take a picture."

He trains the lens on the elevator and part of the street, his eye pressed to the viewfinder, or "chimney." The car he didn't like has since departed and been replaced by a dusty pickup that he thinks is just right.

As he works, I get out a notebook and begin an inventory of the street. Directly opposite, on the corner, is the former Bank of Chebanse, a neat gray sandstone building with a silvery TV antenna sprouting from its roof and a green real estate sign hanging in front. Beside it, to the right, is Hanson's Variety Sundries, then a red-brick café with Stroh's beer announced in red neon in one window and a small black-and-white sign over the door that says GOOD FOOD. The firehouse is beyond the café.

We are on Chestnut Street, I see by the sign at the corner by the bank. Except for the firehouse, the buildings are one story. Above the trees in the distance is the town water tower, the name Chebanse lettered large in blue.

Other cars and a pickup are pulling into the lot. There is much opening and slamming of car doors as a half dozen men pile out for their lunch break. They are in work clothes and mostly young men, some with full beards. They stop talking momentarily as they look Plowden over, then proceed across the street to the café. He appears wholly unaware of them.

On the far side of the tracks, about fifty yards off, is a line of nondescript frame houses of the kind to be seen in every railroad town across the Midwest, or, for that matter, in any number of photographs by David Plowden. I wonder aloud about what buildings might have stood there in the parking lot in days past. "Something did," says Plowden. "You may be sure of that. There's always the feeling that something is gone."

A bell at the railroad crossing starts clanging, and Plowden, obviously delighted, tells me, "We're going to have a dividend." A northbound freight rolls through: four diesel engines pulling what seems to be an endless line of chemical tank cars, empty boxcars, and huge, cagelike cars filled with foreign-made automobiles—108 cars in total, Plowden informs me. "I always count them," he says. The train was a "mixed consist," he

explains, the automobiles coming no doubt from the docks at New Orleans. The four diesel "units" (not engines) were GP 30's or 35's, built by
General Motors.

In the café later, he asks a pretty waitress what beer they have on tap.
She names three or four brands besides Stroh's, and he orders a Coke and a
hamburger. There is a hubbub of voices from the other tables and a clatter
of dishes that he has to talk over. He has the classic long jaw and high color
of an English country squire. He leans forward, elbows on the table,
directly across from me, his dark eyes sparkling. "Imagine! Less than two
hours from Chicago and you're in country like this—in a town like this.
You can't do that from New York, God knows. The land here is more
beautiful than anything I knew in the East. The scale is so enormous. You
feel the elements here." He pauses. "Isn't it fascinating that the skyscraper
developed not on an island, where it was needed, but out here, where
there's infinite space."

·   ·   ·

David Plowden is past fifty and he has been on the road the better part of
his life. He has traveled by rail and highway, in parlor cars and in the
cabs of locomotives when the temperature outside was twenty below, in a
VW microbus filled with wife and children, and, more recently, in the
gray Datsun, usually alone, a tape deck playing Brahms or Fats Waller
("depending on my mood"). He has seen and photographed hundreds of
little backwater places like Chebanse. He loves to talk of days spent
in Davy, West Virginia, for example, or Cement, Oklahoma ("That's Cement," he stresses) or Eleven Mile Corner, South Dakota, recalling the
names of diners and motels and people he met. ("Dalhart, Texas . . . the
man's name was R. W. Willer. He said, 'I'm a leftover of the Dust Bowl!'
He invited me to lunch at his house. . . . We had pork chops. Everybody
sat with their hats on. He introduced me to his whole family—said, 'This
fellow's from New York.' And that's about all he said, and everybody
sat down and ate pork chops.") He has photographed roadways and
main streets and grain elevators, gas stations, ore docks, river steamers
and lake steamers, freighters, ferryboats, tugs, lighters, bridges, power
lines, steel mills, coal mines, bars, parking lots, skyscrapers, subdivisions,
shopping centers and graveyards, freight yards, freight trains, passenger
trains, railroad crossings, railroad stations, and steam locomotives. In
more than twenty years of work, he has produced some of the most
powerful photographs we have of man-made America and of the Mid-

western working farmland he has come to love, it would seem, above everything else.

Much of his work has appeared in magazines, often as special portfolios. *Time* wrote that his photographs tell more about the nation and its manifest values than reams of reports and environmental studies. He has been exhibited at galleries and universities; he is represented in private collections and museums (the Art Institute of Chicago, the Smithsonian, the Library of Congress); he has been compared with Walker Evans, the brilliant chronicler of the Dust Bowl; with the painter Edward Hopper; and with Eugene Atget, the great French photographer of the last century. Like Atget, wrote Owen Edwards in *American Photographer*, Plowden has found "that the camera is a fine device for the remembrance of things passing."

But the major display of his talent is in his books. They are the lifework. He has produced eight in which he did both the photographs and the text, the most recent of which, *Steel*, appeared in 1981, and five others for which he provided the illustrations.

A Farewell to Steam, published in 1966, was the first of those he considers entirely his own, and was followed four years later by the sumptuous *Lincoln and His America*, in which he also included old photographs. *The Hand of Man on America*, his most popular book, appeared in 1971. It was based on a major exhibition of his work at the Smithsonian and included the picture he is probably best known for—that of the Statue of Liberty rising, ghostlike, from a weedy, rubble-strewn New Jersey wasteland. ("As a photographer," he wrote in the introduction, "I have turned to the way I know best to express my distress over our appalling indifference and misplaced priorities.") *Floor of the Sky*, about the Great Plains, was published in 1972.

Bridges: The Spans of North America (1974) represented six years of photography and research, financed in part by a Guggenheim fellowship, and some twenty-nine thousand miles of travel. As a visual testimony to the grandeur of engineering and as a concise history of American bridge design and construction, it is unequaled by anything in print, a work of imagination and scholarship that would qualify him as someone of note had he done nothing else. In the most personal of his books, *Commonplace*, also published in 1974, he abandoned the heroic forms of engineering for ordinary side-street, back-door America, and *Tugboat* (1976) is an exuberant little book about the doings of the *Julia C. Moran* and her crew on a single day in New York Harbor.

If one is looking for a repeating theme or dominant symbol in his work, the most obvious is the railroad, and the story of his career, at a glance, would appear to be that of the small boy who loved trains and loved taking pictures of them and so grew up to be an important photographer of all that is linked to the railroad and to that distant day when the steam locomotive dominated the landscape.

In fact, his first attempt at a photograph, at the age of ten, was of a train. He was waiting with his mother on the platform at Putney, Vermont, but when the train came around the bend—"whistling and puffing and roaring down the river into Putney"—he was so frightened he handed the camera back to her. "You take the picture," he said. A few weeks later, with a new Box Brownie she had given him, he had better luck.

His first published photograph appeared in *Trains Magazine* in 1954, when he was still in college. It was of the Great Northern Railroad's celebrated train *The Empire Builder*, and Plowden went to Pennsylvania Station in New York to pick up his first copy of the issue. "I thought everybody in the station should come up and shake my hand," he remembers, "and I was very disappointed when they didn't." His first job after college, the only "regular" job he ever had, was on the Great Northern. "Then when I began studying photography seriously, at Rochester [New York] under Minor White, he told me the first thing I had to do was get my trains out of my system. 'Go and do your engines,' he would say. 'You will never do anything else unless you get those engines done. Now go and leave and do them.' "

But for all he feels still about his engines, for all he knows about the whole panoply of American railroading past and present, this is no mere train buff turned photographer; these are not the photographs of some rather uncomplicated or typical American boy who, in middle age, pines for the nighttime wail of Old 97. David Plowden is a deeply thoughtful, perceptive, complex and often troubled man—also a romantic, also humorous, temperamental, stubborn and brave and contradictory. He both adores and abhors the machines and the industrial spectacle he memorializes in his work. He longs for "real country," as he says, and yet lives in dread of being "sent off to some awful place where I'm supposed to photograph a moose." He is a profound patriot—as deeply and sincerely patriotic as anyone I know—and at the same time feels himself an alien in most of the land he travels. He will tell you people are his real interest, yet people rarely appear in his photographs.

Even the small towns that he returns to repeatedly for his subject matter both charm and repel him. "I always feel that I love these towns and I always say, 'What am I doing here?' I mean, these places sort of—they give you the feeling as you pass through them—'*Let's get the hell out of here!*' . . .

I never wanted to be in these little places. I've always been fascinated by them, but I'm always terribly glad when the train pulls away—I leave them there and I'm on a wonderful train, and I can go to the dining car and have a good meal or a good drink. Or I can get into my nice car and put the camera down and get the hell out of town. I just don't want to be there—in any of them!"

The devotion and energy he gives his work are extraordinary. In private he will speak of it as a calling or mission. Yet he cares little for "camera talk" of any kind. "I think I know less about photography than I do the things I photograph. I suppose I'd like to feel that I'm a historian."

He is propelled, driven, by a sense of time running out and the feeling that he must not just make a record, but confer a kind of immortality on certain aspects of American civilization before they vanish. "I feel it's essential to do it. I feel somehow or other that it's a mission . . . that it has nothing whatsoever to do with my own being, but that it's something quite apart from me. Somehow or other, I happen to have this—whatever the hell you want to call it—talent or gift or obsession or fanaticism or madness or whatever to go out and do this. And, really, it has very little to do with Plowden the family man, or Plowden the friend, or Plowden anything else. I am doing this and I am absolutely consumed with the sense that it has to be done."

Again and again he has arrived to photograph a certain boat or building or bridge when another week, or even another day, would have been too late. He has photographed the last steam-powered stern-wheel working boat on the Mississippi, the last run on the last day of the Hoboken Ferry. The Scranton railroad station, the SS *Algosoo*, the old Pittsburgh Point Bridge, are no more. "You know where that is?" he will say, pointing at a photograph of the beautiful Point Bridge. "That's gone!"

He is not himself of mid-America or anything like it. Born in 1932, in the midst of the Depression, he was raised in an atmosphere of affluence and high liberal ideals in an apartment house on the Upper East Side of Manhattan. The Plowden side of the family has its ancestral base in Plowden, England, where some nine hundred years of Plowdens are buried in the same plot, while his maternal grandfather, George P. Butler, made a fortune on Wall Street around the turn of the century, mainly by merging railroads.

A great-uncle named Reid is said to have brought golf to this country. Another uncle was the American diplomat Ellsworth Bunker, and Grandmother Plowden, a formidable, fearsome figure, spoke five languages, usually picking one you did not know if she wished to put you in your place.

Plowden was born in Boston, not New York, because his parents were on their way to France—and there was a summer place at Putney. Among his earliest memories is being on the train to Vermont and asking his mother over and over, "Are we in real country yet?"

Still, he found his vocation, found himself, in a pursuit of negligible social status and feels his best in the gritty workaday world.

"I have always lived in two worlds," he explains, and recalls the experience, after Yale, of working on the Great Northern. He had been assigned to Wilmar, Minnesota, ninety miles west of Minneapolis–St. Paul. He was assistant trainmaster on a staff of two and boarded with a family that had a hardware store. But weekends were another matter. His mother had put him in touch with distant relatives who lived in style on Summit Avenue in St. Paul and whose house became his home away from home— "I kept my tuxedo there." He would come in from Wilmar by freight train Friday nights, shed his work clothes in a locker room, jump in a taxi, and go off to Summit Avenue and the tuxedo and a round of parties, where, as he says, F. Scott Fitzgerald was still alive as far as everybody was concerned.

"I was born—well, not exactly in a tuxedo—but I was born there [on Summit Avenue] in a sense. I loved the parties, sure, of course I did. It was a lot of fun—but I never found the people very interesting."

He had not found Yale very interesting either, or any of the schools he attended before Yale. In all there were eight—the Home School ("we polished candlesticks") and the Walt Whitman School, both in Manhattan; Greenfield Hill public school in Fairfield, Connecticut; then a one-room school in Woodstock, New York, where his father was in summer stock; Collegiate, again in Manhattan; Choate, from which he ran away ("I hated it, hated Connecticut; couldn't stand the smell of burning leaves"); Trinity in Manhattan; and finally the Putney School in Vermont. He was a good student all along, but personally indifferent. At Putney he learned how to use a darkroom.

At Yale he majored in economics, loathing every moment. "A phalanx of uncles had to be coped with. I suppose it had a lot to do with the fact that my father had not been so successful. I felt such an affinity with him— so much more than the others."

His father, the actor, was the idolized one. Alone of the male side of the family, his father stood by him, insisting he was meant for other things. But his father was also ill much of the time.

His mother, too, Plowden says, was a never-failing source of encouragement. "I remember when I was twelve or thirteen, she would take me out to the railroad yards in Secaucus, New Jersey, and she would sit there all afternoon so I could photograph."

It was at Yale, in freshman English, that I first met Plowden, though I saw little of him then and sometime later he dropped out, took a year at Columbia. When we ran into each other next, it was in New York nearly ten years later. He was married, living in Brooklyn, and having a difficult time trying to make his way as a photographer.

•   •   •

"A steel mill! There's nothing more photographable than a steel mill. . . . To me, it's the most awesome spectacle we have. . . . I mean, can you believe it! It's like a miniature volcano—all contained—made by us. . . . There's nothing more terrifying than being in a steel mill. You've been in a steel mill; you know what the hell it's like!"

We are back in the car, continuing south on I-57. For a while we have talked about favorite books. "Conrad," he said at once. "All of Conrad. And Willa Cather." And favorite photographers. He named Paul Strand and Walker Evans. I asked how he felt about Stieglitz. "Funny about Stieglitz—isn't it awful—but I never liked Stieglitz—*never, never* . . . I've always felt he was terribly self-conscious. For Christ's sake, don't say that around anyone or I'll be run out of my profession."

"You've already run out, haven't you?" I said. "You ran out."

"Yes, I ran out."

"You never got in?" We were both laughing.

"Listen, I never got in. I'm a heretic. That's what the man who hired me said. He hired me because I'm a heretic. And he said, 'I want you to teach your heresy down here.' "

"What's so heretical about you?"

"Well, I guess I feel that photography is not a holy cow. . . ."

We moved on to favorite painters. "Well—Cézanne," he said after a pause. "And Monet." What about the Americans, I asked. "Hopper," he said. "Hopper, I would say definitely. I actually adore Hopper—I love him."

Did he think Hopper had been an influence on him? I disliked the question, but felt I must ask.

"No. I have not been influenced by Hopper at all. I think Hopper and I probably love the same things. But I started photographing and doing things long before I was really aware of Hopper. It's so hard to say whether you're influenced by someone or not. Of course, you want to say, 'No, certainly not; I'm my own man, and my own person, of course—I've never been influenced by anybody.' Sure, I suppose I've been influenced by Hopper and Walker [Evans] and all those people I admire tremendously. I don't think you can help it."

"Are you working in their tradition?"

"I hope so."

"Carrying the torch?"

"I hope so—in a way. It's a hell of a torch to carry. Yeah—I hope I am."

I wondered how much interest he has in films and if he had ever seen any that seemed to be doing what he does. He mentioned *Days of Heaven* and *The Last Picture Show*. But when I asked if he had any favorites, he all but shouted with delight, "The Marx Brothers—my favorite of all people in the world. I love the Marx Brothers. I would drive a thousand miles. . . . I know every piece—I know everything—*A Night at the Opera*—the scene in the dressing room—the stateroom—where they're all in there. . . ."

But now we have turned to steel mills.

"It's like being in hell," he says. "Absolutely terrifying place! And yet, can you believe that we've been able to do that? And look at the goddamn mess it makes of everything! Look what it's done to the poor guys who work there—look at the pollution, the filth! Look at the bodies of the people who work in these places. And yet, at the same time, these men who work there are intensely proud. And I think there are some who are proud of doing it because they know how goddamn dangerous it is. They're almost at war. It's almost like this American thing of always being at war, always having a war to fight. We're always fighting the frontier; we're always fighting the mine, trying to get the coal out of the ground. We're always beating ourselves against things, and I think that's so much the American spirit. And you get out here and it looks beautiful now, but Jesus Christ, in an hour and a half we might have a tornado, a hailstorm. This guy's field"—he is pointing to a cornfield to the right—"will be laid flat, cut to ribbons. Now he's pitting himself against it. Look at that water standing in that field there. See that below—he had to replant all that. That was all wasted away. . . .

"The guys at Dessie's Bar [a place in Virginia that he has photographed], they're the guys who hack the coal out. There was one guy there whose son took me around, and the son said, 'My daddy goes in that mine six miles every day and he works *on his knees*.' And they all have black lung and they all live filthy, goddamn broken lives—they're all horrible places to work in. . . .

"There's a picture in the book of a fellow who was slagging the steel— you know, throwing the slag off the top of the ingots with all those showers of sparks; and when he finished, he came rushing out and he ripped open his coat, and he said, 'Look, mosquito bites, mosquito bites.' And there were scars from all of the sparks, and he was proud of it—this great guy. These people are heroic. The locomotive engineer . . . the farmer who is out pitting himself against the weather and against the goddamn bugs and everything else all the time—to me they're much more real than the guy who makes the money and sits in the office . . . I find myself more sympathetic to them. I always have. . . . I suppose it's also because I can't imagine anything duller than sitting in an office all day long."

We have left I-57 and are cutting cross-country, heading west, inland, on all but empty section roads. "One of my students, a guy from Taiwan, couldn't believe it when he saw this. I was out here with a class and he wasn't photographing. He said, 'I can't deal with this. I've never seen land like this.' "

The road is as straight as a landing strip and walled in on both sides by corn eight feet high, higher, mile after mile after mile. When the road rises and there is a break in the corn, we can see enormous distances—six, maybe ten miles; I can't tell because the scale of everything is so different. I feel like the student from Taiwan. There are no fences and the few houses barely show above the corn.

"All right, David," he explains. "This is the Corn Belt! Right in the middle of it!"

He wants to stop and get out, but he is waiting for another rise where we can see. We are doing about sixty. It is beginning to look as though the sun might break through for the first time all day. A grasshopper, or something, splatters against the windshield. A soybean field appears suddenly on the right. In the middle, maybe five hundred yards from the road, a lone, small figure of a man is working with a hoe. Then, as abruptly, he and his field are gone, and we are in corn again.

There is a lot of blue sky suddenly. And now the sun is out and brilliant beyond expectation, changing the look of everything. Plowden likes the change. "All the time, the whole thing is light," he says. "And the light out here . . . well, look, from one horizon to another, it's the sky."

The air rushing past the window is noticeably hotter, but I am struck even more by the smell. I have smelled growing corn before but never anything like this.

"And just listen," says Plowden, his voice dropping almost to a whisper. "It doesn't make any noise . . . you'd think that anything that was in such abundance would yell."

A sign says that what we are seeing is Lester Fister's Hybrid Corn.

We hit a long, slow rise and at the crest, at a crossroad, he pulls off on the shoulder. We are at the junction of 400 East and 2200 North, according to an incongruous street sign.

We get out, and the wonderful smell is nearly overpowering. I hear an airplane faintly in the distance. Otherwise there is little or no sound. Again we can see for miles, the roads running off exactly to the four points of the compass. We are immersed in corn smell and silence and Illinois summer. A mile up the road the sun is hitting what must be a metal barn roof. In nature there are no straight lines, I seem to remember reading somewhere, and here everything runs straight—roads, fields, roof lines— yet you feel an elemental force in the corn itself, as if the land has never really been tamed.

I check my watch. It is two-fifteen, less than twenty-four hours since Plowden met me at O'Hare.

His face is alight with pleasure, "We're 'smack dab in the middle of the country,' as Sandra says. No matter which way you look, it's America."

Sandra, his wife, is the former Sandra Schoellkopf of Buffalo, whom he married five years ago after an earlier marriage—to Pleasance Coggeshall—ended in divorce. Plowden has four children, two grown from his first marriage, a young son and daughter from his second marriage.

He must have a souvenir of this spot, he announces. I think he means to pilfer a green ear of Lester Fister's Hybrid. Instead he is setting up for a picture. "You know, half the pictures are souvenirs."

He talks now while he works, only it is talk broken by periodic pauses, sometimes in midsentence, so that it comes out like this:

"Hear the cicada? . . . The light . . . is certainly going to . . . be possible . . . in about two seconds. . . . Clouds are like pieces of concrete. . . . Is that car coming or going? . . . I can't tell. . . . Now hear the rustle . . . when the wind starts. It's almost eerie . . . out here . . . when you're by yourself . . . and the wind begins to blow on the corn."

It is an impossible picture, he concludes. There is no way to convey the sensation of such space. I am sure he is right.

Half an hour later we are in Gilman, again on the Illinois Central Gulf, and he has already made several shots from a spot beside Jed's Yazoo Mowers ("Sales and Service"), where Main Street crosses the tracks. There is more to Gilman than Chebanse. A James Bond movie, *For Your Eyes Only*, is playing at the Palace up the block. There is a Ben Franklin, a Montgomery Ward. Plowden is concentrating on the stark, silver-gray side wall of Roeder's Hardware, which is in the immediate foreground. I ask what he meant when he said clouds are like pieces of concrete.

"When you get that great white blob up there"—he points to what seems to be a perfectly beautiful cloud hanging over the store—"in a still black-and-white picture, it's going to be just as important as that car that's moved in there"—in front of the store—"and it's going to make just as much difference as that white car"—farther off down the street—"in the whole composition."

He likes this corner. The words Roeder's Hardware are painted in elegant old style across the upper left-hand side of the blank wall. "It's just fun. It's just pure fun! I mean, it's a wonderful sign. And a wonderful old tin building and this funny old main street . . . and the window makes it [a small first-floor window on the right] . . . I can't resist it. . . . You know what I really love about doing this? In a sense I preserve this little place—I caught it, and it won't disappear. It's been held. There's something about this particular moment, this particular unique little corner—and it's not going to go. . . . I love that feeling; I love that feeling of getting this place. You know, when you talk about everything disappearing and time going by and . . . it's sort of a nice feeling to think that even if that tin place burns down like that building in front of the town up there"—he has seen something I haven't—"maybe, maybe these pictures will be preserved just the way we have all of those pictures from other times that somebody else took the trouble to do. And to me, to be part of that tradition is very, very important."

Several minutes pass and nothing is said. Two or three more cars have pulled in and parked near the front of the store.

"Now, you see how it works with all those cars lined up . . . you see, the single car there didn't work out at all." He makes several more shots. "I really love that feeling . . . to hold, to preserve some of this. . . . You're seeing me at home. This is my turf. This is the kind of thing I would rather do than anything else. I always just gravitate to these old sort of . . . always along the railroad and always out in this country. It's home—I just poke around."

We pay a call at the Gilman *Star* and introduce ourselves to the editor and publisher, George Elliott, who stands at the front counter with us chatting about crops and Gilman and his paper. He bought it soon after the Second World War and has been doing "just fine." We buy two copies and leave, Plowden having taken no pictures of Mr. Elliott or his office and having said nothing about being a photographer.

"I always feel it's a terrible imposition," he says afterward in the car. "If I had taken his picture he would have become a character. We were equals at the time."

I ask if this is the sort of day he would be having if he were alone. Yes, he says, except that about now he would find a cool spot in a graveyard somewhere and take a nap.

We continue west, never out of corn country, except in the little towns. Plowden studies the sky and predicts perfect light by evening. At Piper City he slows to a crawl—looking, looking, looking. "These towns are like postage stamps. They're just pasted down on the land." We pass a playground under shade trees, a nice old house with a big screened porch. "Piper City," he says softly. "Look at this one right here . . . the house behind the iron fence . . . that's a marvelous house. It's after 1870 . . . because look at the panes of glass, in fours." A smaller house with some young girls sitting on the porch looks, he says, like the house Ronald Reagan lived in in Dixon, to the northwest. "Piper City," he repeats again.

At Chatsworth he likes what he sees enough to get out and walk around. We go into a junk shop. He is interested in souvenir ashtrays, and he finds three he likes, as well as some postcards and a rusty outdoor thermometer with a crack in the glass. The proprietors, Mr. and Mrs. William Durante, strike up a conversation. We learn that they once owned the Biograph in Chicago, the motion picture theater where Dillinger was shot and killed. It explains, they say, the pictures they have hanging of Dillinger and FDR. A vacant movie house across the street is also their and also, like the pictures of Dillinger and FDR, for sale. We all study it through the window. The price is $15,000, they tell Plowden. It is his chance to make a killing in show business, says Mrs. Durante, and we all laugh, Plowden the loudest.

At Forest, where we get gas, he reports that we have driven 170 miles, and we start south on Route 47, a two-lane cement road that he considers one of the most beautiful roads in America.

"The shame is, most people never travel a road like this, never see this kind of country, or, if they do, don't bother to look because it's not their idea of scenery."

In another hour we have passed through Strawn and Sibley and detoured to circle an idle line of freight cars, Plowden trying and failing to get an angle he likes. We have been off on a dirt road between empty fields, scaring up hundreds of small bright yellow butterflies—sulphur butterflies, according to Plowden—and we have swung back onto 47, heading straight through to Gibson City.

"I remember once in a dining car, the steward had all the shades pulled down, and we were going across Kansas or Oklahoma, someplace along there. And I pulled up the shade—and I was almost the only person in the car—and the fellow came by again and pulled the shade down. He said, 'There's nothing to see out there, son.' He said, 'It isn't worth looking at.' I was outraged. I pulled it up, figured I was a patron. But I think so many people feel that way about this country—that it isn't worth looking at. And they're the people who don't know it. I think the people who live here love it. But I think people who don't know aren't aware of this. You know, they're going to the Rockies or they're going to Sun Valley, or they're on their way to ski or to see the Grand Canyon. It's so sad . . . I used to call up the AAA—used to be a member—and ask them to route me someplace, and then I would go the other way. I still feel that way."

Gibson City disappoints him. Gibson City has dressed up its Main Street. Somebody has sold its merchants on the idea of visual uniformity. Instead of the usual chaos of signs, every shop and store is labeled in the same orange lettering on a milk-chocolate background. "Suburban. Awful," Plowden mutters, and we swing north and east on Route 54, which will take us back to I-57.

The light on the fields and distant farm buildings is beautiful beyond anything we have seen all day. Ahead, according to the map, is Roberts. It will be our last stop, Plowden decides.

•   •   •

"What are the principal aggravations of your work?"

"Aggravations? My own shyness."

"What a wonderful answer."

"My own feeling of reticence to go and say, 'Here I am. I'm here to photograph your land.' You know, 'Taking a little bit of your home—a little bit of your soul. I want to steal a little bit.' I feel that way. I feel a terrible imposition. I feel that it's a tremendous privilege to go to somebody's place and to photograph it. I don't do it lightly. . . . I don't have that thick skin that I should have as a photographer—walk right up and walk right in, you know, the old *Daily News* approach. Get your picture at all cost. I can't do that. . . . If I'm going to photograph somebody, that to me is part of the dialogue. I mean, it's part of having talked to that person, to have known that person for a few minutes. I'm not going to run up behind him and grab a picture with a long lens. I'm going to sit down and talk to him and say, 'I want to photograph you. Let's talk.' And to me it would be dishonest to do it any other way."

"What part of it is drudgery? Any of it?"

"Yes. A lot of it is drudgery. A hell of a lot is drudgery. The developing of the film is sheer, absolute donkey work. All of the business of after the prints are made and having to go through all of the hypo and the second hypo and the hypo eliminator and all of the washing and the drying and the spotting of the pictures to remove the dust spots that you couldn't remove—you know, that you couldn't get off the film. All that to me is just rote work. You know it and you do it, but it's not interesting, except that you know you're making something."

"What else?"

"Driving. Long distances by yourself. And it seems as if I spend almost more time sitting behind the wheel of a car than anything else."

"Overnight stays?"

"Oh, Jesus—in motels! That's the worst of all. . . . The only thing that sustains me is to get to the motel to call Sandra. You know, 'How are you?' 'I'm here.' The first thing I give her is my phone number, just to know she knows . . . and to me those are desperate moments."

●   ●   ●

Roberts is still another tiny tree-shaded country town and, by the looks of its vacant store windows, very nearly dead. But with the light the way it is now, there is something almost magical about Roberts. Main Street is short and wide. There is not a soul to be seen and no cars on the street now other than our own. A child's wagon is standing alone on the sidewalk. It all looks like a stage set. The late evening sunshine glows on the dingy, old storefronts like theatrical lighting.

Plowden loves it and gets right to work, showing no sign of fatigue. He moves the camera and tripod from point to point up the side of the street where the wagon stands. He is shooting steadily. I walk on the other side, where I won't be in the way. I think of the stories of Wright Morris and of Larry Woiwode's *Beyond the Bedroom Wall*. I think of something Plowden himself wrote in his preface to *Commonplace*—that we will not find the look of America in places like Williamsburg or Virginia City, Montana. "Only actors will we find, and a set designed by wishful thinking." And there he is across the street, the actor's son working on what is so plainly an empty set, albeit of another kind.

Only last night, in his study at Winnetka, as we were looking through some of his prints, he was talking about the people in a photograph in which there are no people. "It speaks of people," he said. "That street speaks of all the people who were there—always. And I want people . . . I want them to hear their own footsteps as they walk down that street and to occupy that particular space without my filling it with characters. Because I think you would be more interested in them—the characters—than in their space. But if the space is there . . . the street is there by itself . . . I think you will occupy it. It's like a stage set, *you* become the actor."

It is seven-fifteen. But it is another half hour before he stops and we go. The sun now is a crimson ball above the corn fields. "Oh, I love this light," he says. "This is the time I love. You really feel the earth turning."

I am assuming that that is it for the day, but ten miles farther along he sees a square white barn tucked among the corn to the side of the road, and he brakes and stops.

The barn won't work for him, he decides after we are out of the car. The picture is on the other side of the road, the panorama to the west, where the sun is very nearly down. We are standing in the grass on the shoulder. Another car speeds past. He gets the camera and tripod.

The temperature has dropped and the smell of the corn in the cooler air is even more wonderful than before. Birds are flying overhead—veering specks too high for me to know what they are—and the sky is very pale, nearly colorless, turning pale pink down near the band of soft gray-green haze that marks the horizon. The trees there, on the horizon, and a scattering of farm buildings and a silo seem to float in the haze, suspended and unearthly, as if in a mirage. And it is this, the long fading horizon, that Plowden is shooting, the shutter of his camera making one slow clunk after another.

"That's the one," he says, back behind the wheel of the car. "That's the photograph, the best."

"Of the day?"

"Of the day."

About nine, at a roadside restaurant beside I-57, just before Kankakee, he calls Sandra to say we are on the way home.

V

ON WE GO

CHAPTER FOURTEEN

Washington on the Potomac

THE ONLY one of our presidents who stayed on in Washington after leaving office was Woodrow Wilson, and for all his celebrated professorial background he certainly did it in style. Ten of his friends chipped in ten thousand dollars each to cover most of the cost of a house of twenty-two rooms on S Street, just off Embassy Row. S Street was quiet and sedate then and it remains so. But once, on Armistice Day 1923, twenty thousand people came to cheer Wilson. They filled the street for five blocks. I have seen the photographs. He came out finally, tentatively, for his last public appearance. He stood in the doorway while they cheered and sang, a pallid, frail old figure wrapped up in a heavy coat, Edith Bolling Wilson at his side, the vibrant, assertive second wife, who, many said, secretly ran the country after his stroke.

I think of her when I pass by. I wonder if, in fact, she was the first woman to be president. And I think about the crowds on that long-gone November day, in that incredibly different world of 1923. What was in their minds, I wonder, as they looked at their former commander in chief? What did they feel for that old man? Are some still alive who were there and remember?

"I am not one of those that have the least anxiety about the triumph of the principles I have stood for," Wilson said in a brief speech. A headline in *The New York Times* the same day was spread across three columns: HITLER FORCES RALLYING NEAR MUNICH.

I pass the Wilson house only now and then. The way to see Washington is on foot, and I like to vary my route. Early mornings are the best time, before the traffic takes over. The past seems closer then. The imagination roams freer.

I try to keep a steady pace. Harry Truman said that for a walk to do you any good, you ought to move along as though you mean it. As a captain in Woodrow Wilson's war he learned a military pace of 120 steps a minute. I try, for the exercise, but also because I am writing a book about Truman and, who can say, maybe starting my mornings as he did will help. In an hour you can cover a lot of ground.

Washington is a wonderful city. The scale seems right, more humane than other places. I like all the white marble and green trees, the ideals celebrated by the great monuments and memorials. I like the climate, the slow shift of the seasons here. Spring, so Southern in feeling, comes early and the long, sweet autumns can last into December. Summers are murder, equatorial—no question; the compensation is that Congress adjourns, the city empties out, eases off. Winter evenings in Georgetown with the snow falling and the lights coming on are as beautiful as any I've known.

I like the elegant old landmark hotels—the Willard, now restored to its former glory, the Mayflower, with its long, glittering, palm-lined lobby, the Hay-Adams on Lafayette Square, overlooking the White House. And Massachusetts Avenue, as you drive down past the British Embassy and over Rock Creek Park, past the Mosque and around Sheridan Circle. This is an avenue in the grand tradition, befitting a world capital.

The presence of the National Gallery, it seems to me, would be reason enough in itself to wish to live here.

In many ways it is our most civilized city. It accommodates its river, accommodates trees and grass, makes room for nature as other cities don't. There are parks everywhere and two great, unspoiled, green corridors running beside the Potomac and out Rock Creek where Theodore Roosevelt liked to ride horseback or take his rough cross-country walks. There is no more beautiful entrance to any of our cities than the George Washington Parkway, which sweeps down the Virginia side of the Potomac. The views of the river gorge are hardly changed from Jefferson's time. Across the river, on the towpath of the old C&O Canal, you can start at Georgetown and walk for miles with never a sense of being in a city. You can walk right out of town, ten, twenty, fifty miles if you like, more, all the way to Harpers Ferry where you can pick up the Appalachian Trail going north or south.

Some mornings along the towpath it is as if you are walking through a Monet. Blue herons stalk the water. You see deer prints. Once, in Glover Park, in the heart of the city, a red fox stopped directly in front of me, not more than thirty feet down the path, and waited a count or two before vanishing into the woods, as if giving me time to look him over, as if he wanted me never to wonder whether my eyes had played tricks.

Even the famous National Zoo is a "zoological park," a place to walk, as specifically intended in the original plan by Frederick Law Olmsted.

It was Olmsted also who did the magnificent Capitol grounds and who had the nice idea of putting identifying tags on the trees, giving their places of origin and Latin names. I like particularly the tulip trees (*Liriodendron tulipifera*), one of the common trees of Washington, which lines the main drive to the east front of the Capitol. There are red oak, white oak, silver linden, a tremendous spreading white ash, sugar maples, five kinds of American magnolias, a huge Japanese pagoda tree. A spectacular willow oak on the west side has a trunk three men couldn't put their arms around. In spring the dogwood in bloom all around the Capitol are enough to take your breath away.

There are trees and there is sky, the immense, overarching sky of the Mall. What American city has anything to compare to the Mall? At first light on a summer morning, before the rush hour, before the first jets come roaring out of National, the dominant sound is of crows and the crunch of your own feet along the gravel pathways. The air, still cool from the night, smells of trees and damp grass, like a country town. Floodlights are still on at the old red Smithsonian castle, bathing it in a soft theatrical glow, like the backdrop for some nineteenth-century gothic fantasy. The moon is up still, hanging in a pale sky beyond the Washington Monument, which for the moment is a very pale pink.

•   •   •

I am always moved by the Mall; by the Monument, our greatest work of abstract sculpture; by the Lincoln Memorial with its memories of Martin Luther King, Jr.; and by the Vietnam Memorial. I don't like the Hirshhorn Museum. It's ugly and out of place. And I don't like the ring of fifty American flags around the base of the Monument, because they seem so redundant. (How much more colorful and appropriate, not to say interesting, it would be to replace them with the fifty flags of the fifty states.) But I love the steady flow of life in every season, the crowds of tourists from every part of the country, all parts of the world. One Saturday morning I stopped to watch a high school class from Massachusetts pose for a group portrait in front of the colossal equestrian statue of Grant at the east end of the Mall, the Capitol dome in the background. They looked so scrubbed and expectant, so pleased to be who they were and where they were.

I keep coming back to look at the statue and its companion groups of Union cavalry and artillery. Grant on his mighty horse, his face shadowed by a slouch hat, looks brooding and mysterious. He and the side groups are the work of a prolific sculptor who is hardly remembered, Henry Merwin Shrady, whose father, George Frederick Shrady, was Grant's physician. Henry Merwin Shrady had no romantic misconceptions about war. He spent twenty years on his memorial to Grant—twenty years "laboring on details of action and equipment, which have passed the scrutiny of military men as well as artists," I read in one biographical sketch—and he died of overwork before it was dedicated. To me it is the most powerful of all the statues in Washington, and I wonder that it is not better known.

Though I have lived in a number of other places, Washington has been the setting for some of the most important times of my life. I saw it first when I was about the age of those students from Massachusetts, traveling with a school friend and his family. I had seldom been away from home in Pittsburgh and could hardly believe my eyes, hardly see enough. We got about by streetcar. It was something like love at first sight for me. At the Capitol we were given passes to the Senate gallery and warned not to be disappointed if only a few senators were on the floor. There was almost no one on the floor and one man was reading a newspaper. No matter. I was overcome with a feeling I couldn't explain, just to be in that room. I would happily have stayed all afternoon.

The next visit was about five years later, while I was in college, only this time I was head over heels in love with a girl, who, fortunately, also wanted to see the sights. We stood in line for the White House tour, drove down along the Potomac to Mount Vernon. It was March, but felt more like May. The tulips were out at Mount Vernon, and the river, I remember, looked as blue as the ocean. That night, all dressed up, we had dinner at the old Occidental Restaurant, next door to the Willard.

In 1961, after Kennedy took office, still in our twenties, we came back again. I had a new job as an editor with the U.S. Information Agency, then under the direction of Edward R. Murrow. Only now we came with three small children. On summer evenings, my office day over, we would meet to walk around the Tidal Basin, the baby riding in a carriage. One Saturday afternoon at the Library of Congress, I found my vocation.

•   •   •

In 1983 we returned, and found that in the intervening time, Washington had become a changed city. There was more variety, more going on besides politics and government, more music, better restaurants, more theater. The addition of Kennedy Center made a tremendous difference.

There were more resident composers, painters, filmmakers, and writers. *Smithsonian* magazine, *The Washingtonian*, and *The Wilson Quarterly* were being published in Washington, in addition to the *National Geographic*, *The New Republic*, and *U.S. News & World Report*.

All Things Considered, radio at its best to my mind, is a Washington-based production of National Public Radio, and WETA, Washington's public television station, producer of *The McNeil-Lehrer Report* and *Washington Week in Review*, had launched *Smithsonian World*, the project which, with my work on Truman, had brought me back again after twenty years.

Much goes on in history and biography. The biographers Edmund and Sylvia Morris keep an apartment near the Library of Congress; he is working on volume two of his life of Theodore Roosevelt while gathering material for a biography of Ronald Reagan; she is writing the life of Clare Boothe Luce. Rudy Abramson of the Washington bureau of the Los Angeles *Times* is doing a biography of W. Averell Harriman. Albert Eisele, author of a superb study of the intertwining careers of two old Washington hands, Hubert Humphrey and Eugene McCarthy, called *Almost to the Presidency*, is writing the life of Cardinal Cushing. And Daniel J. Boorstin is finishing a sequel to *The Discoverers*, his opus on the human quest to understand the world.

Not everyone, I realize, cares for Washington as I do. "Neither Rome nor home," somebody once said. New Yorkers can be particularly critical, impatient with the pace, annoyed by the limits of the morning paper. Government buildings have a way of depressing many visitors, including some of my own family. I remember a woman from the Boston *Globe* who wrote at length about what a huge bore it all is. A one-industry town was her theme, which wasn't exactly new or true.

There is no local beer, no home baseball team. The tap water tastes pretty bad until you become accustomed to it. The cost of living is high, parking is a headache, the cab drivers may be the worst on earth.

And of course there is more than one Washington. There is lawyer-corporate Washington, in the sleek glass boxes along Connecticut Avenue, student Washington, journalist Washington, and black Washington, worlds I know little about. Violent crime has become a national issue. Its "inner city" ghetto, its slums, are a disgrace, like all slums, but here especially, "in view of the Capitol dome," as is said repeatedly.

What I'm drawn to and moved by is historical Washington, or rather the presence of history almost anywhere one turns. It is hard to imagine anyone with a sense of history not being moved. No city in the country keeps and commemorates history as this one does. Washington insists we remember, with statues and plaques and memorials and words carved in stone, with libraries, archives, museums, and numerous, magnificent old houses besides the one where Woodrow Wilson lived.

Blair House, catty-corner to the White House on Pennsylvania Avenue, is an example. The morning of April 18, 1861, in its small front parlor, Robert E. Lee sat with Francis P. Blair, Sr., who, speaking for Abraham Lincoln, offered Lee command of the Union Army. I never walk by without thinking of this—and of the historians who dismiss the role of personality in history, the reverberations of a single yes or no.

Blair House was built in 1824 and has been owned by the government since World War II, when, the story goes, Eleanor Roosevelt found Winston Churchill pacing the upstairs hall at the White House in his nightshirt. She decided the time had come for some other kind of accommodation for presidential guests. Later, the house served as quarters for the president himself, President Harry Truman, while the White House was being restored.

One autumn afternoon, right where you walk by Blair House, the Secret Service and the White House police shot it out with two Puerto Rican nationalists who tried to storm the front door and kill Truman. Truman, who was upstairs taking a nap in his underwear, ran to the window to see what the commotion was about. One assassin was dead on the front steps, a bullet through the brain. Private Leslie Coffelt of the White House police, who had been hit several times, died later. On the little iron fence in front of the house a plaque commemorates his heroism.

Or consider the Octagon House, three blocks over at 18th and New York. The Octagon, which is actually hexagonal, is a contemporary of the White House and one of the architectural gems of Washington, in the federal style. It is occupied, appropriately, by the American Institute of Architects, and, like the Wilson House, open to the public.

In 1814, after the British burned the White House, James and Dolly Madison and their pet macaw moved into the Octagon for a stay of six months. The peace treaty officially ending the war of 1812, the Treaty of Ghent, was signed in the circular parlor over the main entrance. The house has a magnificent circular stairway, all its original mantels, most of its original woodwork, its original marble floor in the foyer. The architect was William Thornton, the first architect of the Capitol.

Reportedly there is also a secret tunnel in the basement leading to the White House. It is one of those old Washington stories you hear again and again, like the story of alligators in the sewers of New York. It is even given as gospel in the excellent American Guide Series book on Washington. But the tunnel doesn't exist, sad to say. Nor apparently is there an Octagon ghost, as reported repeatedly. The original owner was a rich Virginia planter named John Tayloe. Supposedly he had a beautiful daughter who, thwarted in love, threw herself from the stairway to her death on that marble floor, and her ghost has haunted the house ever since. As it happens, Tayloe had fifteen children, none of whom is known to have committed suicide, and for twenty-odd years, anyway, nobody has heard or seen a sign of a ghost.

I can't help but wonder about the spirits of Jefferson and Jackson, Lafayette, Daniel Webster, and others known to have dined or slept in the house. And what of Dolly herself, in her rose-colored Paris robe, her white turban with its tiara of ostrich plumes? An eyewitness to the signing of the Treaty of Ghent said that the "most conspicuous object in the room" was Mrs. Madison, "then in the meridian of life and queenly beauty . . ."

On the high rise of R Street in Georgetown is a palatial red-brick house with white trim, large as a small hotel and all very Italianate, which was once a summer residence for Ulysses S. Grant and later owned by Rear Admiral Harry H. Rousseau, one of the builders of the Panama Canal. In the 1930s it was taken over as bachelor quarters by a band of exuberant young New Dealers known as the Brain Trust, with Tom ("Tommy the Cork") Corcoran as their leader. One of them remembers a night when a friend dropped by bringing his own grand piano. "A moving van arrived and three or four fellows got the piano up the stairs and into the living room. Tom and his friend played duets all evening. Then the boys packed up the piano and put it back into the moving van."

There is John Kennedy's house, also in Georgetown, at 3307 N Street, and the house on Massachusetts Avenue off Dupont Circle where for decades Alice Roosevelt Longworth held court. Across the street stands the monstrous, gabled brick pile that once belonged to Senator James G. Blaine, "Blaine of Maine," a brilliant rascal who nearly became president in 1884. It was a puzzle to many of his time how somebody with no more than a senator's wages could afford such a place.

The elegant headquarters of the National Trust for Historic Preservation, at 18th and Massachusetts, was once Washington's most sumptuous apartment house. Andrew Mellon, who served three presidents as secretary of the treasury and who gave the country the National Gallery, occupied the top floor. On G Street on Capitol Hill, near the old Marine barracks, you can find the little house where John Philip Sousa was born. On the crest of the hill at Arlington, across the Potomac where the sun goes down, stands the columned Custis-Lee Mansion. From its front porch you get the best of all panoramas of the city.

• • •

Some of the history that has happened here I have seen with my own eyes. When John Kennedy's funeral procession came up Connecticut Avenue, the foreign delegations led by Charles de Gaulle, I watched from an upstairs room at the Mayflower Hotel. It had been reserved as a vantage point by the St. Louis *Post-Dispatch*, so that Barbara Tuchman might describe the scene much as she did the funeral of Edward VII in the opening chapter of *The Guns of August*. Marquis Childs of the *Post-Dispatch*, a friend, had been kind enough to include me. So I shared a window with Mrs. Tuchman. "Look at de Gaulle, look at de Gaulle," she kept saying, as he came striding along in his simple khaki uniform, taller than anyone, his face a perfect mask.

On the afternoon when the Senate voted for the Panama Canal Treaties, I was watching from the gallery, and later that evening, as Washington was lashed by a regular Panama deluge, I was among the several hundred people who crowded into the State Dining Room at the White House to celebrate, to see Jimmy Carter enjoy one of the few happy moments of his administration.

Much of what I feel about the city comes from books I have loved. The story of the Brain Trusters and their piano, for example, is from a collection of reminiscences edited by Katie Louchheim called *The Making of the New Deal*. If the Wilson house stirs a chain of thoughts on my early morning ventures, it is mainly because of Gene Smith's *When the Cheering Stopped*.

I am never in the National Portrait Gallery, once the Patent Office building, that I don't think of Walt Whitman's account in *Specimen Days* of how the wounded and dying men from the battles of Bull Run and Fredericksburg were crowded among the glass display cases for the patent models. Passing the Capitol as a new day is about to begin I think of how, in *The Path to Power*, Robert A. Caro describes young Lyndon Johnson arriving for work:

> But when he turned the corner at the end of that street, suddenly before him, at the top of a long, gentle hill, would be not brick but marble, a great shadowy mass of marble—marble columns and marble arches and marble parapets, and a long marble balustrade high against the sky. Veering along a path to the left, he would come up on Capitol Hill and around the corner of the Capitol, and the marble of the eastern facade, already caught by the early morning sun, would be gleaming, brilliant, almost dazzling. . . . And as Lyndon Johnson came up Capitol Hill in the morning, he would be running.

Like millions of readers, my view of the Senate and its protagonists has been forever colored by Allen Drury's *Advise and Consent*. Lafayette Square, for all its obvious charms, means even more because it is the setting for the Henry Adams novel *Democracy*.

Then to read Louis J. Halle, Jr.'s beautiful *Spring in Washington* is to have your eyes and spirit opened to a world that has nothing to do with government people or official transactions or anything much connected with the human hive of Washington. Written in the last year of World War II, when the city's sense of its own importance had reached a new high and the author himself was serving as an official at the State Department, the book is an informal, philosophical guide to the local natural history. It is a small classic still in print after forty years. "I undertook to be monitor of the Washington seasons, when the government was not looking," the author begins modestly.

Sometimes when I go looking for places that figure in favorite books, the effect has considerably more to do with what I have read than what remains to be seen, for, alas, much in the city has been destroyed, torn down in the name of progress. In *Specimen Days* Whitman writes of standing at Vermont Avenue and L Street on August mornings and seeing Lincoln ride by on his way in from Soldier's Home, his summer quarters. Lincoln, dressed in plain black "somewhat rusty and dusty," was on a "good-sized, easygoing gray horse" and looked "about as ordinary" as the commonest man. "I see very plainly Abraham Lincoln's dark brown face, with the deep-cut lines, the eyes, always to me with a deep latent sadness in the expression," writes Whitman. "We have got so that we exchange bows, and very cordial ones." A lieutenant with yellow straps was at Lincoln's side. The rest of the cavalry escort followed, two by two, thirty men in yellow-striped jackets, their sabers drawn, everyone moving at a slow trot.

Waiting for the light to change on the same corner, on a thoroughly present-day August morning, I look in vain for Whitman's Washington. The early traffic grinds by toward Lafayette Square. The buildings around, all recent and nondescript, include banks and offices and something called the Yummy Yogurt Feastery. Across the street, rearing above the tops of the cars, is a huge abstract sculpture made of steel. No signs of those other times. No sign of the man on the easygoing gray horse. . . . And yet, it happened *here*. This is no ordinary corner, never can be. "The sabers and the accoutrements clank," Whitman says, "and the entirely unornamental *cortège* as it trots toward Lafayette Square arouses no sensation, only some curious stranger stops and gazes." Maybe that's me now, the curious stranger.

The most engaging guide to the city's landmarks is *Washington Itself* by E. J. Applewhite, which is both well written and full of delightful, little-known facts. Thanks to Mr. Applewhite, a former official of the Central Intelligence Agency, I now know as I did not before that the statue of Winston Churchill in front of the British Embassy has one foot planted firmly in the extraterritoriality of the embassy's Crown property and the other over the boundary in U.S. territory, in tribute to Churchill's British-American parentage. I know that the Government Printing Office is the city's largest industrial employer; that the eight glorious columns inside the old Pension Building are the tallest ever built in the Roman style, taller even than those at Baalbek; that the Mayflower Hotel is by the same architectural firm, Warren and Wetmore, that did Grand Central Terminal in New York.

If asked to name my favorite book about the city, I would have to pick Margaret Leech's Pulitzer Prize–winning history, *Reveille in Washington*, first published in 1941, a book I have read and reread and pushed on friends for years.

It is Washington during the Civil War, a chronicle of all that was going on at every level of government and society. I read it initially in the 1960s, in those first years of living here, and it gave me not just a sense of that very different Washington of the 1860s, but of the possibilities for self-expression in writing narrative history. Like Bruce Catton's A *Stillness at Appomattox*, it was one of the books that started me on the way, first reading Civil War history, then thinking more and more of daring to try something of the kind of my own—if ever I could find a subject.

The subject turned out to be the Johnstown flood of 1889, and the fact that I found it in Washington, found the work I wanted most to do, has, I'm sure, a lot to do with my affection for the city.

A number of old photographs were spread out on a big oak table in the Picture Collection of the Library of Congress at a point when my wife and I happened by one Saturday. They had been recently acquired by the library, and one of the curators, Milton Kaplan, took time to tell us about them. A Pittsburgh photographer had managed somehow to get into Johnstown with all his glass plates and heavy paraphernalia only a day or so after the disaster, when almost nobody was getting through. In one picture a whole tree was driven through a house like a javelin. I didn't know it then, but I had begun my first book.

I had also "discovered" the Library of Congress, the greatest "treasure house" we have, and I have been drawn to it, I have been inspired and fortified by it ever since, no matter where I was living. Any city that has the Library of Congress is my capital. Some of the best, most productive days of my life have been spent in its manuscript collection or working with its newspaper files. It is one of the wonders of the world. The statistics are staggering—twenty million books, of which less than a fourth are in English, nearly six million pieces of sheet music, more than one million recordings of music and the spoken word, the papers of twenty-three presidents, the papers of Clara Barton and James G. Blaine, the Wright brothers, Clare Boothe Luce, Margaret Mead, and J. Robert Oppenheimer, Sigmund Freud, Lillian Gish, and George Washington Goethals. Its Madison Building is the largest library building in the world. I prefer the old building, the Jefferson Building, as it is now known, with all its Beaux-Arts marble extravagance and beautiful workmanship. The domed Main Reading Room is one of the most spectacular interior spaces in America.

It was because he wanted to be near the Library of Congress that Woodrow Wilson chose to retire in Washington. Very understandable.

The combination of the Library of Congress, the National Archives, and the Smithsonian, all within walking distance of one another, more than justifies the city's reputation as an unrivaled center for research. And they are only the largest and best-known of numerous libraries and research facilities within the city limits. There are a half dozen universities with excellent libraries. The Folger Shakespeare Library is here. The Columbia Historical Society, devoted to the history of the District of Columbia and housed in a splendid old brewer's mansion, has a library of fifteen thousand volumes, collections of maps, prints, manuscripts, memorabilia, many thousands of rare old photographs. The Society of the Cincinnati has a research library devoted to the Revolutionary War that includes some twelve thousand volumes and letters from nearly all the principal figures of the war.

At the main public library, the Martin Luther King Library downtown, you can now work with the morgue file of the defunct Washington *Star*, long the city's leading paper. Each of the military services has its archives. As do the government departments and agencies. A new fourteen-story National Agricultural Library at nearby Beltsville, Maryland, has become the "most extensive collection of agricultural information in the free world: more than 1.8 million volumes and growing." Should ever you wish to know about asphalt or child care, coal, cotton, firearms, drugstores, banking, peanuts, or civil engineering, or almost anything else you can think of, there is probably a national association to provide what you need. In the Yellow Pages I also find a National Academy of Astrologers.

                    •   •   •

A further source needs to be mentioned. It is the large supply of living memory, all that is tucked away in the minds of those older Washington residents who were witness to or actually took part in the events of earlier times. They are here in amazing numbers, and it has been my experience that they like to share what they know and remember. They will give generously of their time; and you don't have to chase across half the country to find them.

In my work on Truman I have talked with perhaps fifty men and women who knew him or worked with him (or against him in some instances), all people living in Washington—retired journalists, former White House aides, senators and Senate staff, the wife and son of a former secretary of state. And I have more to see, since each invariably tells me of others I mustn't overlook. And how much will be lost when these people are gone.

One man knew not only Truman but Roosevelt, Churchill, Stalin, and Eisenhower as well. He is not one whose name you would recognize. Passing him on the street, you would take no notice. Part of his job was to be inconspicuous. He is a retired Secret Service agent. "You must have been asked to talk about these things many times," I said somewhat apologetically about midpoint in our conversation. "No, Mr. McCullough," he answered. "Nobody has ever asked me about any of this."

• • •

Of nearly equal importance to the political historian or biographer, or anyone trying to understand the past, is what might be called the living model. People are the writer's real subject, after all, the mystery of human behavior, and a historian needs to observe people in real life, somewhat the way a paleontologist observes the living fauna to better interpret the fossil record.

This is very important. And all varieties of the old political fauna of Washington past are around today, alive and mostly thriving—the glad-handers and nostrum sellers, the doctrinaires, the moneybags, the small people in big jobs, the gossips, the courtesans and power-moths of every kind and gender, as well as the true patriot, the devoted public servant, the good, gray functionary down in the bureaucratic ranks, who, so often, is someone of solid ability.

Harry Truman used to talk of Potomac Fever, an endemic disorder the symptoms of which were a swelled head and a general decline of common sense. Were you only to read about such cases, and not see them with your own eyes, you might not appreciate what he meant.

Ambition, the old burning need for flattery, for power, fear of public humiliation, plain high-mindedness, a sense of duty, all that has moved men and women for so long in this capital city moves them still. The same show goes on, only the names and costumes are different.

It helps to remember how much good creative work has gone on here down the years in so many fields. Washington was the home of Alexander Graham Bell, Oliver Wendell Holmes, Jr., and the historian Frederic Bancroft, who also developed the American Beauty Rose. Bruce Catton wrote *A Stillness at Appomattox* here. Rachel Carson wrote *The Sea around Us* and *Silent Spring*.

Two further observations: First, I am struck more and more by the presence of Abraham Lincoln. He is all around. It is almost as though the city should be renamed for him. Most powerful, of course, is the effect of Daniel Chester French's majestic statue within the Memorial, our largest and, I suppose, our most beloved public sculpture. But there are three other Lincoln statues that I know of, one in Judiciary Square, another in Lincoln Park, a third in the Capitol Rotunda. Elsewhere in the Capitol are two Lincoln busts, five paintings of Lincoln, and down in the crypt a colossal marble head, an extraordinary work by Gutzon Borglum that deserves a better place where more people will see it. Lincoln is at the National Portrait Gallery—in spirit upstairs in the grand hall, scene of his first inaugural ball, and on canvas in a portrait by George P. A. Healy that dominates the hall of the presidents. There is Anderson Cottage at Soldiers' Home on North Capitol Street, Lincoln's summer White House, where, until the time was right, he kept the Emancipation Proclamation locked in a desk drawer; and the so-called Lincoln Bedroom at the White House, where he never slept but where he signed the Proclamation. A duplicate of the Healy portrait, Lincoln pensive, his hand on his chin, hangs over the mantel in the State Dining Room. A duplicate of the Lincoln bed in the Lincoln Bedroom is the bed Woodrow Wilson died in at the house on S Street. Pew 54 at little St. John's Episcopal Church on Lafayette Square, the Church of the Presidents, is marked with a silver plate as the Lincoln pew.

There is Ford's Theater with its flag-draped Lincoln box and, downstairs in the basement, a Lincoln museum, containing the clothes and large black boots he was wearing the night of the assassination. Across the street, in the Petersen House, is the room where he died the following morning. Maybe his presence is felt most of all in the rise and dominance of the Capitol dome, which he insisted be completed during the Civil War to show that the Union continued.

The second observation is really a question: Why do so many politicians feel obliged to get away from the city at every chance? They claim a pressing need to get back to the real America. To win votes, many of them like also to deride the city and mock its institutions. They run against Washington, in the shabby spirit made fashionable in recent presidential campaigns. It is as if they find the city alien or feel that too close an association with it might be somehow dishonorable. It is as if they want to get away from history when clearly history is what they need, they most of all, and now more than ever.

What if, instead of rushing off to wherever it is they come from, some of them were to spend a morning at the Wilson House or on the Mall with their fellow citizens touring the National Museum of American History? Or what if they took time, say fifteen minutes, at the National Gallery to enjoy and think about George Caleb Bingham's *The Jolly Flatboatmen*—that one painting? Might not that too be a way of reaching the real America?

I have no sense that the people they represent fail to appreciate the city or to feel its spell. They come in ever increasing numbers, by the tens of millions. They climb the sweep of marble steps at the Supreme Court, pose for a picture by the Grant statue. They move slowly, quietly past the fifty-seven thousand names in the polished black stone wall of the Vietnam Memorial. They pour through the Air and Space Museum, the most popular museum in the world, craning their necks at the technical marvels of our rocket century. We all do. We all should. This is our capital. It speaks of who we are, what we have accomplished, what we value.

CHAPTER FIFTEEN

Extraordinary Times

THE SPAN of years since 1936 has been the most troubled, unsettling, costly, adventurous, and surprising time ever. There is no period to compare to it. More has changed, and faster, more has been destroyed, more accomplished than in any comparable interval in the five thousand years since recorded history began.

To a very large degree it has been a time of horror, of war after war, wars to stop war, religious wars, wars of "liberation," many more than fifty wars in fifty years, including the worst war of all time, the shadow of which is still with us. Terror and atrocity have been made political policy and carried to hideous extremes. But it has also been a time of marvels and of unprecedented material progress for much of humanity. To many areas of the world it has brought the exhilarating awareness that change is actually possible, that things don't have to stay the same.

These have been the years of Stravinsky and Picasso, Faulkner and Eugene O'Neill, Ella Fitzgerald and the Golden Gate Bridge. Present advances in such fields as medicine and communications seem to belong to a different century from that of 1936. Since 1980, to cite one stunning example, there has not been one case of smallpox anywhere on earth.

•　　•　　•

The colossal sums spent on research and development, the links between government and science, industry and science, the onrush of scientific discoveries have made change of all kinds accelerative, like gravity, and the effect is felt everywhere. Science has transformed the way we live, how long we live. It has meant the steady spread of improvements of a kind new to human experience, and it has brought a level of fear that is also new. Physicists, biologists, and astronomers have become shapers of great world events as much.as, or more than, generals and politicians, and this too is new.

Fifty years ago the center of world power and interest was Europe. On the maps of Africa, Asia, and the Middle East there were no countries called Tanzania or Zaire. Or the People's Republic of China. Or Vietnam. Or Israel.

Furthermore, fifty years ago the physical limits of the human adventure were still defined by the geography of the earth alone.

One simple measure of how many changes have taken place in everyday life in America is our vocabulary. A college dictionary from 1936, for example, does not contain such words as *automation* or *antibiotics*, *ecosystem*, *Chicano*, *nursing home*, or *condominium*. No one then had ever heard of a zip code or jet lag. The word *gay* was defined as "full of, or inclined to, mirth," or "bright-colored." *Program* was a noun, not a verb.

America then had no Pentagon. The United States Army numbered all of four hundred thirty-eight thousand men, which put it in twenty-first place, behind, among others, the armies of Argentina and Switzerland.

With the country in the grip of the Great Depression, nine million people were out of work. The poorest were desperately poor. Nearly 40 percent of American families had annual incomes of less than $1,000. In places like the coal fields of Kentucky, there was seldom enough to eat. Some families were living on weeds.

Nineteen-thirty-six was a year of ominous headlines. Hitler marched unopposed into the demilitarized Rhineland. Spain erupted in civil war. The Italian dictator Mussolini, using planes, mustard gas, and two hundred fifty thousand troops, crushed Ethiopia, while his son, Vittorio, crowed over the victory. Bombing Ethiopian cavalry was "exceptionally good fun," he told the press.

It also was the year that Franklin Roosevelt, speaking at the Democratic National Convention in Philadelphia, told the country, "This generation of Americans has a rendezvous with destiny."

Two of the century's most crucial developments were not in the headlines, however. One was entirely unknown to the public, the other beyond the comprehension of all but a very few. A future that almost no one could have imagined in 1936 was already taking form in two European settings with nothing in common except their proximity on the Baltic Sea.

The first was a highly secret research installation begun that year by the Germans at the island village of Peenemunde for the purpose of launching experimental rockets. Unlike the modestly financed pioneering work on rockets by physicist Robert Goddard in the United States, Peenemunde was a high-priority military effort—enormous, amply supported, well staffed, and with a brilliant young engineer named Wernher Von Braun newly appointed as "technical overlord."

The second, less than 120 miles from Peenemunde, was Copenhagen's Institute of Theoretical Physics, a center of free inquiry open to scientists from all over the world, where in 1936 the subject was nuclear fission. As those involved would remember, the institute was the place to be at one of the most exciting junctures in the history of science. As time would tell, the history of science was to be very largely the history that mattered.

The institute's director—and its inspirational force—was the much-loved Nobel Prize–winning physicist Niels Bohr, who had once thought it pointless to expect any new source of energy from the atom. Yet, in January 1939, Bohr reported to a Washington, D.C., conference of theoretical physicists that the uranium atom, when split, would produce a power millions of times greater than anything known on earth. It was possibly the most important piece of information of the century. Bohr, however, mumbled so that nobody understood what he was saying. When his friend Enrico Fermi stood up and offered a clarification, the room suddenly emptied, scientists rushing to the nearest telephones to alert their universities and laboratories, while the few reporters present sat wondering what was going on.

In August Albert Einstein addressed a historic letter to Roosevelt warning that a terrible new kind of bomb could be made and that Germany had already stopped the sale of uranium from the mines in Czechoslovakia. He urged a speeding up of scientific research under government direction. Roosevelt, in league with the British, initiated what would become the top-secret Manhattan Project at a cost of $2 billion, a sum undoubtedly equal to all the money spent until then on scientific research. Politics and physics had been joined irrevocably.

The war began September 1, 1939, when German armored divisions smashed into Poland. By the time it was finished, it had become "total war." It was the cataclysmic upheaval of all time and the most important event of the century.

Eventually, more than eighty million people were in uniform and possibly as many as fifty-five million people were killed. And something new had been added to the annals of organized slaughter: the dead included tens of millions of civilians.

In June 1941, six months before Pearl Harbor, Hitler made the fateful decision to attack Russia. If we had only the statistics of battle losses, we would have to conclude that World War II was primarily a titanic struggle between the two totalitarian empires of Germany and Russia. Not counting an estimated seven hundred eighty thousand of their civilian dead, the Germans probably lost more than four million men—more than the battle deaths suffered by China and Japan combined. The Russians appear to have suffered as many as seven million deaths in battle. U.S. fatalities, some three hundred thousand, seem minuscule by comparison, but they were still nearly three times the American dead in World War I.

•   •   •

The war ended in 1945, and 1945 was the watershed year of the twentieth century. One kind of world ended, another began. Roosevelt died, Hitler committed suicide, Churchill was voted out of office. The United Nations was founded. An independent republic of Vietnam was formed with Ho Chi Minh as president. The end of the war was a time of huge celebration and thanksgiving, but it was also the point at which mankind saw as never before its own capacity for evil. It was the year the death camps were revealed, and it was the year of the bomb.

Although Hitler's plan for the "complete elimination of Jews from European life" had been reported years earlier, only when a number of the camps—Buchenwald, Dachau, Belsen, Auschwitz—were liberated shortly before the German surrender was the truth known. Eisenhower, seeing his first "indisputable evidence" at a camp near Gotha, insisted on being shown everything, because "I felt it my duty to be in a position from then on to testify at first hand about these things in case there ever grew up at home the belief or assumption that 'the stories of Nazi brutality were just propaganda.' "

Documentation came with the Nuremberg trials. Ten million human beings had been exterminated factory-fashion. Approximately six million were Jews. Another word not found in the 1936 dictionary had to be invented to label the process: *genocide*. Prisoners, including children, were shot, hanged, beaten to death, starved to death, buried alive, and systematically sent to gas chambers. Photographs of the survivors that appeared in magazines like *Life* are never to be forgotten.

Because the outcome of great events becomes so well established in our minds, there is a tendency to think things had to go as they did. But there is nothing inevitable about history. The defeat of the Nazis, the war's overriding mission, was never a certainty. Recall the dark winter of 1941–1942, when the Germans had advanced nearly to Moscow, the British ships *Repulse* and *Prince of Wales* were at the bottom of the South China Sea, our forces on Bataan had surrendered and German U-boats were sinking ships within sight of the New Jersey shore. The importance of the defeat of the Nazis can hardly be overstated.

The date of the blinding flash at Alamogordo, New Mexico, the day the first atomic bomb was detonated, was July 16, 1945, six years and not quite six months after Niels Bohr's announcement in Washington. Whether the use of the new weapon on Hiroshima and Nagasaki was necessary will never be settled to everyone's satisfaction. Based on the estimate that the planned invasion of Japan would result in possibly a half million American casualties and many times that for-the Japanese, however, the decision seemed necessary at the time. The bombs were dropped to end the war, and they did.

In the last analysis, the deciding factor in the war was America's tremendous industrial power, and at the war's end that power was still intact. With World War II, U.S. history had become world history. Europe's—Great Britain's—time had passed. "America at this moment stands at the summit of the world," Churchill told Parliament the summer of 1945. For four years, until the Russians exploded an atomic bomb in 1949, the United States was without equal or challenge.

•   •   •

The next decades were earthshaking: the mounting tensions of the Cold War, the rise of the Third World, the astonishing revival of West Germany and Japan and the final stage of the Chinese Revolution, which has directly affected the lives of one-fifth of the human race. Mao Tse-tung became one of the looming figures of the age.

The world grew smaller and more dangerous. Crisis and more war followed—the Berlin Airlift, the Korean War, the Hungarian Revolution, the Suez crisis, the chilling Cuban missile crisis and the repeated bloody challenges to the existence of Israel.

• • •

Among the consequences, for better or for worse, was the steadily increasing power of the American presidency. Harry Truman, a lifelong student of history, made history as few presidents ever have—including Franklin Roosevelt, who had exercised more power than any president since Lincoln. The Truman Doctrine of 1947, "to support free peoples who are resisting attempted subjugation," set a course that can be said to have saved Europe and to have led to Vietnam. Truman launched the Marshall Plan, established NATO, sent U.S. troops into Korea, and proceeded with the hydrogen bomb. In the years since Truman, the size, complexity, and influence of the executive branch have only expanded.

• • •

"When you're at war you think about a better life; when you're at peace you think about a more comfortable one," said a character in Thornton Wilder's play *The Skin of Our Teeth*. In postwar America prosperity was no longer "just around the corner," it had arrived. The Great Depression seemed a memory of olden times. For all the energetic programs of the New Deal, it was World War II that had finally ended the Depression. Now it was the mounting cost of the Cold War arms race that helped keep the economy booming, though nobody liked to think of defense as the welfare state.

A shift of population that had begun during the war grew to surprising proportions over the next thirty-odd years, becoming one of the nation's greatest migrations. Millions of people, black and white and mostly poor, left the rural South for the big cities of the North and West.

The GI Bill made possible a college education for millions of veterans who otherwise could never have met the cost. A federal interstate highway program—the largest construction effort on record—hastened the growth of suburbia and thus had more impact on home building than even the federal housing program. Women entered the work force in greater numbers; in time, the women's movement took hold.

Television arrived. Television conquered. It has been said to represent an advance in communications comparable to the invention of print. We don't know yet. But how greatly our perception of history has been affected by it! How many of the telling moments of our time are remembered because of what we saw on television: There was the point in the Army-McCarthy hearings when the Boston lawyer Joseph Welch turned and said, "Have you no sense of decency, sir, at long last?" There was Eisenhower's surprising farewell address from the White House warning of the influence of the "military-industrial complex." There were the Nixon-Kennedy debates, Watergate, the return of the hostages from Iran, the travels of Pope John Paul II and the endless Vietnam war on the nightly news. And, above all, the tragedy at Dallas, the scenes of which, like those of Martin Luther King, Jr. at the Lincoln Memorial, have been replayed so often they have become part of the experience of a generation that was not alive to view them firsthand.

Television was only one manifestation of a much larger phenomenon, the advance of science and technology. Peenemunde produced the giant V-2 rocket, the first true ballistic missile, and the Manhattan Project produced the atom bomb. Importantly, World War II also produced in crude form what we call the computer. And it is the modern computer in combination with the rocket and the bomb that makes possible the intercontinental ballistic missile, and thus the threat of annihilation that hangs over us all. The rocket delivers the bomb, the computer delivers the rocket. But World War II also contributed radar and jet aircraft. In the 1950s came the polio vaccine and the Pill; afterward, microchips and lasers, all effecting enormous change. The deciphering of the genetic code in the 1960s could prove to be as important to the course of history as the splitting of the atom.

Few people picture this as an era of geographical exploration in the old sense, yet the largest topographical feature on earth was delineated and mapped in the late 1950s. The midocean ridge system is an underwater mountain range some forty thousand miles in length with valley-to-peak elevations up to two miles. From this discovery and studies of the ocean floor has emerged a revolution in the earth sciences: the new geological theory of plate tectonics that envisions the crust of the earth as composed of immense shifting sections.

Unprecedented advances have been made in astronomy, in our understanding of the architecture of the human brain. Most dramatic of all has been the venture in space. It eclipses all prior voyages of discovery. The rocket, our most terrifying tool of destruction, has taken us on the adventure of the century. The rocket is the symbol of the times.

The American space program began, literally, where German rocket development left off. Wernher Von Braun and a staff of one hundred twenty or so German rocket scientists were brought to the United States from Peenemunde after the war, and it was the V-2 that they began working with in the late 1940s. Times had changed.

• • •

The first satellite in orbit was the Russian *Sputnik* of October 1957. A month later a second Russian satellite carried a small black-and-white dog named Laika, demonstrating that life was possible in outer space. The first human being to go, the Russian cosmonaut Yuri Gagarin, orbited the world on April 12, 1961. The following year John Glenn circled the globe three times and saw four sunsets in four hours, fifty-five minutes.

"These are extraordinary times," John Kennedy said when he went to Congress in 1961 to ask for the money to put a man on the moon. From Laika to the flight of Apollo 11 and Neil Armstrong's walk of July 20, 1969, was only twelve years. The cost of the moon flight was $25 billion.

Events close at hand are hard to judge without the proportion time lends. But two stupendous failures of science and technology in 1986, the tragedy of the space shuttle *Challenger* and the disaster at Chernobyl, are clearly history of major consequence. If nothing else, they surely must mark an end to the hubris of those who see mankind as master of the universe. (The explanations of what happened refer often to human error, as if there were any other kind.)

Real progress there has been, in much of everyday life. Anyone who doubts this need only imagine—or recall—a visit to a 1930s dentist. The prospects for many old American cities are noticeably improved. Countless items in common use—from cameras and home computers to cars and running shoes—are far superior to what was previously available. College enrollment is up. Life expectancy keeps increasing.

Still, much of the history of recent decades has been a lesson in limitations. Vietnam painfully demonstrated the limits of American power. We have seen our environmental blunders bring appalling consequences, not just for seabirds and river systems, but for ourselves. The poisoning of the Missouri town of Times Beach with dioxin is but one example.

• • •

We have known little but disappointment and frustration in trying to solve the problems of crime and drugs. We have an educational system that produces high school graduates who have no idea where Egypt is or in which half of the century World War I occurred.

Real earnings for middle-income families, the majority of Americans, are declining. Economic gains for black Americans have fallen far short of the promise of the civil rights movement of the 1950s and 1960s. A census study shows that white Americans have accumulated eleven times the assets of blacks and that nearly a third of black households have no wealth at all.

In the world at large, there are now more dictators than in 1936. Nor has genocide been confined to the Nazis. In Cambodia, following the victory of the Khmer Rouge in 1975, as many as two million people were murdered. To the long list of assassinated world leaders that began with Mohandas Gandhi in 1948 has now been added the prime minister of Sweden, Olof Palme.

These are the sobering facts of our much reported, but imperfectly understood, present. What will future historians make of it all? Maybe little of this will figure as large as we might expect. Maybe the critical event of the era will be the rise of Islam or the new theory that all matter is composed of strings. Or maybe it will be something going on about which we know no more than was known of Peenemunde in 1936.

Quite possibly it will be our own flourishing numbers—the human population of the world, which in the summer of 1986 passed the five billion mark—and such consequent problems as the ravaging of irreplaceable resources. It is estimated that the tropical rain forests of the world are being destroyed (mostly to make room for agriculture) at the rate of an area the size of Nebraska every year, and since these forests are home to more species of terrestrial life than anywhere else, their destruction could in the long run be among the most tragic of mistakes.

Who and what have affirmed the human spirit in this fifty years of unprecedented change?

Roosevelt, in peace and in war; Churchill, as few leaders ever have ("The nation had the lion's heart. I had the luck to give the roar," he said on his eightieth birthday); Anne Frank, whose *The Diary of a Young Girl*, the great book of World War II, will be read as long as there are books; Rosa Parks, who refused to get up and move to the back of the bus in Montgomery, Alabama, on December 1, 1955; Polish Solidarity leader Lech Walesa; the unmanned spacecraft *Voyager II*, a product of the human mind that departed earth nine years ago, traveled three billion miles, and in January 1986 succeeded in photographing the planet Uranus, in the dark, while moving at a speed of about forty thousand miles an hour; and Niels Bohr, who had a horseshoe nailed over his front door for luck and who, when questioned by a skeptical colleague on whether he believed in such superstition, responded, "Oh, no, but I am told that it works even if you don't believe it."

CHAPTER SIXTEEN

Recommended Itinerary

I ONCE KNEW an able and accomplished man who had been fired from his first job after college because his employer decided he was deficient in positive attitude. "You'll never go anywhere," he was told as he departed. Unable to find another job, he spent the next several months seeing the world and, remembering the old employer and those parting words, he took particular pleasure in sending him a postcard from each stop along the way, from one foreign capital after another, to let him know just how far he was going.

I want you of the graduating Middlebury class of 1986 all to go far.

I want you to see Italy—Florence, in particular—at least once in your lifetime. I hope you can spend an hour in front of the great, five-hundred-year-old Botticelli at the Ufizzi, *The Birth of Venus*. Do it for the unparalleled pleasure of it, but also so you will have the experience to draw on whenever overtaken by the common hubris of our time, which is that our time outranks all others in all attainments.

I hope by the time you are my age you will have been to Edinburgh, little Edinburgh, and walked its stone streets and read its great thinkers and considered their impact on our own Founding Fathers.

Go to Palenque—Palenque, the stupendous Mayan ruin in the beautiful Mexican province of Chiapas. Climb the long stairway of the central

pyramid-tomb to the very top and, with the main palace and other monuments spread before you, try to keep in mind that what you are seeing is
only a fraction of what once was and that all of it was built under the rule of
one man who lived more than a thousand years ago, a king called Pacal, a
name virtually unknown to North Americans, except for a handful of
scholars, yet plainly one of the most remarkable leaders in the whole
history of our hemisphere. He had to have been. You need only see
Palenque to know that.

• • •

I hope you go to Italy and Scotland and to places like Palenque because
I think you will afterward see and understand your own country
more clearly. That is an old idea, I know—that the country you learn most
about by traveling abroad is your own—but then some old ideas bear
repeating.

But you must also go please to Monticello. Walk through the vegetable
garden that Jefferson carved out of the south side of his "little mountain."
Tour his extraordinary house, see his trees, enjoy the view, so much of
which still looks as he saw it. But pay particular attention to the vegetable
garden and remember what it tells you about patriotism.

It is eighty feet wide and one thousand feet in length. He grew no fewer
than 450 varieties of vegetables, fruits, nuts, and herbs. Four hundred and
fifty varieties! The garden was begun in 1774, which makes it older than
the United States. He was constantly experimenting, trying "new" vegetables like okra and eggplant and Arikara beans brought back from the Lewis
and Clark expedition. He grew fifteen varieties of peas alone.

In his perfect hand in his garden diary he recorded all that he planted
there, where, when, and the time it came to his table. He considered
agriculture a science to be taken seriously. But his patriotism was also
involved. "No greater service can be rendered any country," he once said,
"than to introduce a new plant to its culture"—that from the man who
wrote the Declaration of Independence!

Patriotism in a plant. How different from what the Hollywood impres-
arios have in mind for their centennial tribute to the Statue of Liberty.

Your travels should take you through the great heartland of Illinois,
Missouri, and Kansas. And you must get off the interstates. You must ride
the side roads where the small towns are, and the farmland, where main
streets are boarded up and you soon grow tired of counting the abandoned
farms because there are so many. What kind of people are we if we turn our

backs on the land and the people who have worked it for so long in all seasons?

Go to eastern Kentucky. See with your own eyes what the strip miners are doing, still, for all the ballyhoo about reclamation. The reports you have read about reclamation are largely lies. Go see the rape of the land that continues every day, not in far-off, who-gives-a-damn-about-it, good-for-nothing, backwoods hillbilly Kentucky, but *your* Kentucky, *your* country.

Look at people when you travel. Talk to people. Listen to what they have to say.

•   •   •

Imagine a man who professes over and over his unending love for a woman but who knows nothing of where she was born or who her parents were or where she went to school or what her life had been until *he* came along—and furthermore, doesn't care to learn. What would you think of such a person? Yet we appear to have an unending supply of patriots who know nothing of the history of this country, nor are they interested. We have not had a president of the United States with a sense of history since John Kennedy—not since before most of you were born. It ought to be mandatory for the office. As we have a language requirement for the Foreign Service, so we should have a history requirement for the White House. Harry S. Truman, who never had the benefit of a college education but who read history and biography and remembered it, once said, "The only new thing in the world is the history you don't know."

If nothing else, seeing the country should lead you to its past, its story, and there is no part of your education to come that can be more absorbing or inspiring or useful to your role in society, whatever that may be. How can we know who we are and where we are going if we don't know anything about where we have come from and what we have been through, the courage shown, the costs paid, to be where we are?

Put Antietam on your list. Go to Antietam in Maryland and stand on the hillside near the old whitewashed Dunker church and try if you possibly can to imagine what happened there that terrible day, September 17, 1862. Once, last summer, sitting in a garden restaurant in Washington with a friend from out of town, she told me how moved she had been by her visit to the Vietnam Memorial. Had I seen it? she wanted to know. I said I had. I had gone the first time late in the afternoon of a day spent at Antietam.

"What is Antietam?" she said. She is a graduate of one of our great universities. She is an editor of the op-ed page of one of our largest, most influential newspapers. It was a bright summer afternoon and people at the adjoining tables were all happily eating and chatting.

"Antietam," I said. "Maybe you know it as Sharpsburg." She hadn't any idea of what I was talking about. I said there are 57,000 names on the Vietnam Memorial and the Vietnam War lasted eleven years. At the Battle of Antietam in one day there were 23,000 casualties. In one day. It was not just the worst, bloodiest day of the Civil War; its toll in human life exceeded that of any day in our history. It happened hardly more than an hour's drive from where we were sitting, and she had never heard of it.

•   •   •

I feel so sorry for anyone who misses the experience of history, the horizons of history. We think little of those who, given the chance to travel, go nowhere. We deprecate provincialism. But it is possible to be as provincial in time as it is in space. Because you were born into this particular era doesn't mean it has to be the limit of your experience. Move about in time, go places. Why restrict your circle of acquaintances to only those who occupy the same stage we call the present?

For a lift of the spirits walk over the Brooklyn Bridge, one of the surpassing masterworks from our past and as strong and enduring a symbol of affirmation as I know. There is something wonderful about a bridge, almost any bridge, but it is our greatest bridge.

Or go to a tiny graveyard on the Nebraska prairie north of the little town of Red Cloud and look about until you find a small headstone. It reads "Anna Pavelka, 1869–1955."

By every fashionable index used to measure success and importance, Anna Pavelka was nobody. Three weeks ago my wife Rosalee and I were among several hundred visitors who arrived in a caravan of Red Cloud school buses to pay her homage. Who was she and why did we bother?

She was born Anna Sadilek in Mizzovic, Bohemia, present-day Czechoslovakia, in 1869. In 1883, at age fourteen, she sailed with her family to America to settle on the treeless Nebraska prairie in a sod hut. Some time later, in despair over the struggle and isolation of his alien new life, her father killed himself. As a suicide he was denied burial in the

Catholic cemetery. They buried him instead beside the road and the road makes a little jog at the spot there still.

Annie afterward worked as a "hired girl" in Red Cloud. She fell in love. She left town with a railroad man she hoped to marry, but was deserted by him and forced to return. She bore an illegitimate child. Later, she married John Pavelka, also of Bohemia, who had been a tailor's apprentice in New York, a city man, and who knew little of farming. She ran the farm and she bore him, I believe, eleven more children. She spent her life on the farm there on the prairie.

And that's about all there is to the story—except that she adored her children and her farm and she was also known to a younger woman from Red Cloud named Willa Cather who transformed her life into a very great and enduring American novel called My Antonia. The Antonia of the story—the Anna Sadilek Pavelka of real life—was a figure of heroic staying power. But it is her faith and joy in life, her warmth that matter most. "At first I near go crazy with lonesomeness," says her city-man husband at the close of the novel, remembering his first years in Nebraska, "but my woman is got such a warm heart."

Anna Pavelka reaches out to us because of what Oliver Wendell Holmes called "the transfiguring touch" of Willa Cather's art, because of what she, through Willa Cather, says about the human spirit.

Take the novels of Willa Cather when you go to Nebraska. Bring Faulkner when you're going south. Take Cather, Faulkner—take books wherever you go. Read. Read all you can. Read history, biography. Read Dumas Malone's masterful biography of Jefferson and Paul Horgan's epic history of the Rio Grande, Great River. Read Luigi Barzini's books on Italy and America. Read the published journals of those who traveled the Oregon Trail. Read the novels of Maya Angelou and Robertson Davies; read Wendell Berry, Wallace Stegner, and the poems of Robert Penn Warren. As much as you have read in these four years, it is only the beginning. However little television you watch, watch less. If your experience is anything like mine, the books that you read in the next ten years will be the most important books in your lives.

·   ·   ·

When to go? Always a question. I think of a comment by the late George Aiken about the pruning of trees. "Some say you shouldn't prune except at the right time of year," he said. "I generally do it when the saw is sharp."

George Aiken, of Vermont, as I hope you know, was one of the best things that ever happened to the United States Senate. Wherever you go, don't forget Vermont. Don't forget this lovely town and these mountains and the people who live here.

Go with confidence. Prize tolerance and horse sense. And some time, somewhere along the way, do something for your country.

CHAPTER SEVENTEEN

Simon Willard's Clock

SIMON WILLARD was never a member of Congress in the usual sense. Simon Willard of Roxbury, Massachusetts, was a clockmaker early in the nineteenth century and he did it all by hand and by eye.

> In cutting his wheel teeth [reads an old account], he did not mark out the spaces on the blank [brass] wheel and cut the teeth to measure, but he cut, rounded up and finished the teeth as he went along, using his eye only in spacing, and always came out even . . .
> It is doubtful if such a feat in mechanics was ever done before, and certainly never since.

The exact date is uncertain, but about 1837, when he was in his eighties, Simon Willard made a most important clock. I will come back to that.

On a June afternoon in 1775, a small boy stood with his mother on a distant knoll, watching the Battle of Bunker Hill. Seven years later, at age fourteen, he was a diplomatic secretary at the court of Russia's Catherine II; at twenty-eight, minister to the Hague. He was minister plenipotentiary to Russia at the time of Alexander I. He saw Napoleon return from Elba. He was a senator, secretary of state, and finally president. He had seen more, contributed more to the history of his time than almost anyone of his time.

But then, as no former president ever had, John Quincy Adams returned here to the hill to take a seat in the House of Representatives, in the Twenty-second Congress. Adams was thrilled at the prospect. "No election or appointment conferred upon me ever gave me so much pleasure," he wrote in his diary. And it was here that this extraordinary American had his finest hours.

He took his seat in the old House—in what is now Statuary Hall—in 1831. Small, fragile, fearing no one, he spoke his mind and his conscience. He championed mechanical "improvements" and scientific inquiry. To no one in Congress are we so indebted for the establishment of the Smithsonian Institution. With Congressman Lincoln of Illinois and Corwin of Ohio, he cried out against the Mexican War, and for eight long years, almost alone, hooted and howled at, he battled the infamous Gag Rule imposed by Southerners to prevent any discussion of petitions against slavery. Adams hated slavery, but was fighting, he said, more for the unlimited right of all citizens to have their petitions heard, whatever their cause. It was a gallant fight and he won. The Gag Rule was permanently removed.

Earlier this year, at the time of the inaugural ceremonies, I heard a television commentator broadcasting from Statuary Hall complain of the resonance and echoes in the room. What resonance! What echoes!

John Quincy Adams is a reminder that giants come in all shapes and sizes and that, at times, they have walked these halls, their voices have been heard, their spirit felt here. Listen, please, to this from his diary, from March 29, 1841:

> The world, the flesh, and all the devils in hell are arrayed against any man who now in this North American Union shall dare to join the standard of Almighty God to put down the African slave trade; and what can I, upon the verge of my seventy-fourth birthday, with a shaking hand, a darkening eye, a drowsy brain, and with all my faculties dropping from me one by one, as the teeth are dropping from my head—what can I do for the cause of God and man. . . . Yet my conscience presses me on; let me but die upon the breach.

And how he loved the House of Representatives:

> The forms and proceedings of the House [he writes], this call of the States for petitions, the colossal emblem of the Union over the Speaker's chair, this historic Muse at the clock, the echoing pillars of the hall, the tripping Mercuries who bear the resolutions and amendments between the members and the chair, the calls of ayes and noes, with the different intonations of the

answers, from different voices, the gobbling manner of the clerks in reading over the names, the tone of the Speaker in announcing the vote, and the varied shades of pleasure and pain in the countenances of the members on hearing it, would form a fine subject for a descriptive poem.

Some nights he returned to his lodgings so exhausted he could barely crawl up the stairs. In the winter of 1848, at age eighty, after seventeen years in Congress, Adams collapsed at his desk. A brass plate in the floor of Statuary Hall marks the place.

He was carried to the Speaker's office and there, two days later, he died. At the end Henry Clay in tears was holding his hand. Congressman Lincoln helped with the funeral arrangements. Daniel Webster wrote the inscription for the casket. . . .

Many splendid books have been written about Congress: Harry McPherson's *A Political Education*; Allen Drury's *A Senate Journal*; Alvin Josephy's *On the Hill* and *Kings of the Hill* by Representative Richard Cheney and Lynne V. Cheney; *Rayburn*, a fine recent biography by D. B. Hardeman and Donald Bacon; and *The Great Triumvirate*, about Clay, Webster, and Calhoun, by Merrill Peterson. Now, in this bicentennial year, comes volume one of Senator Robert Byrd's monumental history of the Senate.

But a book that does justice to the story of Adams's years in the House, one of the vivid chapters in our political history, is still waiting to be written, as are so many others.

Our knowledge, our appreciation, of the history of Congress and those who have made history here are curiously, regrettably deficient. The truth is historians and biographers have largely neglected the subject. Two hundred years after the creation of Congress, we have only begun to tell the story of Congress—which, of course, means the opportunity for those who write and who teach could not be greater.

There are no substantial, up-to-date biographies of Justin Morrill of Vermont, author of the Land Grant College Act . . . or Jimmy Byrnes, considered the most skillful politician of his day . . . or Joe Robinson, the tenacious Democratic majority leader whose sudden death in an apartment not far from here meant defeat for Franklin Roosevelt's court-packing scheme . . . or Carl Hayden of Arizona, who served longer in the Senate than anybody, forty-one years.

We have John Garraty's life of Henry Cabot Lodge, Sr., but none of Henry Cabot Lodge, Jr. Search the library shelves for a good biography of Alben Barkley or Speaker Joe Martin and you won't find one. They don't exist. The only biography of Senator Arthur Vandenberg ends in 1945, when his career was just taking off.

The twentieth-century senator who has been written about most is Joe McCarthy. There are a dozen books about McCarthy. Yet there is no biography of the senator who had the backbone to stand up to him first— Margaret Chase Smith.

"I speak as a Republican," she said on that memorable day in the Senate. "I speak as a woman. I speak as a United States Senator. I speak as an American. I don't want to see the Republican Party ride to political victory on the four horsemen of calumny—fear, ignorance, bigotry, and smear."

We have books on people like Bilbo and Huey Long, but no real biographies of George Aiken or Frank Church.

Richard Russell of Georgia, one of the most highly regarded influential figures to serve in the Senate in this century, used to take home old bound copies of the *Congressional Record*, to read in the evenings for pleasure. He loved the extended debates and orations of older times and would remark to his staff how strange it made him feel to realize that those who had once counted for so much and so affected the course of American life, even American ideals, were entirely forgotten.

You wonder how many who pour in and out of the Russell Building each day, or the Cannon Building, have any notion who Richard Russell was? Or Joseph Gurney Cannon? There is no adequate biography of either man.

As Speaker of the House and head of the Rules Committee, Uncle Joe Cannon of Danville, Illinois, once wielded power here of a kind unimaginable today. He was tough, shrewd, profane, picturesque, and a terrible stumbling block. It was the new twentieth century. The country wanted change, reform. Uncle Joe did not. "Everything is all right out west and around Danville," he would say. "The country don't need any legislation."

When a bill came up to add a new function to the U.S. Commission of Fish and Fisheries, making it the U.S. Commission of Fish and Fisheries and Birds, Cannon protested. He didn't like adding "and Birds" . . . "and Birds" was new and different and thus unacceptable.

The insurrection that ended Cannon's iron rule, a revolt here in this chamber in 1910, was led by George Norris of Red Willow County, Nebraska. There have been few better men in public life than George Norris and few more important turning points in our political history. Yet how few today know anything about it.

How much more we need to know about the first Congress when everything was new and untried.

How much we could learn from a history of the Foreign Relations Committee.

Imagine the book that could be written about the Senate in the momentous years of the New Deal. Think of the changes brought about then. Think of who was in the Senate—Robert Wagner, Burton K. Wheeler, Hugo Black, Alben Barkley, Huey Long, Tom Connally, Vandenberg, Taft, George Norris, Borah of Idaho, and J. Hamilton Lewis, a politician of the old school who still wore wing collars and spats and a pink toupee to match his pink Vandyke whiskers.

It was "Ham" Lewis who advised a newly arrived freshman senator named Truman from Missouri, "Harry, don't start out with an inferiority complex. For the first six months you'll wonder how the hell you got here, and after that you'll wonder how the hell the rest of us got here."

For some unaccountable reason, there is not even a first-rate history of the Capitol, nothing comparable, say, to William Seale's history of the White House. This magnificent building grew in stages, as America grew. It is really an assembly of different buildings, representative of different times, different aspirations, and the story should be told that way.

We are all so accustomed to seeing our history measured and defined by the presidency that we forget how much of the story of the country happened here.

Beside Congress, the presidency seems clear, orderly, easy to understand. The protagonists are relatively few in number and they take their turns on stage one at a time.

Congress seems to roll on like a river. Someone said you can never cross the same river twice. Congress is like that—always there and always changing. Individuals come and go, terms overlap. The stage is constantly crowded. The talk and the rumpus go on and on. And there is such a lot of humbug and so much that has been so overwhelmingly boring.

But let no one misunderstand, and least of all you who serve here, we have as much reason to take pride in Congress as in any institution in our system. Congress, for all its faults, has not been the unbroken procession of clowns and thieves and posturing fools so often portrayed. We make sport of Congress, belittle it, bewail its ineptitudes and inefficiency. We have from the beginning, and probably we always will. You do it yourselves, particularly at election time. But what should be spoken of more often, and more widely understood, are the great victories that have been won here, the decisions of courage and vision achieved, the men and women of high purpose and integrity, and, yes, at times genius, who have served here.

It was Congress, after all, that provided the Homestead Act, ended slavery, ended child labor, built the railroads, built the Panama Canal, the interstate highway system. It was Congress that paid for Lewis and Clark and for our own travels to the moon. It was Congress that changed the course of history with Lend Lease and the Marshall Plan, that created Social Security, TVA, the GI Bill, fair employment laws, and the incomparable Library of Congress.

It is not by chance that we Americans have built here on our Capitol Hill, side by side, with the center of government, our greatest library, a free and open repository of all books and ideas in all languages from all parts of the world.

In two hundred years, 11,220 men and women have served in the House and Senate, and while the proportions of black Americans, of women, of Hispanic and Asian Americans, and native Americans have not, and do not now, reflect the country at large, it is nonetheless the place where all our voices are heard. Here, as they say—here as perhaps we cannot say too often—the people rule.

We need to know more about Congress. We need to know more about Congress because we need to know more about leadership. And about human nature.

We may also pick up some ideas.

Considering the way defense spending has been handled in recent years, we might, for example, think of reinstating an investigating committee like the Truman Committee of World War II, which saved billions of dollars and thousands of lives.

If we are unwilling to vote the taxes to pay for the war on drugs, to save our country, why not sell bonds as we did in two world wars?

Above all we need to know more about Congress because we are Americans. We believe in governing ourselves.

The boy should read history, the first John Adams wrote to his wife, Abigail, about the education of their son, John Quincy. History. History. History. We must all read history, and write and publish and teach history better.

Who were those people in the old bound volumes of the *Congressional Record?* What moved them? What did they know that we do not?

Our past is not only prologue, it can be bracing. In Emerson's words, "The world is young: The former great men [and women] call to us affectionately."

•   •   •

I have decided that the digital watch is the perfect symbol of an imbalance in outlook in our day. It tells us only what time it is now, at this instant, as if that were all anyone would wish or need to know. . . . Which brings me back to Simon Willard.

In the years when the House of Representatives met in Statuary Hall, all deliberations were watched over by the Muse of History, Clio. She is there still over the north doorway. She is riding the winged Car of History, as it is called, keeping note in her book. The idea was that those who sat below would take inspiration from her. They would be reminded that they too were part of history, that their words and actions would face the judgment of history, and that they could count themselves part of an honorable heritage.

There is alas, in this chamber, no such reminder—only the television cameras.

Clio and the Car of History are by the Italian sculptor Carlo Franzoni of Carrara. The clock in the foreground is by Simon Willard. It was, as I said, installed about 1837. Its inner workings, cut freehand by Simon Willard, ticked off the minutes and hours through debate over the Gag Rule, the annexation of Texas, the Mexican War, tariffs, postal service, the establishment of the Naval Academy, statehood for Arkansas, Michigan, and Wisconsin, matters related to immigration, the Gold Rush, statehood for California, the fateful Kansas-Nebraska Act, and the final hours of John Quincy Adams.

It is also a clock with two hands and an old-fashioned face, the kind that shows what time it is now . . . what time it used to be . . . and what time it will become.

And it still keeps time.

On we go.

Index